JANE JACOBS

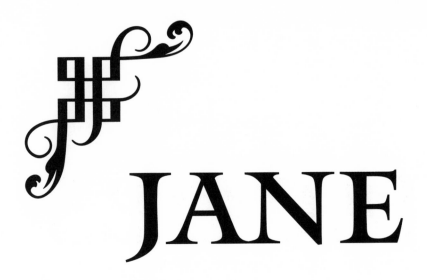

JANE

HarperCollins*Publishers*Ltd

JACOBS

Urban Visionary

Alice Sparberg Alexiou

Jane Jacobs: Urban Visionary
Copyright © 2006 by Alice Sparberg Alexiou

Published by HarperCollins Publishers Ltd

First Edition

HarperCollins books may be purchased for educational, business,
or sales promotional use through our Special Markets Department.

HarperCollins Publishers Ltd
2 Bloor Street East, 20th Floor
Toronto, Ontario, Canada
M4W 1A8

www.harpercollins.ca

Library and Archives Canada Cataloguing in Publication
Alexiou, Alice Sparberg, 1951-
Jane Jacobs : urban visionary / Alice Sparberg Alexiou.

ISBN-13: 978-0-00-200802-0
ISBN-10: 0-00-200802-5

1. Jacobs, Jane, 1916-. 2. City planning. I. Title.
HT166.A418 2005   307.1′216′092   C2005-905454-9

HC 9 8 7 6 5 4 3 2 1

Printed and bound in the United States

For Nick, who found his soul in New York

CONTENTS

ACKNOWLEDGMENTS

The germ of this book began when I watched Ric Burns's wonderful documentary *New York*. Burns devotes a segment to Jane Jacobs and the battles that she fought, and won, in Greenwich Village, telling her story with such passion and admiration that I knew immediately that I had to write about this woman who stood up to Robert Moses.

I wish most of all to thank my husband, Nicholas Alexiou, who with his superb intellect helped me shape my thoughts and whose love kept me sane as I was banging out this book. Also my sons, Alex and Joseph, whose interest both in my subject and in the progress I was making made me feel proud and happy. My parents, Lester and Esther Sparberg, all my life have encouraged me to go after whatever seems important to me, just as Jacobs's parents did for her. My brother, Andrew Sparberg, a city planner and urbanite par excellence who knows every bridge, tunnel, and street in New York, knew the answers to all my obscure questions about his beloved city. My sister-in-law, Donna Comer Sparberg, a native Bronxite, shared memories with me.

A special thank-you to Sam Freedman, the author of numerous books and a professor at the Columbia University Graduate School of Journalism. Sam mentored and encouraged me and so many other writers, and continues to do so in his yearly book-writing seminar at Columbia. Also to my wonderful agent, Wendy Schmalz, who never lost faith in me. To Marlie Wasserman, my editor at Rutgers University Press, for her patience, guidance, and humor. Ditto to Jim Gifford, my editor at HarperCollins Canada. Thanks also to Lyman Lyons for copyediting, and to Marilyn Campbell, director of the prepress department, and Christina Brianik, assistant to the director, at Rutgers University Press. To Roberta Israeloff for hours of conversation and insights. To Chris Jensen for his friendship and legal expertise.

At Boston College, Richard Keeley, John Atteberry, and the staff of the Burns Library helped me in all phases of this project, and I especially thank them for their enthusiasm and generosity. In Toronto, Herschel Stroyman, Thomas Adams, Larry Solomon, Christopher Hume, Richard Gwyn, Bobbi Speck, Robert Fulford, and David Crombie answered my many questions and directed me to sources. Sally Gibson guided me in my research at the Toronto archives; ditto for Sandra Alston at the University of Toronto's Fisher Rare Book Library. I am especially grateful to University of Toronto professors David Hulchanski, Jim Lemon, and Larry Bourne, who read and critiqued sections of my manuscript. The conversations I had with them and their colleagues Shoukry Roweis and Frank Cunningham as their guest at the University of Toronto faculty club also helped me immensely. I was also the guest at the home of Nathan Glazer, who spoke extensively with me about Jane Jacobs. He, too, read parts of my manuscript.

For the section on the Bronx, I am indebted to Eddie Bautista, Yolanda Gonzalez, and Petr Stand.

Thanks also to: Eric McLuhan, Derrick de Kerckhove, Jon Petersen, Eileen Travers, David Warsh, Fred Kent, Arthur Stoliar, Carmen and Avram Greiss, John Simon, Herbert Gans, Ellen Simon, Gene Sklar, Judy Kirk Fitzsimmons, Alexandra Whyte, Jason Epstein, Kenneth Jackson, Dolores Hayden, Robert Fishman, Donald Miller, Roberta Brandes Gratz, Eric Allison, Ron Shiffman, Robert Wojtowicz, Margot Gayle, Carol Gayle, Robert Lucas, David Osborne, Marshall Berman, Gayle Feldman, and Joseph X. Flannery. All gave of their time to speak with me, and helped make it possible for me to write this book.

JANE JACOBS, 1916–2006

On April 25, 2006, as this book was about to be printed, Jane Jacobs died in Toronto, two weeks shy of her 90th birthday. This book examines the ideas of Jane Jacobs, one of the great thinkers of our time.

INTRODUCTION

On a May evening in 2004, hundreds of people streamed into Great Hall, a huge Gothic-style auditorium at New York's City College. They filled up all available seats, but still more people continued to arrive, who then found places to stand along the side aisles or in the back. They had come to hear a lecture by Jane Jacobs, whose 1961 book *The Death and Life of Great American Cities* completely unnerved experts and ultimately changed the way we view cities. The audience waited patiently as Jacobs, eighty-eight, leaning hard on her cane and helped by her son Ned, slowly struggled up the stairs at the side of the stage. She sat down at a table and, hunched over her typewritten notes, spoke to the audience for two hours without interruption. With her spiky white hair and deep wrinkles, her blue eyes twinkling behind her glasses, she was seated all alone above the audience on the large stage, looking like an ancient wise woman and filling up the huge hall with her firm, clear voice. People listened intently as she took them on a roller-coaster ride through a panoply of subjects that included the future of skyscrapers, economic development, the decline of agrarian culture, suburban office clusters, the social philosopher Lewis Mumford, the greening of city spaces, and the ongoing debates over rebuilding Ground Zero—all

Radio Row, Cortlandt Street, Manhattan, 1936. Photo by Berenice Abbot. Miriam and Ira D. Wallach Division of Art, Prints, and Photographs, The New York Public Library, Astor, Lenox and Tilden Foundations.

described through the prism of time, the advertised theme of her speech.

Time, Jacobs said, means past, present, and future. The future category is the one most easily disposed of because nobody can know what the future will be. Then she took this typical Jacobs observation, deceptively simple and seemingly obvious, and ran with it. Nobody can predict outcomes. But the enduring model of supply and demand in economics assumes exactly that. And that erroneous assumption leads to economic stagnation, such as we are seeing today. Jacobs cited the two World Trade Center towers as just one example of the point she was trying to make. When the towers were going up, many were saying that there was already too much office space in New York. The critics were correct. The towers were a financial disaster. Offices stood empty. "The perfect plaza remained bleak and characterless." The World Trade Center did not conform to its "perfect predetermined end result."

As Jacobs's mind raced, the audience held on tight and kept up with her. Multilayered as her presentation was, her ideas were all coming together. The city, she was now saying, is an ecosystem. It needs protection from destructive outside forces, and it must be allowed to grow. For example, the building of the World Trade Center in the late 1960s wiped out "Radio Row," a cluster of electronics stores along Cortlandt Street that constituted "a prehistoric Silicone Valley." "Who knows," mused Jacobs, "what would have happened if the area had been left alone?"

Jacobs has been thinking about what cities are and how they work for most of her life. Cities, she wrote in *Death and Life,* pose the same kinds of problems as the life sciences. And like the sciences, they consist of many variables that are "interrelated into an organic whole." She castigated planners for trying to impose artificial order, as if cities were recalcitrant children who must be forced to obey those who think they know better. "This book," the first sentence reads, "is an attack on current city building and rebuilding." Forty-plus years after its publication, *Death and Life* still resonates. It is required reading in many college courses. The historian Kenneth Jackson, author of *Crabgrass Frontier,* has used the book in almost every class he has ever taught. It has been translated into many languages, including Japanese, Dutch, Italian, and Portuguese. *Death and Life* is now part of the Modern Library series, a distinction Jacobs shares with such great American writers as Edith Wharton, Henry Adams, and Walt Whitman. Jacobs's work is undisputedly a classic that must be read over and over again.

Like any classic, the passing of time only highlights the book's message. For example, deploring the neglected condition of lower Manhattan in 1961 and arguing for mixed use before anybody had heard of the concept, Jacobs wrote that the area's waterfront "should become a great marine museum—the permanent anchorage of specimen and curiosity ships, the best collected to be seen and boarded anywhere." New restaurants, she added, would then open nearby. The area would come to life. And to that, she continued, why not add cultural events? How about theater? Or opera?

Jacobs wrote these words more than twenty years before the development of South Street Seaport. Her words continue to resonate today, as New York struggles over the question of how to rebuild lower Manhattan in the wake of 9/11. The passing of time only highlights the freshness of *Death and Life*. How appropriate, on that spring evening at City College, that eighty-eight-year-old Jacobs talked about time. "I don't want disciples," she told her audience as she was ending her speech. "I want people with independent minds to read my books."

Jacobs has been thinking independently throughout her long life. She takes long-held assumptions and looks at them in original ways. She challenges expert opinions with breezy confidence. She asks questions that stare us in the face, questions that are so obvious but that we, if not for her, do not see. Often her answers provoke controversy. In *Death and Life* Jacobs criticized the building of high-rise projects to house the poor. She based her criticism on direct observation. This panacea for the pressing issue of inadequate housing, Jacobs said, had turned out in fact to be a disaster. But a lot of powerful people were vested in the construction of public housing, and attacked Jacobs mercilessly upon publication of her book. In 1979 she gave a series of lectures on Canadian radio in support of Quebec's secessionist movement, challenging the assumption that separation would be a bad thing.

To date, Jacobs has written seven books. Without question, the most influential is *Death and Life*—at least so far. Her passion has remained cities, but her later works focus on economics. She explores such questions as how cities fuel economies and the moral nature of commerce. How lucky we all are that she has lived so long. Like some biblical prophet, Jacobs forces us periodically to examine our lives and environment. Moreover, she has put her words into action. In the 1960s she led several successful grassroots fights in New York against large-scale building projects. One would have destroyed much of Greenwich Village, replacing wonderful old buildings with high-rises. Jacobs also helped defeat the Lower

Manhattan Expressway, which Robert Moses had been trying to build for many years.

In Canada, where she and her family moved in 1968, Jacobs is a famous and beloved figure to whom mayors and prime ministers often turn for advice. In the United States, however, except for her acolytes, her name is no longer well known. But her influence there is felt all over. People have ideas that originated with her, but don't know the origin.

Jacobs formulated the ideas that she set forth in *Death and Life* as a young mother living in New York's Greenwich Village during the postwar period, when popular wisdom had it that American cities were in a state of crisis. Downtowns were dying while people were fleeing in droves to the suburbs. Those left behind were increasingly poor, and people of color. Public transportation systems were starved, as federal highways were being built.

Jacobs, then working as an editor at an architectural magazine, observed firsthand that public policy, instead of reversing, was actually exacerbating these trends. Under the 1949 Federal Housing Act, known as the Title I program, millions of federal dollars were pouring into cities for the large-scale bulldozing of slum neighborhoods, to be replaced with high-rise projects. Nowhere was this policy more enthusiastically pursued, or on such a wide scale, than in New York City, where Title I was controlled, according to Robert Caro, "absolutely" by Robert Moses. Such an influx of public money invited corruption. The property where slums existed was often valuable, and developers correctly smelled huge profits. Moreover, "slum" was a subjective term. Neighborhoods that looked scruffy to officials were being wiped out in the name of that postwar ideal called urban renewal.

But often these blocks, filled with families and their small businesses, were perfectly viable. New York's huge bureaucracy made it all but impossible for the displaced to fight back. Now and then, some tried. The merchants of Radio Row, for example, appealed all the way to the Supreme Court to try to stop the Port Authority from razing their block. The Authority's supporters complained of harassment and castigated them for standing in the way of progress. The merchants lost.[1]

Today, we take for granted the wisdom of renovating old factory buildings into malls or condos, or of making once-decaying waterfronts like those in Baltimore and New York into wonderful public spaces. Community groups plant gardens in empty lots and buy abandoned apartment buildings from the city for one dollar and fix them up. Public housing is now built on a human scale, not as high-rises. We have respect for the past, as embodied in buildings, in a way that we didn't before. Since 1965, New York has had a landmarks law. But when Jacobs was writing *Death and Life,* there was none. Some of the structures then being torn down were not only salvageable but irreplaceable. The most egregious example, of course, was McKim, Mead and White's masterpiece, Pennsylvania Station, with its vaulted steel-and-glass ceilings and mammoth marble columns, modeled after the Baths of Caracalla in Rome.

In *Death and Life* Jacobs described in detail how powerful forces were hurting cities, both physically and metaphysically. She discussed the importance of neighborhoods, and what made one block friendly, but another deadly. She talked about the need for old buildings, and faulted restrictive zoning regulations as often harmful to a neighborhood's vitality. She castigated the high-rise housing project; the design, she wrote, was not only ugly, but wrecked a neighborhood's soul. To be sure, she wasn't the only one thinking or writing about such problems. Already in 1950, the esteemed Lewis Mumford, who was then architectural critic for the *New Yorker,* was criticizing the projects for "the bleak uniformity of the huge black prisms the tenants occupy."[2] But Jacobs's words affected us like nobody else's. "Under the seeming disorder of the old city, wherever the old city is working successfully, is a marvelous order for maintaining the safety of the streets and the freedom of the city." So begins a much-quoted passage that runs for four pages, in which she compares the daily rhythms of her Greenwich Village neighborhood to "an intricate sidewalk ballet." Her command of language takes our breath away.

There is, however, a glaring but seldom-mentioned shortcoming in Jacobs's otherwise brilliant book: she barely mentions race, clearly a required subject in any serious discussion about cities. Moreover, race was already under the microscope when Jacobs was writing *Death and Life*. We will return to the subject of Jane Jacobs and race later in the book; for now, suffice it to simply note her silence.

When I was contemplating writing this book, I telephoned Jacobs in Toronto. She told me, curtly, that she wouldn't cooperate. It's too time consuming, she said. It takes time away from my writing. Besides, she has said elsewhere, I haven't done anything much. I'm just a writer. Jacobs has asked Random House, her longtime publisher, not to facilitate my or any other would-be biographer's task.

But a life so remarkable needs to be told. We want to know, who is this woman? Besides writing the seminal book about cities in our time, she organized successful community battles in New York against hugely powerful interests. She continued her grassroots activism after moving to Canada in 1968, and never stopped. Now in her late eighties, she still turns out for civic meetings in her beloved adopted city, Toronto, lending her support to the issues she considers pressing. Such happened on a freezing, snowy night in the middle of January 2004 when she, along with her neighbor Margaret Atwood, turned up at a meeting, complete with gaily colored, papier-mâché ear trumpet, to lend her support to a group of Yorkville residents angry over a proposed high-rise building in their neighborhood. And she continues to write, banging out her books on an old Remington typewriter in her study.

Her oldest son, Jimmy, a physicist, and his family live down the block from her. Her other son, Ned, a musician, and his wife live in British Columbia. So does her daughter, Burgin, an artist, and her husband. Jacobs's husband, Robert, who had fought every civic battle alongside his wife, with whom she had discussed all the ideas that went into her books—"by this time I do not know which ideas in this book are mine and which are his," Jacobs had written in the prologue to *Death and Life*—died of lung cancer in 1996. "I know that my wife is more eminent than I am," he once said. "I'm proud of that and I am so proud of her."[3]

And so is her adopted city. Toronto adores her, but adulation, she claims, makes her nervous. She has always refused to take credit for her successes. It's not just me, it's everybody who fights alongside me, she says. Just go out yourself and get involved. Go to your zoning board meetings. Think for yourselves. And while you're at it, give 'em hell.

Jacobs has always resented having to fight the government. It takes time away from my writing, she says. Understandable. But it is hard to believe that so brilliant a leader does not derive satisfaction from her run-ins with authority—especially one with a sense of humor. As fearsome a fighter as Jacobs is, she always has a twinkle in her eye. When she lived in New York, she once wrote out her monthly utilities check to "Consolidated Pollution" in protest against the air pollution caused by Con Edison. (The check, by the way, was cashed.)[4]

No company, no individual, no matter how powerful, was off limits to Jacobs. She feared nobody—not even Robert Moses. "Because of the forty years of adulation of the newspapers—and of the public that read the newspapers—for forty years nothing could stand in Moses's way," wrote Robert Caro in the introduction to *The Power Broker*, his Pulitzer Prize–winning book about New York's great and awful figure, whose parks and roads and bridges utterly transformed the city. "No Mayor or Governor dared to try to breast the wave of public opinion in whose curl Moses rode. One President tried. Franklin Delano Roosevelt, the bitterest enemy that Moses ever made in public life, attempted as President to exact vengeance for humiliations previously received at Moses's hands. But although he made his move at the very zenith of his own popularity and prestige, the President found himself forced to retreat by a storm of acclaim for Moses that rolled not only through New York but across the country."

But Jane Jacobs stood up to Robert Moses.

Jane Jacobs, by the power of her words, not only derailed Robert Moses's Lower Manhattan Expressway, but changed the way we view cities. Once we read her books, the world looks different, and always will.

CHAPTER ONE

From Scranton to New York

People sometimes assume that Jane Jacobs, the former Greenwich Village activist and passionate lover of cities, is Jewish. But she comes from old Protestant stock, born Jane Isabel Butzner in Scranton, Pennsylvania, the heart of coal-mining country, in 1916. Some of her ancestors arrived before the American Revolution. They came from Bavaria, Holland, England, and Scotland, settling in Pennsylvania and Virginia. An ancestor on her mother's side, Robert Boyd, arrived in America in 1738 from England, and served as a captain in the French and Indian War. A paternal ancestor fought in the Revolutionary War and was killed in the battle of Bunker Hill. Her maternal grandfather, James Boyd Robison, was a Union captain in the Civil War and a survivor of Libby Prison in Richmond, one of the Confederacy's notorious prisoner-of-war camps.

Jane was the third child of Bess Robison Butzner, a nurse, and John Decker Butzner, a hard-working and highly respected physician. She, in fact, was delivered by her father, to whom she bore a strong resemblance with her tall frame and aquiline nose. She has often talked about the tremendous influence that John Butzner exerted upon her intellect. He was, she has said, an original and deep thinker who encouraged his children to think for themselves. She

Scranton, Pennsylvania, ca. 1935. Lackawanna Historical Society.

recalls him theorizing that mental illness had physical causes, certainly a radical view during the 1920s and 1930s when he was practicing medicine. As a child, she once asked her father what the purpose of life was. He told her to look at the oak tree outside the window. "It's alive," Dr. Butzner said. "What's its purpose?"[1] Dr. Butzner had other interests as well, such as sports. He especially loved to follow baseball and boxing, and encouraged his children to do athletics. All did; both Jane and her older sister were on the school swimming team.

Jane's parents grew up in small towns, became educated, and moved to the big city. Bess Robison, the daughter of a successful lawyer, was first trained as a teacher before becoming a nurse. John Butzner grew up on a family farm in Virginia, before the state had public education. He and his cousins were "home schooled" by female cousins. Later, thanks to the legacy of a wealthy uncle, Marshall Decker, most of the brood left the family farm and became highly educated. John Butzner attended the University of Virginia, where he received both his bachelor's and medical degrees. He and Bess Robison met in Philadelphia at the hospital where he was interning and she was the supervising night nurse.

In 1905 they moved to Scranton, where John established a busy practice. He owned an automobile, a little red Ford, which he used for making his house calls, as doctors did in those days. But, Jacobs has pointed out, it was only for making his rounds that he used a car. If you wanted to go downtown, you took the streetcar. Scranton had an extensive system, the first all-electric streetcar system in the United States, and for that reason was known as "Electric City." Jane's first address in Scranton, listed on her birth certificate, was on Electric Street. The streetcars were, Jacobs would later recall, splendid specimens. With her eye for detail, she described how they looked: they were "painted fuchsia or silver or sky blue, and had flowered chintz seat covers."[2]

She loved the city. She used to look forward to going to the dentist because she got to ride the streetcar downtown. Life in the city, the Butzners told their children, was far superior to the country. Scranton had three vaudeville theaters, a science museum, and a library housed in a wonderful building styled after the Musée de Cluny in Paris. Jane and her three siblings were raised in a lovely old house, the largest on their block. But by the time she was a teenager, Scranton was slipping into economic decline, as were Buffalo and Pittsburgh and other then-great cities of the Northeast that had gotten rich off coal and steam and steel. Scranton's coal had been all mined out. The automobile replaced the trains. Racked by unemployment, Scranton's population was shrinking.

Growing up there, Jacobs told a reporter in 1993, was perhaps one of the reasons she would later think hard and then write about what made some cities stagnate but others prosper. She would come up with an original hypothesis: cities are living organisms, and their economies are reciprocating systems.[3] If any part of a city's economy stops, so does the entire system.

As a child, she was already taking the mental notes that would form the basis for her original thinking. She was always thinking about how things worked. Once when she was nine, she listened, incredulous, as a teacher explained to the class that cities always grow up around waterfalls. "I absolutely didn't believe this because there was a waterfall in Scranton—it was lovely but it didn't have anything to do with the economy of Scranton. Mines were the thing in Scranton. I was very suspicious. I didn't think the waterfall could account for it." Jane immediately told her teacher that she was wrong. There was, she said, a waterfall in a park near her house. And it had nothing to do with the city.

Throughout her school years, Jane did just enough work to pass her courses but no more. She did learn a lot, she concedes, from her teachers in the first and second grades. But by the time she got to the third grade, she discovered that she could read anything and thereafter tuned out her teachers. All her life, she would remain a voracious reader. For the time being, she began sneaking books into the classroom, holding them under her desk so as to be able to read during lesson time. It must have been tough for young Jane at school, with a mind that was racing way ahead of her teachers. Sometimes she wrote poems and stories. Among her papers at Boston College are two letters written in the late 1920s by Thomas Lomax Hunter, publisher of a small local newspaper and apparently a friend of Dr. Butzner. Hunter praises the nine-year-old Jane for two poems—"The Flapper" and "A Bedtime Story"—that she has submitted and he has published. He is certain, he writes, that she will continue her writing and have an impact on the world.

Jane sometimes alleviated the boredom she suffered at school by getting into mischief. She would blow up paper bags in the school cafeteria and pop them, a stunt that once landed her in the principal's office. Or she would spit on the stairway rail and slide down, to the delight of the kindergarten children below. Once she entertained a pack of her friends by running up the down escalator in the Scranton Dry Goods store. "When we were kids," wrote a Scranton newspaper columnist who knew Jane when they were both children, "she was a free spirit, clever, hilariously funny and fearless." There was the time when Jane's unsuspecting teacher told the class to raise their hands and promise to brush their teeth every day for the rest of their lives. It happened that Dr. Butzner had just the previous day advised his daughter, age seven, never to promise to do anything for the rest of her life while she was still only a child. Promises, he told her, are serious. What her father had said made sense to her. She refused to raise her hand. She also told her classmates that they should not promise, either. Her teacher, enraged at the child's cheekiness, lost her temper. She threw Jane out of classroom. Jane walked out of the school building and wandered along some railroad tracks. Then she went home to her mother to eat her lunch. She doesn't tell us what her mother said to her during that lunch. How we'd love to know.

Jacobs throughout her life has often talked about her parents with great affection. They both encouraged her independence and never undermined her confidence. Jacobs says that her teachers, however, tried to do so. When the seven-year-old Jane returned to school after lunch on the day she had mouthed off to her teacher, the latter made no mention of what had happened. Jane, clearly, had won the battle. If anything, the incident only served to increase her already-healthy self-esteem. It wonderfully illustrates her incredible nerve that she was already displaying as a child, which would one day enable her to stand up to anybody in the world, even Robert Moses.[4]

Jane inherited her spirit of rebellion from both sides of her oldline Protestant family. Some ancestors had pursued the American ideals of life, liberty, and the pursuit of happiness in very concrete ways. "I was brought up to believe that simple conformity results in stagnation for a society, and that American progress has been largely owing to the opportunity for experimentation, the leeway given initiative, and to a gusto and freedom for chewing over odd ideas," Jane wrote in 1952. "I was taught that the American's right to be a free individual, not at the mercy of the state, was hard-won and that its price was eternal vigilance. . . . I am grateful for that upbringing."[5]

Her maternal grandfather, James Boyd Robison, was a successful lawyer who nevertheless supported grassroots movements. He ran for Congress in 1872 on the Greenback-Labor ticket, a fact that made later generations proud. Jane had even inherited a scrapbook of his campaign. Her father came from a family with some pretty radical ideas. Some of the Butzners refused to fight in the Civil War because they did not believe in secession or slavery; after the war, they even became Republicans. Her father went to medical school at the University of Virginia, as did his brother William, who became a lawyer. Another cousin became a Baptist minister. Not only the men, but the women, too, were educated. One female cousin became the director of a sanatorium; another, a college professor in Georgia. Another relative was a Quaker who, in Jacobs's words, "believed in women's rights and women's brains." This woman published her own work under her own name, refusing to use a masculine nom de plume as custom then dictated.

A maternal great-aunt, Hannah Breece, one of twelve children, was a schoolteacher in Pennsylvania who went on to study anthropology instead of marrying. She was assigned by the U.S. Department of the Interior to teach Native Americans in the Southwest, where she traveled by covered wagon from reservation to reservation. From there she went to Alaska—she was forty-five, the year was 1904—and remained there for fourteen years, teaching in various locations that included fishing camps and a reindeer station. Conditions were terrible. Winters were so cold that food placed in a skillet froze if it was not sitting right on the stove's hottest spot. In the summer the mosquitoes were so thick that she had to wear a hat with a veil, which was tied under her arms. Hannah's students suffered from poverty and malnutrition. One winter she witnessed a whooping cough epidemic. Traveling in Alaska in winter meant by dog sled; in summer, by kayak. While on the water she wore a kamleika, a waterproof poncho-like garment with a hood. Hers was made of bear intestines.

During her years in Alaska, Hannah, a staunch prohibitionist, started a one-woman temperance movement. Alcoholism was widespread in the native population. Once, upon discovering a barrel of home brew in the tent of a fishing camp, she ordered some men to heave it all out. They obeyed her. Hannah later put together a memoir of her years in Alaska. At age seventy-seven, she entrusted it to her niece Jane Butzner, then twenty-one, with the hope that Jane could help her get it published. Jane eventually did get it published—in 1995.[6]

Female role models like great-aunt Hannah shaped Jane Butzner's perceptions about women and what they were capable of. "I grew up with the idea that I could do anything. Nothing was going to be barred from me if I wanted," Jacobs told the *Boston Globe* in 1993. Nothing, that is, within the prescribed female occupations, like nursing or teaching. To be sure, she resented the fact that most professions were male dominated. "But I didn't resent it in this corrosive way because it wasn't affecting me internally." The reason, she said, was her parents: they treated her and her brothers the same. Moreover, Jacobs said, she grew up during the 1920s, following the long wave of feminism that culminated in the passage of the Nineteenth Amendment, which gave women the vote. The 1920s, Jacobs said, were nothing like the 1950s. During those postwar years, she and other women professionals were told that they shouldn't be working outside the home.

Upon Jane's high school graduation, her parents told her that they had saved money for her to go to college if she ever wanted to. But Jane had enough of school: "I was so damn glad to get out of school I couldn't even think of going to college." The year was 1933. She took a stenography course so as to be able to support herself. She also spent six months in rural North Carolina with an aunt, Martha Robison, who ran a Presbyterian community center and mission. Then she worked, unpaid, at the local newspaper for a year, writing up "the meetings of the Women of the Moose, and the Ladies' Nest of Owls No. 3," and putting together the "Agony" column, for which she composed letters both to and from. The experience, Jacobs said, constituted her journalism school. And then it was time to move on.[7]

The year was 1935, the depths of the Depression, and there was no work to be found in Scranton. There was no question of remaining there. What would she do, wait around to get married? Not Jane, daughter of the progressive-minded Butzners. What better place to seek her fortune than New York? Jane had visited New York when she was twelve. Arriving by ferry from New Jersey into the financial district on a weekday, she was, she would later recall, "just flabbergasted at all the people in the streets . . . the city was just jumping." Now, at age nineteen, she was eager to go back. Besides, her older sister Betty was already living there. Betty a few years earlier had graduated from design school in Philadelphia, and was now working as a salesgirl at the Abraham & Strauss Department Store in Brooklyn. That made her one of the lucky ones with a job.

The two sisters moved into a sixth-floor walkup near the Brooklyn Bridge. Jane began job hunting. She aspired to be a newspaper reporter, a downright nervy ambition for a young woman in those days, unless you were satisfied with the women's club beat. Serious reporting was for men only, the newsroom as much their sanctuary as any locker room. But for now, she needed to support herself. Thanks to the stenography course she had taken, after a few months of searching Jane landed a job as a secretary for a candy company. For the next five years she held various secretarial positions. She worked for a clock company, then a drapery hardware company, and afterward a steel distributing company. And sometimes she was out of work. When funds were low, she and Betty survived on Pablum, a baby cereal, and bananas.[8]

In her spare time or in between jobs, she was eagerly exploring New York. "I was gradually learning the city, in a very disorderly way," Jacobs would recall some seventy years later.[9] Sometimes she went by subway, which cost a nickel in those days. Or she and Betty would ride about on rented bicycles. Jane was young and there was so much to marvel at, such as the crowds and all those skyscrapers, the architectural form that defined New York. "Manhattan has been compelled to expand skyward because of the absence of any other direction in which to grow. This, more than any other thing, is responsible for its physical majesty," E. B. White would write in his 1949 *Here Is New York,* a valentine to his city. Even now, in the middle of the Depression when most new building construction had stopped, the Empire State Building was going up. There was poverty all around, but cars were clogging the streets and New York never stopped moving. Robert Moses was overseeing the construction of the Henry Hudson Parkway and the Triborough Bridge, and the unemployed were being put to work rebuilding New York's long-neglected parks and playgrounds and turning neglected shorelines into public beaches.

New York, huge as it was, though, was made up of individual neighborhoods, perhaps three blocks long and two wide, and virtually self-sufficient, E. B. White would write. "Thus, no matter where you live in New York, you will find within a block or two a grocery store, a barbershop, a newsstand and shoeshine shack, an ice-coal-and-wood cellar (where you write your order on a pad outside as you walk by), a dry cleaner, a laundry, a delicatessen (beer and sandwiches delivered at any hour to your door), a flower shop, an undertaker's parlor, a movie house, a radio-repair shop, a stationer, a haberdasher, a tailor, a drugstore, a garage, a tearoom, a saloon, a hardware store, a liquor store, a shoe-repair shop." So strong is the sense of neighborhood, White wrote, that when a New Yorker walks two blocks from his corner, he feels that he is in a strange land.

Immigrants gave individual neighborhoods distinct identities. In the 1930s much of New York's population was foreign-born, and they were eternally renewing New York as they were reinventing themselves. Immigrants created a continual state of flux where new ideas were always bubbling up and finding places to take root, whether on the streets or in places of higher learning such as City College, which educated immigrants' children and nurtured their left-leaning ideologies. Or at the New School, all the way downtown in Greenwich Village, founded in the 1930s as "The University in Exile" by refugee Jewish intellectuals from Nazi Germany.

But New York was also a terrible, cruel place, especially during Jane's early years there. When she arrived in 1935, Mayor Fiorello La Guardia was trying to hold together a desperate city where every day dozens of unemployed men lined the grungy blocks around Union Square, selling apples out of boxes. A million and a quarter New Yorkers were on the dole. Bread lines snaked around corners.

In Klein's, one of the bargain department stores ringing the square, you could buy a child's coat for a dollar with a matching hat for a quarter. If you could afford a cup of hot chocolate for a dime at the nearby Childs Restaurant, you felt like a millionaire. Down on the Bowery, homeless men down on their luck filled the flophouses every night, paying twenty cents for a bed. More than half a million New York families, including a million children, were living in slums, some even in the same appalling "old law" tenements that photojournalist Jacob Riis had documented forty-plus years earlier in his shocking book *How the Other Half Lives*. People who had seen poverty all over the world, including Europe and South America, said that no slums, anywhere, were as awful as New York's. The average population density in New York slums—that is, the population per acre—was more than twice the national average.

In old-law tenements, only the street-facing rooms had windows. Back rooms faced an air shaft. Individual apartments had no toilets or place to bathe inside. Families shared a single toilet in the hallway or even an outside privy in the rear yard. One *New York Post* reporter followed fifteen city councilmen as they, in a show of concern for their constituents, toured some Lower East Side tenements. After the group had visited three apartments, only three men remained. The rest made early exits because they couldn't stomach what they were seeing. At 30 Scammel Street was a rear tenement predating the Civil War, with a foul toilet in the hall; a railroad flat at 10 Henry Street had side windows that "looked out on a bleak air shaft one foot wide or so." One of the occupants, a twenty-one-year-old son, Harry, made seven dollars a week in a factory. In his spare time he drew pictures. "His favorite, a country scene showing little homes nestling under trees, hangs on a bedroom wall and it's labeled 'a perfect dream'" (*New York Post*, April 17, 1938).

New York's poor had nowhere else to live besides tenements. After the 1920s, developers had stopped constructing low-cost housing, and the reason was basic: owning such properties was not profitable. Up to now, private enterprise ruled New York. Neither the state nor the federal government offered any help in solving the city's housing crisis. In contrast, European governments had been subsidizing low-income housing since the late nineteenth century. People everywhere were now talking about the government's responsibility to provide decent shelter for its citizens. In the climate of the 1930s and President Franklin Roosevelt's New Deal, few questioned that this was the right thing to do.

The Federal Theatre Project in New York even produced a play on the subject as part of its "Living Newspaper" series. For the title, playwright Arthur Arent borrowed a phrase from Roosevelt's second inaugural speech in 1936. "I see one-third of a nation," FDR intoned, "ill-housed, ill-fed, ill-clothed." Arent's *One Third of a Nation* sold forty thousand tickets even before it opened. During its run, the *New York Post* reported, tickets were going "like a tenement fire." In the play, the main character, Angus Buttonkooper, goes on a tour of New York's slums in 1850 and then again in 1938. Each time, Buttonkooper finds the same terrible conditions.

"I mean, the picture never changed: Lousy, stinking holes, called homes in 1850—and in 1938, the same holes, still occupied by human beings. No great change. Just talk, reports, pleas, occasional outbursts of public resentment. Laws that hardly helped," Arent told a *New York Post* reporter in answer to the question of what motivated him to write his play. At the end of *One Third of a Nation*, Buttonkooper makes a direct plea to the government to house the poor. Private enterprise, says Arent, clearly cannot; who hasn't come to that conclusion by now? The play was so successful that in 1938 Paramount Studios made it into a movie starring Sylvia Sidney.

New York, in fact, had taken the lead in housing reform. One of Fiorello La Guardia's first acts as mayor was to create the New York City Housing Authority in 1934. The Housing Authority immediately went out to document conditions in New York's slums. The following year, La Guardia asked Roosevelt for $150 million to be used for slum clearance and building new housing. Langdon Post, the chairman of the Housing Authority, told the *New York Times* that the new housing program would take ten years to complete. It would, he assured everybody, "wipe out the slums of today." There was, he said, no better way to spend public money than clearing slums. The passage of the United States Housing Act in 1937, which allocated $100 million in federal funds to build decent shelter for the poor throughout the nation, mandated the elimination of "unsafe or unsanitary dwellings." Which de facto meant that you had to destroy old buildings before receiving any federal funding to build anew. Given the state of housing in New York City, the logic of the law seemed irreproachable. Ironically, New York's first public housing project, First Houses on the Lower East Side erected in 1936, consisted of renovated old-law tenements.

But with the passage of the Housing Act, there would be no more renovating, only razing. And nowhere would that provision be more enthusiastically carried out than in New York. During La Guardia's tenure as mayor (1933–1945), ninety-five hundred tenement houses would be torn down. In 1938 two Public Works Administration projects went up, in Harlem and Williamsburg, Brooklyn. People lined up for blocks just to get an application. In 1938 thirty-six thousand people applied for the handful of vacancies available in the thirteen thousand apartments under the control of the New York Housing Authority.[10]

As New York's housing problems continued to fester, Jane Butzner would observe, and think. Her sister years later recalled going with Jane specifically to examine an early housing project in Brooklyn. Jane, said Betty, was already wondering how well the building design was working for the occupants.[11]

One day, after spending a fruitless morning at an employment agency, Jane hopped on the El and took a ride with no particular destination in mind. When the car pulled into the Christopher Street stop, she got off simply because she liked the sound of the name. She wandered about the twisty, narrow streets of Greenwich Village, which had escaped the gridiron plan imposed upon the rest of Manhattan. So in the Village, you had to give people landmarks, not directions, to any given destination. There was something special about this place, with its down-to-earth scale and jumble of buildings. Except for a few blocks here and there, and the north side of Washington Square, with the elegant 1830s Greek Revival houses that were the setting for Henry James's famous novel, the

Village was decidedly scruffy and comfortable as an old slipper. Old warehouses were interspersed with tenements. People sat on the stoops of the brick row houses, using their streets like their living rooms. Diminutive dormered wood-frame houses looked like doll-houses. The tiny backyards behind them made the Village feel un-like other neighborhoods. Many dwellings were now serving as boardinghouses.

Jane admired the crafts shops, filled with leather belts and big copper earrings. These were New York things; she'd never seen anything like them in Scranton. She couldn't afford to buy any of them, but if she lived here, she could at least look at them. She also liked the grubby way that Village people dressed. "In midtown, I remember I always felt so depressed," Jacobs would recall many years later. "Everyone looked so well-dressed and with-it. But down on Christopher Street, people looked the way I felt." And rents were cheap.

Jane was smitten. Returning to Brooklyn, she told her sister that she'd found this great place, and they absolutely had to live there. The two soon moved into an apartment on Morton Street, where sometimes Jane sat on the building roof, watching the garbage trucks drive about. They stopped at the curbs, and the garbage men leapt off and heaved in the trash that people had piled up at the side-walk. And Jane pondered over the many pieces of New York that, taken all together, made the city work.[12]

The population of Greenwich Village was as mixed as its dwellings and included a large Italian and Irish working class, many of whom worked as longshoremen on the adjacent docks where sailors from all over the world were always debarking. If the sailors needed some funds to tide them over or just somebody to confide in, they knew to head right to McAvoy's Pharmacy at the corner of Christopher and Washington. There, Minnie Belle "Mother" McAvoy, one of New York's few women proprietors, would dis-pense loans to them along with some free advice and her own spe-cial vegetable tonic for hangovers. The intelligentsia hung out at the Minetta Tavern or Romany Marie's tea salon on Eighth Street, where the Moravian-born Marie, dressed in colorful gypsy garb and jangling jewelry, read palms and tea leaves and tenderly offered hospitality to her starving artist patrons, often feeding them or putting them up when they couldn't pay the rent. Marie had been doing this since 1912, the golden age of the Village, which now, in the 1930s, was still nurturing artists and writers.

The Butzner sisters' neighbors included such luminaries as painters Jackson Pollock and Willem de Kooning, novelist Dawn Powell, and poets Delmore Schwartz and E. E. Cummings, both of whom were taken in by the wiles of Joe Gould, the crazy Village fixture known as Professor Sea Gull, who was immortalized by the writer Joseph Mitchell. The homeless Gould came from a wealthy old Yankee family. A Harvard graduate, he prowled the Village streets, claiming to be writing a grand oral history, mooching money off bleeding-heart literati. Gould crashed poetry parties and wandered into all the Village bars, including the White Horse Tavern on Hudson Street, the watering hole of many a famous writer. The hopelessly alcoholic Delmore Schwartz would flee there when he was tired of writing his verses in his dingy little room around the corner, and Dylan Thomas practically lived at the White Horse in between sleeping off booze and his notorious womanizing.[13]

Later, the White Horse would become a favorite spot for Jane to socialize and drink beer with her neighbors. But not now, because money was too short to hang out at bars. Besides, she was too busy working. Or if she had been laid off, which happened frequently, she was pounding the pavement looking for another job. Or she was exploring the city, watching people going about their business and wondering how their businesses worked. And she was writing, even selling some of her stories. She found her subjects just by walking about, letting her mind settle wherever it wanted. She would scribble down notes on whatever scraps of paper she had in her purse. Then she would go home and write.

Cue magazine bought one of her stories, about the variations in New York's manhole covers. Another Jane Butzner story was about the fur business, not something she had planned to write about except that one day she found herself in the fur district, where a man, a Mr. Edgar Lehman, came out of his shop. Jane asked him questions.

She went home and wrote up a story, which she then pitched to *Vogue*—because who, she asked herself, would read about furs? *Vogue* bought it for forty dollars, a lot of money in those days. Then she wrote another story for *Vogue,* this one about the flower district, with a lead paragraph that grabbed the reader by the throat: "All the ingredients of a lavender-and-old-lace-story, with a rip-roaring, contrasting background, are in New York's wholesale flower district, centered around Twenty-eighth Street and Sixth Avenue. Under the melodramatic roar of the 'El,' encircled by hash-houses and Turkish baths, are the shops of hard-boiled, stalwart men, who shyly admit that they are dottles for love, sentiment, and romance."

Vogue bought that story, too, and then another one, about the diamond district, then located on the Bowery between Hester and Canal. The district, wrote the twenty-one-year-old Jane, is "one of the largest and strangest jewel exchanges in the world, where seventy per cent of the unredeemed jewelry pawned in the country is bought and sold. . . . No one seems to know why this district has grown where it has, an island in the most squalid section of New York City. It is adjacent to no allied centers; it exists by itself, surrounded by the almost legendary Bowery life."[14]

In the same year—1937—that *Vogue* published her stories, Jane's father died in Scranton. John Butzner was only fifty-nine. He died in the hospital, where he lay in an oxygen tent surrounded by his four children and wife. The *Scranton Tribune,* eulogizing him "as a most capable physician and high-minded gentleman," added: "The community and the profession which he adorned are the poorer by his passing." "He was a man's man," wrote the newspaper's sports editor, a friend of Dr. Butzner, who was an avid sports fan. "He dedicated his life to the most humanitarian of all endeavors—alleviation of suffering." The death of her father, who had so profoundly influenced her, must have devastated Jane.

The following year she decided to attend college. She enrolled at Columbia University's School of General Studies as a non-matriculating student, which meant that she could study whatever she wanted. For the first time in her life, Jane found to her surprise that she enjoyed school. She even received good grades. Her courses included constitutional law and economic geography. She also took zoology and geology, which, she said, she "passionately loved." After two years at General Studies, Jane was required to matriculate, which would have meant attending Barnard. But the institution rejected her application, despite the good work she had done at Columbia. The women's college based its decision on her terrible high school grades. Jane claimed that she didn't care. Barnard had course requirements, something that she could not tolerate. "I was allowed to continue getting an education," Jane wrote sarcastically in 1961, displaying what would be her lifelong disdain for formal schooling. She never attended college again. But for the rest of her life, she would continuously draw on many of the ideas she had been exposed to while studying Columbia, bang them around in her head, and turn them into her books.[15]

In the meantime, Jane went back to making a living. She found a secretarial position at *Iron Age*, a trade publication for the metals industry, which was now booming because this was the beginning of World War II. Soon she was promoted to associate editor, a real coup for her. Finally, she was working full-time as a writer, but under a boss, Mr. T. W. Lippert, who clearly had it in for her. "I understand that he made loose and untrue allegations about my morals," Jane would write later about her boss. Once Lippert sent her, ostensibly on a work assignment, to a stag dinner that included, in Jane's words, "entertainment to which he was well aware no women were invited." In her file Lippert referred to her as "only a typist" even though she officially occupied an editorial position.[16] Her boss's treatment of her amounted to a clear case of sexual harassment, but it was happening at a time when women had no legal recourse, let alone even a name for the concept.

But even in such a demoralizing work environment, she continued to perfect her writing craft. No matter the subject, her voice came through loud and fresh. "Silver has been the comic opera metal of the War. It has precipitated an enchanting argument over whether or not bus bars are safe from thieves," Jane wrote in a 1943 story about the use of non-ferrous metals during the war. "It has raised a fantastic pother over whether the economic system will be

as stable with silver on loan to war plants as it is with silver under-
ground at West Point. It has produced the incredible Uncle Shylock
suggestion that silver be lend-leased to our allies at one dollar an
ounce, against a United States import price of forty-five cents."
During her time at *Iron Age* she also wrote about unemployment in
Scranton and the depressed Lackawanna Valley. She remained at
the publication for three years. Afterward she found a job as a feature writer for the Office of War Information. At the war's end, she
became a reporter for the State Department and Overseas Information Agency's magazine *Amerika*.

And then she found love.

Robert Hyde Jacobs Jr., like Jane, came from old Protestant
stock. His great-grandfather, Ferris Jacobs Sr., was a doctor who
served in the Union army during the Civil War. His son Ferris Jr.
also served, as a cavalry officer. Robert's grandmother was the first
woman to graduate from Antioch College in Ohio; her father was
a mason who had worked on the original college building. Robert
was an architect who had received his training at Columbia University. The couple met in 1944 through Betty, who was Robert's work
colleague at Grumman, the Long Island defense plant where both
were designing aircraft. Betty invited Robert to a party at her and
Jane's Village apartment.

Nearly fifty years later, Robert recalled that evening: when he
walked through the door, he told a *Boston Globe* reporter, "there she
was, in a beautiful green woolen evening dress, and I fell in love."
Jane concurred: "Cupid really shot that arrow."[17] Two months after they met, the couple married. It was wartime and young couples
were getting married fast. "The only reason we waited that long was
so that I could meet his parents," Jane told the *Boston Globe* in 1993.

The wedding took place in Jane's childhood home in Scranton,
where her mother was still living. It was a modest affair, with only
family members attending. "Miss Butzner will wear a white, street-
length dress trimmed with turquoise and fuschia, and a corsage of
white orchids," Jane Butzner's former employer, the *Scranton Tribune,* solemnly reported on the morning of the wedding, which took
place on May 27, 1944. "The living room, in which the ceremony

will be solemnized, will be decorated with lilacs and roses. Iris and garden flowers will be used in the other rooms."

After a honeymoon spent bicycling through northern Pennsylvania and New York, the newlyweds returned to New York City to start their life together. Jane would continue to observe carefully the city that by now was her home. New York in turn would nurture her mind, and enable her to find her writer's voice.

CHAPTER TWO

Urban Blight

I n 1947 the Jacobses bought a rundown old three-story building at 555 Hudson Street. Their new home had no central heating, and garbage was piled in the backyard. On the ground floor was a small retail space that had last been used as a candy store. Five-fifty-five Hudson stood between a laundry and a tailor shop, both also with upstairs apartments where people lived. This typical Village arrangement went completely against New York City's zoning ethos at the time. Commercial activities, experts believed absolutely, should be separated from where people actually lived. The Village, however, long a place that nurtured rebellious thinking, refused to conform to such a fixed idea about how people should live in its space, just as its meandering little streets had escaped being shoehorned into the grid that was imposed over the rest of the city in 1811.

The couple moved into the apartment above the store and began to fix the place up They cleaned the bricks and turned the backyard into a garden. Their first child, James, was born in 1948. Two years later, Jane gave birth to their second child, Ned. She hired a woman to take care of her children and continued to work as an editor at the State Department publication *Amerika*. Robert Jacobs had left Grumman and was now working at an architectural firm.

Park Avenue and Thirty-ninth Street, Manhattan, 1936. Photo by Berenice Abbot. Miriam and Ira D. Wallach Division of Art, Prints, and Photographs, The New York Public Library, Astor, Lenox and Tilden Foundations.

By staying in Manhattan to raise their children, the Jacobses were bucking the conventional expectations of their time: that a young, white, middle-class couple like them would flee the city to buy a house in one of the sparkling new suburbs that were going up all over America. To be sure, one reason people were opting out of an urban life was the severe housing shortages in the cities. Nowhere was this more so than New York City, where during the war it was impossible to find an apartment, and even more so now because all the young couples who had married during the war began to have children. But even more than the baby boom, the policies of the federal government encouraged the exodus to suburbia. The Federal Housing Administration (FHA) and the Veterans Administration (VA) together administered programs of government-backed mortgages with an interest rate of only 4 percent for World War II veterans. That meant the thousands of young couples and their new babies, now living doubled up in city apartments with the in-laws, could afford to move to a brand-new two-bedroom Levittown house with an eat-in kitchen and backyard.

William Levitt built his developments in New York, New Jersey, and Pennsylvania with the government's blessings and help in the form of a virtually unlimited credit line. The Levittowns came to personify the postwar suburb. To the new families, they were a dream come true. The city, people were now saying with great conviction, was no place to bring up your kids. The city was dirty, and there was no place to play. In cities children used the sidewalks as playgrounds, which everybody knew was dangerous. But the suburbs! Ah, those wonderful, new suburbs! There, children played not on the sidewalks—often there were none—but on the grass. Everybody knew that grass was healthy. The suburbs, people said, were so green and leafy, with fresh air and sunshine. The suburbs were like heaven. And in contrast to the overcrowded, decaying city schools, suburban schools were brand new and clean. People felt safe sending their children there.

But when the new suburbanites raved about how "good" their schools were, "good" implied, among other things, "all-white." The postwar suburb was made completely inaccessible to people of color. Segregating the races was then considered not only normal but desirable. The 1936 FHA underwriting manual specifically instructed institutions not to lend money in areas with "inharmonious racial groups." Levitt could not put up his houses fast enough. When he ran an ad in the paper announcing that 350 new houses would go on sale on a Saturday morning, men camped out Friday night in front of the office for a chance put down the ninety-dollar down payment.

The suburbs did not appeal to the Jacobs family. "Suburbs are perfectly valid places to want to live, but they are inherently parasitic, economically and socially, too, because they live off the answers found in cities," Jacobs would tell a reporter for *Mademoiselle* magazine in October 1962. The Jacobses weren't alone in choosing to stay in the city. Other young middle-class couples were also discovering the Village now, buying up old properties for cheap and renovating them long before people were using the term "gentrification." With the exception of the blocks surrounding Washington Square, the neighborhood was still scruffy, shunned during the previous century's real estate booms by developers who had built luxury housing elsewhere in Manhattan. The Village, where factories and warehouses sat next to little wooden and brick houses, did not appeal to the rich. So after the war, the neighborhood felt like the Wild West, says an old Village denizen who bought his Jane Street house in 1949. The Jacobses thought the Village was a wonderful place to raise their children. People hung out on the sidewalks, where you could see them. You never felt alone there; it was a real community, a place where people both worked and played, and socialized with each other.

What a contrast to the blandness of the suburbs, where all the men got on a train every morning to go to the office in the city, leaving their wives to raise the children and take care of their new houses with their new appliances, all alone. There was nobody on the streets, only cars, which was your only way to connect to other people, whom you met at the supermarket or at your children's school. Few young suburban mothers worked. Those who aspired to a separate professional life were considered freaks, as Betty Friedan so famously described in *The Feminine Mystique.* Friedan called their isolation and unhappiness "the problem that has no name." But Jane, the antithesis of the idealized postwar mother, had no such problem. She never stopped working, even through her childbearing years.

While she was still at *Amerika* she received a questionnaire from the U.S. State Department about her political beliefs and affiliations. The year was 1952, the height of the McCarthy era. J. Edgar Hoover was keeping "smear lists" of organizations that he considered "subversive." All federal employees had to swear a loyalty oath to the American government. Their affiliations, past and present, were scrupulously researched. Your friends or coworkers, scared to death of ending up on the "list," might answer questions the government asked about your personal life. This was the second time the government was investigating Jacobs. She had received a similar questionnaire in 1949. The government doubtless considered Jacobs "suspect" because she had belonged to the American Labor Party during the 1940s, and had joined the Federal Workers Union when she began working for the Office of War Information. Ironically, Jacobs was always strongly opposed to communism. In fact, she had dropped her Federal Workers Union membership in 1945 because it was by then communist dominated.

The questionnaire that Jacobs received demanded, among other things, that she discuss fully her "attitude toward the Communist Party, the Soviet system of government, and the aims and policies of the Soviet Union." "It has been stated that during 1947–1948 the *Daily Worker* was delivered regularly to your apartment at 82 Washington Place, New York City," Jacobs's questionnaire read. "If you have ever received the *Daily Worker* by subscription or other arrangement please relate the dates and circumstances and the nature of your interest in the publication." Not true, Jacobs answered, noting that she had already answered this question in 1949. To her statement, she added acidly: "Incidentally, the source of the misstatement in your present question is apparently not aware of my whereabouts in 1948. I lived at 82 Washington Place for only a very few days of that year. I had planned to move from there to my present address before December 30, 1947, but because of the big snow which blocked our street to automobiles, was unable to move until some time during the first week in January."

In her written replies, Jacobs expounded at some length on her views. The Communist Party in Russia, she wrote, is "a ruthless device for maintaining power, an apparatus for political tyranny." But here in the United States, she wrote, the Party poses no danger. "I have too much confidence in the stability and sense of the overwhelming majority of our people to believe that it is dangerous for us to be exposed to the ideas of the Communist Party."

Many people have associated Jacobs with the American left. This assumption comes in part from her image as a "Village" person, and the fact that she admired certain figures from the left of the political spectrum. One of her heroes, for example, was the muckraking journalist I. F. Stone. But Jacobs has never been political in the sense of supporting one ideology or party over another. Larger ideologies, she firmly believed then and continues to believe, only obscure the realities, which are to be found by looking around, paying attention, and trusting your eyes over what people are merely saying. In that spirit, she always supported the right of labor unions and grass roots movements to exist. "I think it is good for us to have vociferous political minorities and to know how to live with them," she wrote.

But her personal support of any individual cause was always based on her absolutely unbending principles. Jacobs ended her affiliation with the Federal Workers Union, she wrote, "both because I was in disagreement with most of the union's political line and because I thought that, in principle, it is a union's proper function to stick pretty close to earth—to practical labor problems involving workers in its field—rather than to conceive of itself as a grand mastermind of national and international policy."

Jacobs's responses to the 1952 interrogatory give us much insight into her thinking, as this elegantly phrased excerpt makes clear:

> It still shocks me, although we should all be used to it by this time, to realize that Americans can be officially questioned on their union membership, political beliefs, reading matter and the like. I do not like this, and I like still less the fear that arises from it. But I understand the necessity for such questions in the case of government workers in sensitive departments. . . . For my part, I am interested, as a citizen deeply concerned in the preservation of traditional American liberties, in presenting my viewpoint as fully and as plainly as possible. I am not answering the enclosed questions in a spirit of sparring with

you or trying to get away with anything. I want you to know how I feel.

First of all, I was brought up to believe that there is no virtue in conforming meekly to the dominant opinion of the moment. I was encouraged to believe that simple conformity results in stagnation for a society, and that American progress has been largely owing to the opportunity for experimentation, the leeway given initiative, and to a gusto and a freedom for chewing over odd ideas. I was taught that the American's right to be a free individual, not at the mercy of the state, was hard-won and that its price was eternal vigilance, that I too would have to be vigilant. I was made to feel that it would be a disgrace to me, as an individual, if I should not value or should give up rights that were dearly bought. I am grateful for that upbringing.[1]

Jacobs remained at *Amerika* until 1952, when the office was relocated from New York to Washington. She began to job hunt, and soon applied for a position at *Architectural Forum,* a classy magazine to which her architect husband subscribed. The magazine, one of Henry Luce's Time Inc. publications, appealed to a serious readership. It didn't turn much of a profit, but Luce enthusiastically supported it nonetheless because he loved it and was proud of it. Its editors recognized and nurtured talent, encouraging writers to produce cutting-edge stories. *Architectural Forum* devoted entire issues to individual cities, ran such stories as "Louis Kahn and the Living City," and published photo essays by luminaries like Walker Evans. The magazine covered Frank Lloyd Wright before anybody else, devoting an entire issue to him in 1938 that Wright even helped design.

Architectural Forum represented a step up in Jacobs's career. The magazine had a tony office on the top floor of what was then the Time-Life Building at Rockefeller Center. It paid its staff very well. For a tryout, editor-in-chief Doug Haskell gave Jacobs an assignment to write about a candy building at Herald Square. Haskell hired her, giving her the title of associate editor. The architect and writer Peter Blake, who was an *Architectural Forum* editor from 1950 until its demise in 1972, said that Haskell's hiring of Jacobs "was probably his most courageous move." Blake remembers Jacobs as "a wonderfully likable, contentious, opinionated woman." Instead of riding the subway to work, she rode her bicycle from Greenwich Village. Jacobs was assigned the school and hospital beat, subjects about which she knew nothing. "You'll be our school and hospital expert," the editors told her. Years later, Jacobs said, "So always be suspicious of magazines! I didn't know beans about this . . . somebody with a printing press tells you you're an expert."[2]

To make up for her lack of formal training, Jacobs lugged home piles of blueprints from her office for her and her husband to study together every evening after the children were asleep. In this way she learned the vocabulary for her new beat. Robert Jacobs also benefited from these marathon teaching sessions: he discovered that he was interested in hospital design. It would become his lifelong specialty. During the next fourteen years, he would work in three New York firms, where he would help design twenty-two hospitals, including New York Hospital and Hadassah Hospital in Jerusalem.

"Like the work corridor, patient bedrooms are planned to eliminate errand-girl demands on nurses' time." This sentence, from a 1954 story by Jacobs about a new California health center, shows that no matter how ordinary the subject, she wrote about it eloquently. Her editors were so pleased with Jacobs's work that they began assigning her stories about city planning, yet another subject that she knew nothing about.

They had handed her a hot potato.

The mid-1950s was a time of unparalleled prosperity in America. The stampede out of the cities to the suburbs was escalating as more and more people bought cars, which they drove on the thousands of miles of new, federally subsidized roadways that were being built after the passage of the Interstate Highway Act in 1956. But for cities, these developments were a disaster. As the middle class continued its exodus, those left behind in the city were disproportionately impoverished, and people of color. Besides "white flight," there had been another demographic factor: hundreds of thousands of African-Americans had in the last decades moved up north in "the great migration." A huge postwar influx of Puerto Ricans to New York, fleeing the poverty of their motherland, had further swelled that city's minority population.

Federally backed mortgages were restricted to new, single-family dwellings, and this was yet another factor, and a major one, in the downward spiral of American cities during the 1950s. Landlords had no incentive to renovate their residential properties, nor private developers to build new rental housing. In the suburbs, land values were booming; in the cities, they were stagnant or even declining. Downtowns were becoming decaying shells of their former bustling selves as former city dwellers began to shop in the new pedestrian malls that were springing up in their brand-new suburbs. More and more people were driving automobiles as public transportation systems, starved for funds since the Depression, continued to deteriorate. The New York subways, after years of neglect, were dirty and smelly. People associated the subways with crime. Riding them, people told you, was tantamount to risking your life. Everyone knew that only those who had to—that is, only the poor—rode the subways.

The intelligentsia was incessantly wringing their hands over "urban blight." What to do? You couldn't just bomb American cities out of existence, although clearly some people would have liked to, judging by some of the things they were saying. The anti-city sentiment that always ran through the American psyche was now reaching a high point, as people built bomb shelters and worried about the Russians. *Collier's* magazine in 1950 published a flamboyant story about an imaginary atomic attack on New York City by the Soviet Union, complete with illustrations. Entitled "Hiroshima, U.S.A.," the article was "part of a national mass media campaign, made with the complicity of the federal government, which shamelessly contributed to the destruction of whatever remained of credible, urban middle-class life," writes Richard Plunz in his 1990 book *A History of Housing in New York City.* A year after the *Collier's* article, the *Bulletin of Atomic Scientists* proposed "defense through decentralization"—in other words, breaking up large cities and dispersing them in order to blur the targets of possible nuclear attacks.

But the government had not turned its back on the cities. On the contrary, it was doing something tangible, and on a huge scale, in keeping with the postwar propensity to think and act big. In 1949, as the white middle class continued its flight from the cities to the new suburbs thanks to the easy availability of federally backed mortgages, Congress passed the Federal Housing Act, which allotted gargantuan sums of money to build public housing for the urban poor. All across America, bulldozers were knocking down entire blocks of slums, which were then being replaced with huge red brick high-rises. At the same time municipalities were drawing up large-scale plans to revitalize crumbling downtowns with new civic centers. The housing act ushered in an era of what historians of cities would call "master planning," all managed by a local planning "czar." Officials across the country enthusiastically touted public housing construction as the cure-all for cities' social ills. It was going to be a brave new world, right down to the high-rise design of the new housing.

New York City's first public housing projects, erected in the 1930s under the La Guardia administration, were low-rises. High-rise structures at that time were associated with luxury tenants, not the poor. In 1941 New York's first high-rise projects went up: the East River Houses in East Harlem, on the site of a just-cleared slum. Only six of the twenty-eight buildings in the project were high-rises, but after the project was completed, officials realized that housing people in towers was the most cost-efficient way to go. From then on, all public housing would be high-rises, modeled on "the tower in the park" design of the Swiss-born architect Le Corbusier, whose real name was Charles Edouard Jeanneret-Gris. Le Corbusier was his maternal grandfather's name, which he assumed when he was in his thirties, as if he were reinventing himself.[3]

Le Corbusier had radical and fanciful ideas that represented modernism in its purest and most impractical form. (Ironically, Robert Jacobs was a devotee of Le Corbusier's ideas.) Cities, Le Corbusier believed, should not be allowed to sprawl in whatever direction they liked; instead they should be built high, within severe boundaries. His signature "Ville Radieuse" design, which he concocted in the 1920s, consisted of gleaming skyscrapers with roof gardens set far apart in green parks, with aerial highways winding around the peripheries. Everything would be strictly zoned. Pedestrian and vehicular traffic were to be separated. Above all, Le Corbusier was concerned with order. Old cities must be demolished, to be rebuilt anew. His proposed "Voisin Plan" for Paris in 1925 would have wiped out the Marais district, now one of Paris's most chic neighborhoods. In its place, Le Corbusier imagined eighteen skyscrapers and a huge highway.

Visiting New York in 1935, Le Corbusier was dazzled. Manhattan was "a city of skyscrapers, a vertical city. . . . It is the first time that men have projected all their strength and labor into the sky—a whole city in the free air of the sky." But the skyscrapers were not big enough, he said. They should be huge, and fewer of them, spaced farther apart. Le Corbusier hated New York's streets. "I am not able to bear the thought of millions of people undergoing the diminution of life imposed by devouring distances, the subways filled with uproar, the wastelands on the edges of the city, in the blackened brick streets, hard, implacably soulless streets—tenement streets, streets of hovels that make up the cities of the century of money—the slums of New York or Chicago." New York, the architect said, was "a beautiful catastrophe." He proposed that the city's messy, short blocks be eliminated, to be replaced by mega blocks.[4]

"New York's slums must come down. There are hundreds of blocks in New York City where all—or most—of the buildings are not fit to be lived in. . . . Repair or conversion only means throwing good money after bad. Here, on these blocks, a beautiful new city can rise: new places, good for living and working . . . new industrial centers, cultural and medical centers, universities, stadiums, and parks . . . new neighborhoods planned so that people and baby buggies, and boys and girls on bicycles may move safely, and old people can sit in the sun and watch the young ones go by." Le Corbusier's utopian vision is encapsulated in these words, which appeared in a 1950s pamphlet issued by the Citizens Housing and Planning Council, a nonprofit group that worked closely with the New York City

Planning Commission. Housing people in high-rises was considered a vast leap forward, not only philosophically but also aesthetically. Instead of fetid, dark tenements, people were being housed in brand-new apartments that had light and ventilation. The new projects were built in clusters, among patches of grass. The children living there, instead of having to play on dirty city sidewalks, now had lawns, just like their suburban counterparts. Policy makers believed that compared to the slums they were replacing, the projects were heaven, and that the people to be housed there should be grateful.

Jacobs's editors believed fervently in these then-mainstream positions. Cities were to be carefully planned and on a grand scale, following the dictum of the famous Chicago architect Daniel Burnham, designer of the Flatiron Building. "Make no little plans. They have no magic to stir men's blood and probably themselves will not be realized. Make big plans; aim high in hope and work," Burnham is supposed to have said. In this spirit the *Architectural Forum* editors also wholeheartedly supported modern design principles, including urban renewal. "Most of us, myself included, believed that the only solution to urban decay—and the only way to reconstruct cities bombed out in World War II—was to raze large portions of what was left and replace it with something akin to the diagrams drawn up, in the 1920s, by Le Corbusier and others," wrote Peter Blake. "These projects seemed entirely rational in the 1920s, and seemed almost as rational to many of us in the 1950s: because there was likely to be an increasing concentration of people in cities, the way to house and otherwise accommodate them was in high-rise buildings; and because these concentrations of people should not be deprived of sun and air and greenery, it seemed reasonable to house them in tall buildings spaced far apart and interspersed with parks and other outdoor amenities."

In 1951 *Architectural Forum* ran a story, "Slum Surgery in St. Louis," ebulliently praising plans for a $58 million public housing project in St. Louis. Pruitt-Igoe, designed by the architect Minoru Yamasaki, would replace a neighborhood of "ramshackle old houses jammed with people—and rats" with twenty-six eleven-story apartment houses based on Le Corbusier's ideas. "Skip-stop elevator service will be combined with open galleries every third floor to build vertical neighborhoods for poor people in a city in which up to now has lived ninety per cent in single houses. . . . And as instructive as the buildings is the site design: a city-purchased park will be stretched out to wind through the area like a river."

In 1954 the *Architectural Forum* editors wanted Jacobs to do a story about another project that was getting a lot of buzz. They showed her drawings of the plans, which Jacobs found, in her words, "charming." But she had no opinion whatsoever about the ideology behind the high-rise design, which her editors felt so excited about. She was coming to the subject completely cold. The editors had decided to send her to Philadelphia, where chief planner Edmund Bacon was in the middle of a major slum-clearance project. Bacon, whose son Kevin would become the famous actor, had studied with Eliel Saarinen in Detroit and was Philadelphia's equivalent of Robert Moses. Like Moses, he fused his gift for planning with political know-how. Bacon's face would appear on the cover of *Time* magazine in 1964, and he wielded tremendous political power in Philadelphia for three decades. He was, in Jacobs's words, "a big poobah." He changed the face of Philadelphia, then decidedly down-at-the-heels. Bacon is perhaps best known for preserving a deteriorating downtown neighborhood filled with wonderful old colonial houses and transforming it into what came to be called "Society Hill," the very epitome of gentrification. Society Hill notwithstanding, like everybody else at the time he believed wholeheartedly in the bulldozer approach to urban renewal.

Bacon took Jacobs on a tour of a black neighborhood in Philadelphia to show her a recent renewal project. "He took me along a crowded street, where there were a lot of recent arrivals in the Great Migration," Jacobs recalled in a speech she gave in 2004, nearly fifty years after the fact. "Obviously they were very poor people, but enjoying themselves and each other. Then we went one street over [where there were new high-rise projects]. Ed Bacon said, let me show you what we're doing. He wanted me to see the lovely vista. There was no human being on the street except for a little boy kicking a tire. I said, 'Where are the people?' He didn't an-swer. He only said, 'They don't appreciate these things.'"

At that moment, Jacobs realized that the high-rise projects that Bacon was so proud of had been designed with total disregard for the people who would actually inhabit them. "What a revelation this was to me! I had no credentials, him being the expert." So, Jacobs continued, "I set myself up as my own expert." She was able to trust her instincts, she said, because of her upbringing.

"My parents never undermined my confidence."

CHAPTER THREE

Urban Renewal

When Jacobs returned to New York from
Philadelphia, she began arguing with her
Architectural Forum editors. All the hyped new
projects that planners and architects were building in the cities, she told them, bore no relation
to what people actually needed. She was basing
her conclusions on what her own eyes told her,
what she had just seen in Philadelphia. Of course
she had no training as an urban planner. But so what? Hadn't her
editors told her that she was now their expert in urban planning?

Her editors were stunned. Jacobs, wrote Peter Blake in his book
No Place Like Utopia, "was questioning virtually all the basic premises by which modern planners had functioned since the end of
World War II and before." The editors held their ground. Jacobs
had her own theory about why they preferred to believe the "experts," rather than their own eyes. "They wanted to live in an exciting new world," she would later say, "that they would create and inhabit. It gave them some purpose in life."[1] Therefore, they believed
all the hype.

But no matter. Jacobs trusted her eyes and her instincts. All her
life she had been interested in how things worked. When she was a
child in Scranton, she studied the locomotives in the rail yards. At
some point she noticed that the locomotives were being fitted with

The Baruch Houses, 1955, one of may public projects then under construction in New York City. New York City Housing Authority.

skirts over the wheels so one couldn't watch any more how the pistons moved the wheels. From then on she began to notice, in her words, "how everything was being covered up and I thought that was kinda sick." She wondered, "Have we become so feckless as a people that we no longer care how things work?"[2]

So now Jacobs was realizing that the plans that Ed Bacon was superimposing on Philadelphia, and Robert Moses on New York and other planning czars in cities across America, had nothing to do with how cities worked. People, she believed, didn't care how cities actually worked. They only cared how to make them look nice. Like the skirts that hid the wheels of the locomotives.

It all made her so angry. So she set out to get the real story on urban renewal, not the one that the city-planning establishment had sold to the world. She was curious about the professional training urban planners were receiving. She discovered that the spanking new environments they were creating on their drawing boards were purely theoretical, based on mathematical models and architectural ideals like Le Corbusier's. But the planners were giving no thought whatsoever to whether inhabitants of these state-of-the-art housing projects actually liked living in them. Nobody was asking the basic questions, such as, what kinds of living spaces make people feel good? Or, conversely, bad? It was as if those questions didn't matter, the assumption being that those living in these new high-rise wonders were like children who didn't know what was best for them, and should just be grateful to the authorities for building them.

"It soon became obvious to me, as I looked at what was being built and how it was working, that city planning had nothing to do with what was being built and how it was working, that city planning had nothing to do with how cities worked successfully in real life," Jacobs would write in the early 1960s. "I was also astounded to discover that although the professions of planning, housing, zoning, and urban renewal fiddling and promoting were beset with vague misgivings, they were intellectually very moribund. There was almost no inquiry being made into the sense, if any, behind the orthodox theories of planning, housing and urban design. There seemed to be almost no curiosity, except on the most superficial level, about how big cities work."[3]

In January 1955, Jacobs gave birth to her third child, whom she named Mary. (As an adult, Mary changed her name to Burgin, a family surname.) After a brief maternity leave she returned to work. One day, a big bear of a man named William Kirk came to the *Architectural Forum* office to pay a visit to one of Jacobs's editors, who was Kirk's personal friend. Kirk, an ordained Episcopal minister, was director of the Union Settlement, an affiliate of Union Theological Seminary, a bastion of liberal Protestantism. Located in East Harlem, the settlement existed to help the denizens of that desperately poor neighborhood. Kirk and his wife, Mary, devoted themselves completely to this cause. Kirk was so modest that in official correspondence he referred to himself simply as "head worker," instead of his well-earned title of "executive director."

East Harlem, a cacophonous urban landscape, was always a poor area, and now growing increasingly poorer as thousands of Puerto Ricans, fleeing their island's poverty, were settling there to start a new life. Bordered on the west by Fifth Avenue, it started at Ninety-sixth Street and continued north, stretching on the east side past Madison and Park, then all the way to the river. The Second and Third avenues Els roared along their corridors while trucks banged their way up First Avenue. Ugly brown gas tanks lined the banks beside the East River.

Always a port of entry for immigrants, the neighborhood was once mostly German and Irish, then Italian and Jewish. Famous natives included Fiorello La Guardia and Burt Lancaster. Now East Harlem had acquired a new sobriquet, "Spanish Harlem," or "El Barrio." By 1949, the year William Kirk arrived in New York with his family to take the helm of Union Settlement, a thousand newcomers a week were coming in from Puerto Rico. Large numbers of newly arrived African-Americans from the rural South were also settling in the neighborhood. The Italian Harlemites resented the invasion of these others into their turf, resulting in racial tensions that were played out in the form of street fights.

The new arrivals crowded into the tenements, which, having housed wave after wave of immigrants, were increasingly rundown, overrun with rats and cockroaches, and more than ever bursting at the seams. A quarter of a million people were now living in East Harlem, an area measuring 1.2 square miles. Often three to six families were occupying apartments intended for one. The streets, the *New York Times* reported, were dirtier than almost anywhere in the city. Health problems included tuberculosis and the highest infant mortality rate in the city. *Time* magazine reported in 1950 that between fifteen and twenty-five babies a week there were bitten by rats. The housing supply was desperately short; no bank had lent mortgage money in East Harlem since before 1940.

That what was arguably New York's worst slum directly abutted the city's wealthiest neighborhood—to this day, Ninety-sixth Street marks where the Upper East Side ends and poverty begins—was a major embarrassment to New York's political establishment. Consequently, when money for urban renewal began to make its way out of Washington and into New York, much of it went into East Harlem. Starting in 1941 with the erection of the East River Houses, the first public high-rises, huge changes began to engulf the neighborhood. The East River Houses, set between 102nd and 105th streets, and First Avenue and East River Drive, obliterated two streets, forming one large superblock. Thirteen additional projects subsequently went up in East Harlem that like the East River project caused entire blocks to be eliminated. All together, high-rise projects would cover approximately one-third of the neighborhood, two-thirds less than what Robert Moses, chairman of the Mayor's Committee on Slum Clearance, wanted. Moses had literally designated *all* of East Harlem for demolition.[4]

William Kirk was now standing in the *Architectural Forum* office, telling the editors that $3 million in federal money—the equivalent of $30 million today—had so far been invested in East Harlem to build new housing. Yet the problems in the community, were only getting worse. The Union Settlement had been examining the effects of "urban renewal" up close. One of the social workers, Ellen Lurie, had just completed a painstaking study of three hundred families in the Washington Houses, a massive project containing more than fifteen hundred apartments that occupied the area between Second and Third avenues, stretching from Ninety-seventh Street all the way up to 104th Street. Five blocks containing two hundred small businesses had been destroyed to build the Washington Houses.

The results were devastating. The new high-rises, it turned out, were making the environment worse than it had been before "slum clearance." Tenants told Lurie that they were afraid to walk the streets at night, that the new projects were being quickly defaced by vandalism, that police protection within the projects was inadequate. The high-rise design, with its elevators and empty public areas, was only increasing the opportunities for crime. The projects were incubating grounds for teenage gangs, who terrorized the other residents. On the old block, which was now being obliterated, one felt a lot safer. People were on the sidewalks, watching their neighbors and also their neighbors' children. So high-rises made life more difficult for mothers, who could no longer watch their children playing in the street from their windows.

Then there was the problem of their children's schools, which were not only old but now more overcrowded than ever because whoever had decided to build the new high-rises hadn't taken into account the subsequent need for more classrooms. Decision makers, in fact, knew nothing of the East Harlem community's concerns for the simple reason that nobody bothered to ask them anything. "In the vast changes in East Harlem since World War II, the community has never really been consulted by the Planning Committee, the Housing Authority, or the City Administration," Lurie wrote in her report. New York's bureaucracy was so huge, the top so far removed from those supposedly being helped, that the latter had literally no input into well-intentioned actions that were now, as it turned out, destroying their lives.

Kirk in the meantime was toiling ceaselessly to get people to listen to him. He was a master at getting things done via networking. He and his wife had a lot of contacts outside of the neighborhood, and they didn't hesitate to use them. But city officials just weren't listening. The list of Lurie's disturbing findings went on and on. Razing tenements to build new housing projects was forcing people from their homes, which, however shabby, were all they had. The displaced were now dealing with a hellish city bureaucracy, which sometimes shuffled them about from one temporary housing situation to another. Sometimes the replacements that the city found for them were worse than the apartments they had been forced to vacate. Lurie documented the case of one slum family that was relocated to another tenement, but this one with an outdoor toilet.

Moreover, the buildings being destroyed often contained small commercial spaces. Lurie's study documented that at least fifteen hundred, maybe more, small businesses—grocery and hardware stores, bakeries and candy stores, little clothing stores, barber shops, and others—employing more than forty-five hundred people had been pushed out of East Harlem. "Squeezed," as Lurie put it, without any compensation from the city. Not only were local merchants being deprived of their livelihood, but their former customers were now stripped of services. "What was formerly a convenience now becomes a hike. Shopping, which was a time in which neighbors met, now is a long, impersonal, tiring business, especially with young children in tow," Lurie wrote. Moreover, the storefronts had housed not only businesses, but also social and political clubs and storefront churches, all institutions that glued the neighborhood together. Once demolished, they were gone forever.

East Harlem merchants formed an association, and were now pleading with the city to include commercial facilities in plans for the new projects. In principle, those listening agreed. But although the merchants won every argument, they lost every decision made by the city, William Kirk would later write in a 1967 letter to a New York housing official. By then, the number of small East Harlem retail businesses that had been lost to urban renewal would have increased to two thousand. But the city did not even acknowledge the problem. "It is utterly impossible to find any serious study of this question," Kirk would write in a letter to a social-work student in 1962. He added that he had traveled to England, where he found "the approach to dislocation is much more perceptive and mature. All interests are carefully studied . . . it is my impression that the concern and care . . . in the English practice is also found in many places on the Continent."

Urban renewal was ripping out East Harlem's heart. How ironic, Lurie would write later in a 1962 report, that in the late 1940s and early 1950s, civic leaders were telling the Union Settlement that it could soon close its doors because "public housing would solve everyone's problems and redemption would be upon us." Instead, it was annihilating whatever in the neighborhood had been viable.

Lurie wrote: "With longing we nostalgically remembered the old Italian band concerts, the colorful street fairs, the rowdy political rallies." She added: "With slightly sentimental fuzziness, we longed for the cop on the beat who called us all by name . . . the friendly game of stoop ball . . . the neighborhood grocer."[5] For all its pathologies, East Harlem was a real neighborhood in the old-fashioned New York immigrant tradition, where people hung out on the stoops and slept on the roofs during the sweltering summers and lived their lives out on the streets. The little immigrant businesses fed not only the community economy, but its souls, too.

One wonderful example was the ubiquitous Puerto Rican cigar stores, as documented by Jeff Kisseloff in *You Must Remember This,* his collection of oral histories. "While the cigar makers worked, the workers would pay maybe five or ten cents a week and they hired people to read to them," recalled interviewee Alvis Sanchez, who came to the United States in 1942.

The reader would read any kind of newspaper, the union paper, every day, and any kind of books, like *Les Misérables.* . . . When they finish, sometimes they would have a discussion about what they hear. The tobacco shops were the best place for talking, because the cigar makers were very radical, very partial in their politics . . . [in those days there were] over fifty thousand were making cigars in New York in maybe one thousand shops. There were factories and *chinchals*—small shops. . . . At first I worked on 125th and Lexington. There were about twelve people in that shop. In *el barrio* you find on any corner a cigar shop."[6]

But now, urban renewal was destroying the cigar shops.

Jacobs listened with interest to all that Kirk was saying. The two took an instant liking to each other. Kirk invited Jacobs to visit East Harlem with him. They spent several afternoons walking through the streets, talking to people, dropping in on all the anchor points of the neighborhood including the little neighborhood stores that so far had escaped the wrecking ball, like Sy Pinsky's hardware store right around the corner from the Union Settlement. They also took tours in the evening, when Jacobs observed clumps of people watching television sets on the sidewalks. Jacobs later described the scene: "Each machine, its extension cord run along the sidewalk from some store's electric outlet, is the informal headquarters spot of a dozen or so men who divide their attention among the machine, the children they are in charge of, their cans of beer, each others' comments and the greetings of passers-by. Strangers stop, as they wish, to join the viewing."[7]

Jacobs's trips through East Harlem felt to her like "collecting a basket of dry leaves," she would tell a *Milwaukee Journal* reporter in 1962. "I didn't know what to do with them but he [Kirk] was showing me a different way of looking at the city! The social aspect. It opened my eyes. I can remember the people in East Harlem hating a patch of green grass. I couldn't understand why until one of them told me that their tobacco store had been torn down, the corner newsstand was gone, but someone had decided the people needed a patch of green grass and put it there." Except that the patches of grasses weren't being used for anything. They stood empty. Every afternoon after the schools let out, kids raced across the patches. Immediately, the Housing Department police shooed them off. Ellen Lurie noted in her report that this happened every day, literally hundreds of kids being chased off the grass, told to go play on the project playgrounds, that's what they're for. On paper, the playground plans had looked so promising. Finally, urban designers were thinking, a safe place for slum children to play, away from the streets. But the reality was otherwise. The playgrounds did not feel like hospitable spaces, and residents shunned them.

Jacobs would return to her office at *Architectural Forum* and think hard about all she had learned from Kirk. Impressed by the work that the Union Settlement was doing, she joined the board and became an active member, fighting along with Kirk to get the city to pay attention to East Harlem's concerns. How incredible that she found the time, between work and mothering—she had an infant, a five-year-old, and a seven-year-old—to devote to this cause. Plus, she had other distractions that were literally right in her own backyard. Jacobs, along with some of her neighbors, was busy paying close attention to disturbing changes that were now happening around them.

The Village, one-time American bohemia and hotbed of radical politics, and still home to writers and now the center of the abstract expressionist art movement, was still a low-rent mecca where you could get cheap eats at the tiny Italian joints decorated with red-checkered tablecloths and Chianti bottles waxy with candle drippings. It was now looking to developers like a pretty good place to invest. Big-name real estate men were starting to buy up the old buildings. They would evict the tenants. With no landmarks law to stop them, they were razing irreplaceable structures and building in their place luxury "egg-crate" apartment buildings. The venerable Brevoort on lower Fifth Avenue, one of New York's oldest hotels where writers and the moneyed classes used to mingle, had been demolished in 1954 along with the adjoining house, which had once belonged to Mark Twain, and the rest of the block. In their place now rose up a nineteen-story luxury apartment building.

The previous year New York University had knocked down the Federal-style Lafayette Hotel on Washington Square South, where writers—Dawn Powell, John Cheever, A. J. Liebling, and Joseph Mitchell were among the regulars—schmoozed around little marble-topped tables in the mirrored-wall café. And along with the Lafayette, the entire block between Eight and Ninth streets was torn down, including Madame Branchard's rooming house, "the house of genius" that at various times was the digs of Theodore Dreiser, Stephen Crane, Willa Cather, and John Dos Passos. Along this block, NYU, now in a period of rapid expansion, built the huge Loeb Student Center, and either controlled by lease or owned three-quarters of the properties that bordered Washington Square.[8]

Villagers in the mid-1950s were worried about NYU's possible plans for Washington Square, the Village's only open space and everybody's playground. Every day mothers took their children there to play; folksingers with guitars came every Sunday to perform at the fountain, spearheading a nationwide craze for that musical genre. And there was simultaneously another threat to Washington Square, the most ominous of all: Robert Moses, who was now proposing to ram a forty-eight-foot-wide sunken highway right through it, linking Fifth Avenue to West Broadway. The new road was imperative, he was telling Villagers, to relieve traffic in the surrounding streets.

But there was another reason why Moses wanted the road: he controlled, besides everything that had to do with roads and bridges and parks, all the Title I money coming into New York.[9] And Moses had grand plans for the city's urban renewal that included the Village. Immediately after Congress passed the Housing Act in 1949, Moses had ten New York City neighborhoods designated as slums. Included were nine blocks southeast of Washington Square bordered by Houston, Mercer, and West Third streets and West Broadway, a mixed residential and manufacturing area (mostly the latter) where New York's hat industry was concentrated. It now constituted a slum to be cleared and replaced with new apartment houses. Moses's Washington Square roadway would extend Fifth Avenue through the Washington Square Park, linking it to West Broadway, which would then be renamed Fifth Avenue South, where new residences would be built.

The blocks south of the Square to be torn down were not beautiful, but neither did they by any stretch of the imagination constitute a "slum." The word, once in the possession of Robert Moses, seemed to have lost its meaning. And once the label "slum" was applied to your neighborhood, reality was beside the point. For your area to appear on the city's "slum-clearance" map was the kiss of death, a clear signal to owners not to invest another dime in their properties because they were all going to be bulldozed, and it seemed there was nothing you could do to stop it. The residents of the Village tried their best. They would fight the "Southeast Project," as it came to be called, bitterly. But in the end they would lose.

It had all gone by the book. The Board of Estimate obediently had approved Moses's slum designation in 1954, clearing the way for private developers to acquire the condemned property from the city at bargain prices. Which, indeed, was exactly the purpose of

Title I—that is, to encourage private builders to rebuild America's cities. Except that the developers of the Southeast Project did not build low-income, or even middle-income, housing. In a brazen affront to the intent of the law, they built luxury high-rises. For some developers, Title I was turning into a land grab.

But the developers had done nothing illegal. Clearly there were gaping loopholes in Title I. In his book *Public Works: A Dangerous Trade,* Robert Moses gave his own interpretation of Title I: "Title I was never designed to produce housing for people of low income. The critics failed to understand that Title I aimed solely at the elimination of the slums and substandard areas. It did not prescribe the pattern of redevelopment, leaving this to local initiative." The term "urban renewal," then, seemed to have a flexible meaning. How it was used depended on where it was being applied. In the mid-1950s, "urban renewal" meant a very different thing in the Village than East Harlem or other poor minority neighborhoods like the Lower East Side or Brownsville in Brooklyn. There, Title I translated into monstrous high-rise public projects housing tenants who were black or Hispanic. Indeed, another unfortunate effect of urban renewal, as it turned out, was that it was only reinforcing segregation. (In East Harlem, William Kirk was trying to counteract this unfortunate effect by creating Franklin Houses, mixed-income and mixed-race housing projects.)

One hundred and thirty-two families were evicted from their homes southeast of Washington Square, along with one thousand small businesses. Among the buildings demolished was a seventeen-story apartment house of large, rent-controlled apartments filled with professional tenants. In the now-emptied-out six blocks, developers built Washington Square Village, a pair of glazed-brick, seventeen-story, 580-foot luxury towers.

New York University had also benefited from Title I, acquiring a three-block strip on the Square where it would build the high-rise Loeb Student Center and later a library designed by architect Philip Johnson; Village residents, including Jane Jacobs, would vainly fight the latter. Ultimately, NYU would also acquire Washington Square Village in 1964, after Paul Tishman, one of the original developers,

ran into financial trouble. (Tishman sat on the NYU board.) The affair was, pure and simple, a travesty—as was the case of another private university in New York City that also benefited handsomely,
and questionably, from Title I.

In 1955 Fordham, a Jesuit institution, acquired property adjacent
to Lincoln Center through the largesse of Robert Moses, who had
a close relationship with the New York Archdiocese. Thousands of
poor black and Hispanic residents were displaced in order to build
Lincoln Center and Fordham's Manhattan campus. The lucky ones
got rehoused in "the projects." As for the unlucky ones—well, it was
just too bad for them, as was made evident by the testimony of
Charles Abrams in 1962 at a National Housing Conference in Washington, DC: "I think most of these relocation surveys by urban renewal authorities are plain common frauds," Abrams said. "With
more than 70 percent of those evicted being Negroes, how can anyone truthfully say they are getting better housing after eviction—
particularly since only a minor fraction ever gets into public housing?" Abrams was stating an obvious but uncomfortable truth: if
you were black or Hispanic and you lost your home and neighborhood in the name of urban renewal, you had far fewer options than
white people. You couldn't go just anywhere, because most places
would not have you. So perhaps you would move in with a family
member. Or you found a new apartment in another slum. But both
were often worse than the place from which you had been evicted.

Clearly, there was something very wrong with a law that was further ghettoizing Brooklyn and East Harlem's blacks and Puerto Ricans inside huge tower-in-the-park projects, even as it was also forcing middle-class people out of their apartments and out of the city.
One man who had been evicted from his rent-controlled Washington Square apartment told a reporter from *The Nation:* "I've got to
get the hell out of New York. The hell of it is, I don't want to move.
I was born and brought up in New York. I love the city. I don't
want to move out to the suburbs and I have to commute every day,
but I've got to." The man moved to Westchester County.

And there were other Title I scandals besides the Southeast Project. A six-block area on the Upper West Side was acquired on the

cheap by developers in 1951, soon after it was condemned by Moses's Slum Clearance Committee. Supposedly this area would be redeveloped as "Manhattantown," a project consisting of seventeen twenty-story buildings. But nothing was ever built. Instead the new owners either built parking lots after knocking down some of the condemned buildings or left them to deteriorate as they continued to collect rents. In 1954 Manhattantown was the subject of a congressional investigation that concluded the obvious: the property was being milked by speculators. But three more years would pass before the city began the necessary steps to repossess the site, and for the story to get any significant press coverage. Indeed, with the exception of the *New York Post,* the mainstream papers were giving Moses a free pass. Especially the *New York Times,* which had a particularly cozy relationship with him. The *Times* also completely whitewashed NYU's land grabbing. "New York University is moving fast in reclaiming parts of the region adjoining Washington Square before it deteriorates," the paper would trumpet in a January 10, 1961, story praising urban universities "joining battle for neighborhood renewal."[10]

Villagers, however, were a savvy bunch, and they were watching. "Greenwich Village and environs still have a number of flavorful, significant old buildings, but it is a sad truth that visiting architects are walking around photographing them these days, sensing that they are not long for this culture," architectural critic and Village resident Walter McQuade would write in an article that appeared in the *Village Voice* in 1957. "Will Louis Sullivan's office building on Bleecker near Broadway give way to a handball court under the auspices of the IBM of book learning, NYU? Will Stanford White's charming Washington Arch be lacerated by the monumental Mr. Moses?" The sassy, brazen *Voice,* to which Jacobs was an occasional contributor, was paying close attention to what was happening in the Village.

Jacobs and her neighbors loved their community, a place that had long nurtured rebellious spirits. Villagers weren't going to lie down and let Robert Moses dig a road through their beloved Washington Square Park. They had lost the Southeast Project fight, but this one they would win. It would take them six tough years. They would win because they realized something basic: New York's bureaucracy was impossible to penetrate. You only had to look north, to the Bronx, where residents had tried in vain to fight the construction of the Cross Bronx Expressway, which now was literally blasting them out of their homes, to see just how useless it was to try to get anyone in city government to listen to you. Especially Robert Moses.[11]

The Villagers, being an independent bunch, thought of a way to bypass the bureaucrats. Raymond Rubinow, a friend of Jacobs who worked in Greenwich Village, came up with the idea of "The Joint Emergency Committee to Close Washington Square to All but Emergency Traffic." "We were trying to collect and concentrate on this issue, the people who felt as we did on that issue. In order to dramatize this and clarify this, a name like that was necessary, not something like 'The Such-and-Such Association,' you know?" Jacobs would recall many years later in an interview with former *Voice* reporter Leticia Kent.[12] From then on, throughout the 1960s Villagers would form a committee for each specific issue as it came up.

The Washington Square roadway fight during the 1950s marked the beginning of community groups in New York City. In the Village there would be plenty more issues to take on. The easy part, of course, was forming the committee. After that, the real work began, much of it done by mothers. The roadway activists, mostly PTA and park mothers under the leadership of Shirley Hayes, would set up a table near the park and ask passersby to sign petitions against the road. Jacobs recalls that sometimes people would refuse because this was the McCarthy era, when people were afraid to sign anything. The mothers got their children involved in the roadway fight. The kids would go around putting up posters and attend rallies with their parents.

This little grassroots group made local politicians feel the heat. The Committee to Close Washington Square got Bill Passannante, their state assemblyman, who was feeling vulnerable in the face of a coming election, to support their bid to get the park closed temporarily to all but emergency traffic. This was accomplished with great fanfare on a summer day in 1958, complete with a ceremony and the press present. The following day, newspapers ran photos of three-and-a-half-year-old Mary Jacobs and another little girl in front of the Washington Square Arch, tying a ribbon across the road now closed to traffic. The road closing proved so popular that it became impossible for any politician who valued his job to let in the cars again. By summer, Washington Square had been closed permanently to all traffic.

Robert Moses, of course, was livid. When he saw during a hearing on the subject that his roadway plan was going to be derailed, he shouted, "There is nobody against this—nobody, nobody, nobody, but a bunch of, a bunch of mothers!" before storming out of the room.[13] But by that time the mothers had rallied the support of some very powerful public people, including Norman Vincent Peale, minister of the tony Marble Collegiate Church, the architectural and social critic Lewis Mumford, and Eleanor Roosevelt, herself a mother who had once lived on Washington Square.

It had been Robert Jacobs who had thought of pressuring Passannante. Robert had, Jane has said, terrific political instincts. He was, however, a quiet man, preferring to stay in the background. During the next decade, Villagers would wage many more battles to save their neighborhood. Many of the leaders in these fights would be women, and foremost among them would be Jane Jacobs. To be sure, she had leadership qualities. But she learned to play the political game from her husband, her main advisor and inspiration. He preferred to cede the limelight to his wife. "He usually stayed in the background," Jacobs later told Leticia Kent, "and I don't think people realized how important he was to all the fights in Greenwich Village."

You wonder where Jacobs found the energy to do all that she did. As she was drawn more and more into community activism, she continued to cover her city-planning beat at *Architectural Forum*. And then something happened in the middle of the roadway battle, something completely unplanned that turned into her tipping point.

CHAPTER FOUR

The Housewife with
No College Degree

In April 1956 *Architectural Forum* sent Jacobs to Harvard University to speak at a conference on urban design. At first she had refused. Jacobs suffered badly from stage fright, and hated speaking in public. But her editors insisted that she had to, as a stand-in for her boss who was on vacation.

"All right, I'll do it," Jacobs finally told Joseph Hazen, her managing editor. "But only provided I can say what I want." Hazen agreed. Jacobs wrote a ten-minute speech attacking urban renewal. She used what she had learned from William Kirk as her subject, with East Harlem's disappearing corner stores as the hook.

"It was a real ordeal for me," Jacobs would later recall about the speech. "I have no memory of giving it. I just went into some hypnosis and said this thing I had memorized." Standing at the front of a large auditorium, she told her audience that in East Harlem, 1,110 stores had already vanished in the course of rehousing 50,000 people. "Planners and architects are apt to think in an orderly way, of stores as a straightforward matter of supplies and services," Jacobs said. "But stores in city neighborhoods are much more complicated creatures. . . . Although they are mere holes in the wall, they help make an urban neighborhood a community." Jacobs

Jane Jacobs in Greenwich Village, 1962. *The Milwaukee Journal,* 1962.

pointed out that these spaces house not only businesses but institutions like churches and political clubs, all of which spring up naturally and constitute a community's lifeblood. When entire neighborhoods are leveled in the name of urban renewal, these vital places are destroyed as well. Nor, Jacobs said, could they be replicated in the rebuilding process because "the physical provisions for this kind of process cannot conceivably be formalized."[1]

Jacobs's speech, deceptively simple, contained complex ideas basic to her thinking, ideas that she would continue to develop throughout her life. How people use space, she was arguing, whether it is a sidewalk or a hole-in-the-wall store or a vestibule with mailboxes, cannot be dictated from above, whether by planners or architects or city bureaucracies. Her underlying assumption is that individual freedom is life's natural state. In the end, her thinking implies, no higher power can stop people from doing as they will.

"The essence of these enterprises," Jacobs said at the end of her speech, referring to East Harlem's rapidly disappearing small businesses, "is that they have a place indisputably their own. Unless and until some solution for them can be found, the least we can do is to respect—in the deepest sense—strips of chaos that have a weird wisdom of their own not yet encompassed in our concept of urban order." The spaces in the new housing specifically set aside for socializing, Jacobs said, did not work. Few people came to visit their friends in projects. But the project dwellers, in contrast, often went back to whatever was left of their old neighborhoods. "Absolutely the only place that shows signs of working as an adult social area was the laundry. We wonder if the planner of that project had any idea its heart would be in the basement. And we wonder if the architect had any idea what he was designing when he did that laundry."

When Jacobs finished speaking, she sat down to the sound of loud applause. "I had hypnotized myself but I had apparently hypnotized them, too," she would later recall, adding that her speech "was a big hit because nobody had heard anybody saying these things before, apparently."[2] Among those in the audience was the social philosopher Lewis Mumford, the architectural critic of the *New Yorker* magazine and one of the most influential thinkers of his time. Mumford was a real Renaissance man, the author of numerous articles and books on subjects that ran across the spectrum of humane letters. But his main interest was cities; he was considered *the* expert on the subject. He had been a professor at the University of Pennsylvania and was now at MIT, where he held an endowed chair. Mumford looked the part of the public intellectual, tall and nattily dressed, with the voice and mannerisms of a gentleman. One adjective frequently used to describe him was "Olympian"; another was "pompous." Mumford, by then in his mid-sixties, was impressed by the forty-year-old Jacobs. He, too, disliked the "tower-in-the-park" design, whether for public housing or middle-class developments like New York City's Stuyvesant Town. He had often stated as such in "Sky Line," his *New Yorker* column.

Now, listening to her, he must have felt gratified; this young woman, it seemed, adhered to many of his ideas. After her speech, he greeted Jacobs warmly, shaking her hand, telling her how impressed he was with her thinking. *Architectural Forum* printed the speech later that year, a two-page spread complete with photos of an East Harlem housing project. The story elicited a flood of letters in response, praising the author for stating something so obvious that so badly needed saying.

As luck would have it, another important person was sitting in the audience at Harvard the day that Jacobs made her speech. He was William Hollingsworth Whyte Jr. "Holly" to his friends, Whyte was a tall, wiry man with a gentle personality, and a senior editor at *Fortune* magazine, another Henry Luce publication. Whyte had written a series of articles about corporate America for *Fortune* that were soon to be published as what would be his landmark book, *The Organization Man*. This highly original work, which sold over two million copies, described in Whyte's characteristic crackling-good prose the stultifying conformism required in the 1950s' corporate environment. Whyte emphasized that this represented a dramatic change in American thinking. Previously, he wrote, Americans had above all cherished their individualism, as embodied in the old "Protestant Ethic." This ideal, Whyte said, comprised "the thought that pursuit of individual salvation through hard work, thrift, and competitive struggle is the heart of the American achievement." Tocqueville, Whyte said, had noticed how tenaciously Americans held on to their independence, and how suspicious they were of authority.

"Fight the organization," Whyte wrote in his book. "But not self-destructively." He added, "I write with the optimistic premise that individualism is as possible in our times as in others. I speak of individualism within organizational life." Whyte himself started out as an "organization man," the son of a railroad company executive in Philadelphia's Main Line. After graduating cum laude from Princeton, he completed an executive training program at the Vicks Chemical Company just prior to World War II. He then served in the intelligence division of the Marine Corps. But he ended up shunning the business world, instead joining the staff of *Fortune* in 1946, where he developed his talents as a writer and reporter. After writing *The Organization Man,* he would devote much of his life to helping preserve open land that was rapidly getting eaten up by low-density suburbs. He also spent years studying and writing about urban space.

When Whyte heard Jacobs's speech, he felt a meeting of minds. No wonder. So many of their ideas converged, or ran parallel to each other's. Both were deep and independent thinkers who questioned basic assumptions and trusted their own instincts. They both studied human behavior by walking around and looking about, then carefully recording what they had seen. Coincidentally, Whyte's studies of the social life of the city had begun, like Jacobs's, in East Harlem, which bordered on his own street, East 94th, where he lived with his family.

What Whyte and Jacobs were seeing happening to cities—the encroachment of the automobile and the spread of suburbs, both encouraged by the 1949 Federal Housing Act and the 1956 Federal Highway Act—worried them. Yet at the same time, both felt optimistic about the future.

And both loved cities, passionately and unconditionally.

Whyte introduced Jacobs to his colleagues at *Fortune.* He invited her to write a story about downtowns for the magazine's series of articles on cities that would begin the following year, 1957. Jacobs declined. She wasn't, she said, qualified. "I couldn't write two hundred words on the subject," she told Whyte.[3] Whyte's colleagues didn't think Jacobs was qualified, either. After all, who was this woman, the mother of three small children—a "housewife," as people said in those days, with no college degree? She lived in the Village and rode to work on a bicycle. All in all, the *Fortune* staff found Jacobs, Whyte dryly recalled, "a most inappropriate choice." In the face of such universal resistance, Whyte backed down and assigned the story to somebody else.

But Jacobs ended up writing it anyway. The editor to whom Whyte had subsequently given the story couldn't do it after all. And in the Jacobs chain of events, which included, in chronological order, her move to New York, her husband Robert's subscription to *Architectural Forum,* and Whyte's attendance at her Harvard talk, that editor's illness led to Jane Jacobs's tipping point. When Whyte circulated Jacobs's first draft of her *Fortune* story to his colleagues, they were beside themselves.

"Downtown Is for People" attacked the redevelopment plans then in the works for downtowns all over the country. These were big plans, and, as happened with the building of public housing projects, involved the large-scale razing of individual streets. From the rubble would arise "superblocks," enormous buildings placed in paved plazas. "Almost without exception," Jacobs wrote, "the projects have one standard solution for every need: commerce, medicine, culture, government—whatever the activity, they take a part of the city's life, abstract it from the hustle and bustle of downtown, and set it, like a self-sufficient island, in majestic isolation." Jacobs argued that these new centers would not revitalize downtowns, but instead deaden them. The end result, she said, would be to banish the street, the very life force of the city.

In the article Jacobs specifically, albeit politely, criticized the plans for Lincoln Center, another Title I Moses project, which would replace eighteen blocks of what *Architectural Forum* called "squalid west-side slum territory" with what would be the most expensive cultural complex in the world. The project was backed by John D. Rockefeller III to the tune of $75 million.[4] That same year Jacobs would be far more caustic in her attack on Lincoln Center in a speech at the New School for Social Research, calling it "a piece of built-in rigor mortis."[5]

"You've got to get out and walk," Jacobs wrote in the *Fortune* article. "Walk, and you will see that many of the assumptions on which the projects depend are visibly wrong." "Downtown Is for People" did not sit well with C. D. Jackson, *Fortune*'s publisher. When Jackson saw the draft, he was on a congressional train going from New York to Washington, DC. He was so incensed that he couldn't wait to get to Washington to speak with Whyte. Instead, he immediately put in a call to him from the train, which was something you did in those times long before cell phones only for really urgent reasons. "Who is this crazy dame?" he shouted. "How could we give aid and comfort to critics of Lincoln Center?" Whyte tried to reassure his boss. Then he arranged for Jacobs and Jackson, along with some *Fortune* editors, to meet. The two of them, according to Whyte, went at each others' throats. In the end, Jacobs's story ran in the April 1958 issue of *Fortune.*

The response was immediate. Letters to the editor poured in, filled with praise for Jacobs's story. *Fortune*'s letters editor sent around a memo about the good news to the staff at *Architectural Forum.* Whyte had scrawled across the top: "Look what your girl did for us! This is one of the best responses we've ever had!"[6]

The entire *Fortune* series was soon published in book form, titled *The Exploding Metropolis.* A few months after her article ran in *Fortune,* Jacobs received a phone call from the Rockefeller Foundation. They were offering her a grant to expand the ideas from "Downtown" into a book, which she accepted. The news that this feisty young woman with no academic degrees had received such a prestigious grant traveled fast. At Harvard, where she had given the speech in 1956 that had changed her life, a professor named Martin Meier along with another colleague from MIT invited her for lunch with the aim of convincing her to join an institute that they were forming on urban studies. They also had a suggestion for her as to how to write her book: go around to middle-income housing projects with a questionnaire to find out what residents liked and didn't like about their living situation. In that way, they suggested, she could collect the necessary data for her book on cities. Jacobs thanked them and made a hasty exit. She did not for one second consider the job offer she received from two top-notch academics that many an urban-studies professional would have been ecstatic to have. For Jacobs, the proposal amounted to "junk." Neither of the two men, one from Harvard, the other from MIT, had the slightest interest in how cities really worked, she later said.[7]

In a letter to the Rockefeller Foundation that she wrote in July 1958, Jacobs spelled out her ideas for her book.[8] There were currently two popular images of the city—one of a diseased clump of crumbling buildings, and the other "the rebuilt city," consisting of a sparkling, orderly arrangement of parks and buildings. Neither image, she said, was true. But both were so pervasive that they blinded people from seeing what was right in front of them. Her book, she wrote, would correct this error. She would create an accurate image of the city for the reader by walking them through the streets and showing them what was happening on the ground, just as William Kirk had done for her. Thereby people would learn to trust their own eyes, just as she did. And they would discover that the city, for all its seeming messiness, was held together by an underlying order that revealed itself in a network of relationships that was as basic to a city as oxygen to a living being.

Describing her thesis was one thing. The toughest part, Jacobs wrote in her letter, would be finding the best way to present it. In other words, how to tell the story. How to take enormously complex ideas and break them down into words that people would want to read and connect to, so that they would change all the misconceptions that they had up to now about cities. All, of course, without oversimplifying. There was always the danger that people would think they understood what she meant, but they really didn't. She had had this experience after the Harvard speech when "planning people began talking excitedly about 'the corner grocery store.' But all they got out of it was, 'put in a corner grocery store.' That was not at all what I was saying."[9]

She had an idea about how she was going to accomplish her goal. She would use the physical world. She would lead her readers through various aspects of the city and show them how to look at the streets, the parks, the stores. She would teach them how to do something that was so obvious, yet was eluding them: to trust their own eyes. People would then discover the truth about cities.

Later that same summer, Jacobs had lunch with Jason Epstein, a brilliant and ambitious young editor at Random House.[10] Epstein, originally from Boston, had graduated from Columbia in 1949.

Now in his late twenties, he was already one of the most influential editors in the New York publishing world. In 1962 Epstein, along with his then-wife Barbara, Robert Silvers, and the poets Robert Lowell and Elizabeth Hartwick, would found the prestigious *New York Review of Books.* Epstein was interested in doing a book with Jacobs. Probably he was not only intrigued by her ideas, but believed that for Random House to publish something about cities would be a wise business decision. The subject was definitely in the air; newspapers and magazines were reporting regularly on the "urban crisis."

At his lunch with Jacobs, Epstein told her that she could have a contract for her proposed book, which at that time existed only as an idea that she was batting around in her mind. Random House was without a doubt the preeminent American publisher of that time. In the 1930s it had published William Faulkner, Eudora Welty, and James Joyce's *Ulysses,* which had been banned in the United States. Now the editors were taking chances on young writers like James Michener, Philip Roth, and William Styron. That Random House was now offering to publish Jacobs's first book was a huge coup, and she accepted Epstein's offer. She received a fifteen-hundred-dollar advance, an average amount for the time.

The following fall, Jacobs took a leave from her job at *Architectural Forum* and began her book, *The Death and Life of Great American Cities.*

Jason Epstein had first heard of Jane Jacobs through his colleague, the writer and sociologist Nathan Glazer. Glazer would later leave the publishing field for academia, first the University of California at Berkeley and later Harvard, where he is now professor emeritus. Glazer belonged to the elite de facto club known as the New York intellectuals, which were helping shape American thinking in all kinds of ways. The intellectuals had their beginnings at City College in the 1930s, where Glazer and other later-to-be-luminaries such as Alfred Kazin, Irving Howe, Daniel Bell, and Irving Kristol set up the New York Jewish version of a Platonic academy, talking and arguing over literature and, above all, politics. Later they would write about their own and one another's ideas in books and in various journals like *Partisan Review, Commentary, The Nation,* and *The New Republic.*

Glazer, who was on the founding editorial staff of *Commentary,* had first met Epstein in 1952 when Epstein approached David Riesman with the idea of reprinting the 1950 book *The Lonely Crowd,* which Glazer had co-authored with Riesman, for Anchor Books. Epstein had just founded Anchor as America's first serious paperback imprint. Epstein's great ambition was to have the equivalent of England's Penguin, and his venture was wildly successful. Epstein would leave Anchor in 1958, to be immediately snatched up by Bennett Cerf at Random House.[11]

After Glazer edited *The Lonely Crowd* for Anchor—the book became a best-seller—Epstein put him in charge of the imprint's second book list. Glazer began looking for books to publish. One of his finds was *The Exploding Metropolis,* the collection of *Fortune* articles that included Jacobs's "Downtown Is for People." In this way, Glazer was introduced to Jacobs. Glazer, who would go on to become one of America's leading thinkers in the area of social policy, at that time was thinking and writing mostly about cities. He was interested in the issues surrounding urban design. He had grown up in East Harlem, and, like Jacobs, was fascinated with cities. After he and Jacobs met, he contributed an article, "Why City Planning Is Obsolete," to *Architectural Forum* in July of 1958, which she edited.

Glazer contended that planning as it was being practiced was a complete failure because it applied to suburbs, not cities. Glazer was referring to the Garden City movement that Ebenezer Howard began in late nineteenth-century England, which advocated decentralization—that is, reducing cities by building smaller, self-contained communities surrounded by green belts, open areas, and farms. One of the movement's most fervent adherents was Lewis Mumford. Glazer also criticized the idea that "the city could be improved by replacing its chaos and confusion with a single plan." Planners, he wrote, mistakenly see cities' liveliness as "disorder." He talked about the richness of a city center. He also discussed how planners confused a city's size with density. Cities, he said, need density. Reducing population density only increases sprawl. The problem is size; because of the Industrial Revolution, cities became so big that they could "no longer combine great density with access to country, as great cities of the past had done." Jacobs would acknowledge Glazer in her book, and expand on his ideas.

Glazer, William H. Whyte Jr., and Jason Epstein: these three highly influential thinkers, all men, recognized Jacobs's genius, and championed her. Whyte had served as a mentor, taking her under his wing and introducing her to people. He encouraged her to trust her own voice. According to Jacobs, he boosted her confidence, helping her to come out and express herself more publicly in the written word.[12] Through Glazer, who worked with her, Jacobs met Epstein, who would remain Jacobs's editor and close friend for forty-plus years.

By publishing her and talking her up to their colleagues, the three men helped make it possible for the plain-talking woman with the straight gray bangs and black horn-rimmed glasses from Scranton, Pennsylvania—"a Greenwich Village housewife," as the newspapers called her—to become one of the most original thinkers of her day.

CHAPTER FIVE

The Death and Life
of Great American Cities

Jacobs began banging out her book in the fall of 1958. She finished it in January 1961. As she worked, she constantly tested what she was writing against what she was seeing on the streets. She visited St. Louis, where she saw the new, much-lauded Pruitt-Igoe project that was based on Le Corbusier's vision. It was already turning into a miasma of crime and vandalism. She went to Boston, "a lovely old city beneath the tinsel, neon and dirt of the contemporary American mess that time and neglect has made of it," as described by *New York Times* reporter Tom Wicker.[1]

There, sociologist Herbert Gans, an expert on urban housing and poverty, showed her around the North and West ends, both tight-knit Italian working-class neighborhoods. The latter area was in the midst of being wrecked in the name of urban renewal. The North End was still untouched, but the buzz was that soon it, too, was going the way of the West End. Gans, who lived in the West End, had been hired by Massachusetts General Hospital to do a study of his neighborhood. Published as a book in 1962, *The Urban Villagers* was a poignant description of how urban renewal had destroyed a vibrant neighborhood.

And she carefully observed what was going on outside her house at 555 Hudson Street. She was drawn there naturally because her

Advertisement for *The Death and Life of Great American Cities*. Used with permission of Random House.

children were young, attending the local public school and playing on the sidewalks. *Death and Life* was about all cities, but most of all, it was about New York. "To New York City," Jacobs wrote in the dedication, "where I came to seek my fortune, and found it by finding Bob, Jimmy, Ned and Mary, for whom this book is written too." Most of the examples she used to illustrate the ideas she set forth came from New York. "Because that," she tells the reader, "is where I live." But she first noticed or learned about most of those ideas in other cities. Then she tested those ideas, going from one city to another. She ended up at her doorstep on Hudson Street. She acknowledges that New York was where she began thinking about "the intricate social and economic order under the seeming disorder of cites," the basic idea of her book. This idea did not originate with her, Jacobs says in the introduction, but with William Kirk, the self-effacing head of the Union Settlement who for years had tried in vain to get New York City bureaucrats to listen to his arguments against urban renewal. But now Kirk had an advocate, Jane Jacobs, whom he had met by chance, and who was now making his case in her book so eloquently that people would begin thinking differently about cities.

Random House aggressively marketed Jacobs's "explosive new book," which is how they referred to *Death and Life* in a half-page ad that appeared in the *New York Times Book Review.* Leading magazines—*Harper's, Saturday Evening Post,* and *Vogue*—ran excerpts from *Death and Life* in the months preceding the book's publication in November 1961, deliberately timed for the Christmas "recommended reading" lists. Afterward, Jacobs further promoted her book on a speaking tour.

"This book is an attack on current city planning and rebuilding." With this now-famous sentence Jacobs begins *Death and Life,* from there lunging right into her take-no-prisoners prose. She traces the thinking that preceded urban renewal doctrine, beginning in the nineteenth century with the British planner Ebenezer Howard and his Garden City movement. Lewis Mumford, Jacobs continues, was one of Howard's most fervent admirers. Like Howard, Mumford believed that cities, swelling to ever bigger and unmanageable sizes ever since the Industrial Revolution, now were in full-blown crisis. Things could simply not go like this unchallenged. Cities, Mumford believed, had grown into huge, all-devouring monsters, the "megalopolis." In the 1920s a group of planners and architects that included Mumford founded the Regional Planning Association of America (RPAA), an informal movement that advocated decentralizing cities by creating new, smaller "regional cities" in the surrounding countryside.[2]

Mumford outlined much of his thought in his 1938 book *The Culture of Cities,* a long, detailed combination history-and-manifesto on cities beginning in medieval times and ending in the present. "If the destructive forces in civilization gain ascendancy, our new urban culture will be stricken in every part," Mumford wrote. "Our cities, blasted and deserted, will be cemeteries for the dead: cold lairs given over to less destructive beasts than man." Mumford proposed a theory of cities, which he based on the teachings of his mentor, the Scottish biologist Patrick Geddes. Cities, he wrote, go through six stages, starting with the village, then proceeding to an Athenian-type golden age. From there they grow into a megalopolis, at which point decline begins—case in point, New York, with its congestion and blight—before everything finally collapses into the final ghastly "necropolis" stage, when "war and famine and disease rack both city and countryside." The critics loved *The Culture of Cities*, with its neat categorizations and long lists. The book landed him on the cover of *Time* magazine and made him famous.

Jacobs contrasts the Garden City movement and the Decentrists, as Mumford's colleague Catherine Bauer called the RPAA adherents, with Le Corbusier's utopian fantasies of gleaming skyscraper cities. The respective ideas seemed to represent opposite ends of the spectrum; indeed, Mumford, with his love of the countryside, did not like skyscrapers. But for all the apparent differences, Jacobs says, these visions had something basic in common:

> To reinforce and dramatize the necessity for the new order of things, the Decentrists hammered away at the bad old city. They were incurious about successes in great cities. They were interested only in failures. All was failure. A book like Mumford's *The Culture of Cities* was largely a morbid and biased catalog of ills. The great city was Megalopolis, Tyrannopolis, Nekropolis . . . a tyranny, a living death. It must go. New York's midtown was "solidified chaos" (Mumford). . . . How could anything so bad be worth the attempt to understand it?

In other words, Jacobs was saying, these men all hate cities.

What gall Jacobs had, to attack the preeminent thinkers on cities of her time! Not that she had ever lacked for nerve. As a child in Scranton, she had humiliated her teacher, challenging her right in front of the class. And now, just as back then, she had no fear of authority. Just as then, her razor-sharp words and perceptions were right on target. Garden cities, located in the countryside at a safe distance from real cities, and Le Corbusier's skyscrapers set in parks, far away from the noisy streets: both visions expressed a fear of cities. Now Jacobs would allay that fear.

Just as she had promised to her sponsors at the Rockefeller Foundation, in *Death and Life* Jacobs takes readers by the hand, just as her friend Kirk had done for her, and leads them through the city to show them just what she means. Writing in the first person, we feel right there with her. And it is clear that we are in the company of somebody who loves cities. She teaches us how to do something so obvious yet so difficult: to trust what we see instead of believing what experts tell us we must believe. From there, she tells us, you must form your own conclusions. "I hope any reader of this book will constantly and skeptically test what I have to say against his own knowledge of cities and their behavior," she cautions. "If I have been inaccurate in observations or mistaken in inferences and conclusions, I hope these faults will be quickly corrected."

Her basic premise is that cities are, in her words, "thoroughly physical places. In seeking understanding of their behavior, we get useful information by observing what occurs tangibly and physically, instead of sailing off on metaphysical fancies." Jacobs turns the reader's attention to the street. She tells us that people are always demonizing the street, as if it were the root of all that is wrong with a city. They say that children shouldn't play there, or on the sidewalks; that both are dirty and dangerous. But in fact streets and sidewalks make the best playgrounds. In this excerpt from a famous and oft-quoted passage in *Death and Life,* Jacobs takes the reader to her little stretch of sidewalk in front of her Greenwich Village home:

> The stretch of Hudson Street where I live is each day the scene of an intricate sidewalk ballet. I make my own first entrance into it a little after eight when I put out the garbage can, surely a prosaic occupation, but I enjoy my part, my little clang, as the droves of junior high school students walk by the center of the stage dropping candy wrappers. . . . When I get home after work, the ballet is reaching its crescendo. This is the time

of roller skates and stilts and tricycles, and games in the lee of the stoop with bottle tops and plastic cowboys . . . this is the time when teen-agers, all dressed up, are pausing to ask if their slips show or their collars look right . . . this is the time when anybody you know around Hudson Street will go by.

Nothing, Jacobs shows us, is safer than a city street that everybody uses. Jacobs describes such a street: it should not be too long, and needs a mixture of workplaces and residences, which assures that there are always people around because it is their presence that keeps the street safe. Jacobs calls this phenomenon "the eyes on the street," one of several phrases she coins in *Death and Life* that would afterward enter our lexicon. At the time when Jacobs was writing, crime, and the fear of it, pervaded New York. Move to the suburbs, people were saying, to escape the dangers of the city. In the suburbs your children will be safe.

And here is Jane Jacobs the mother, pooh-poohing this popular assumption, writing that her children use the city sidewalks for play, and with her hearty approval. Her younger son, she tells us, takes her by the hand and shows her a tiny space between two buildings where he squirrels away "treasures" he selects from garbage pickups that people have left on the curb. A successful city street, where people sit on the stoop and busybodies hang out the windows, checking out what their neighbors are doing—like the East Harlem blocks that were wrecked in the name of urban renewal—provides children with a secure environment. A neighborhood's security, she writes, cannot be imposed by outside forces.

But the design of huge housing projects that rise up from the ruins of urban renewal, set in mega blocks and surrounded with patches of grass that sit empty and despised by residents, deprives children of the street that is essential to their safety. Without streets there is no place for them to play. The playgrounds in public projects, supposedly the healthy substitute for the supposedly evil streets, do not work as play areas. Instead they threaten, turning into havens for gangs and places where mothers warn their children not to go. Low-income housing projects, Jacobs writes, have

"become worse centers of delinquency, vandalism and general social hopelessness than the slums they were supposed to replace."

She wasn't the first, or the only one, criticizing housing projects.
Lewis Mumford, who early on was one of Robert Moses's most
persistent critics, was questioning the design of public housing as
early as 1950 in his "Sky Line" column in the *New Yorker.* That same
year, the Citizens Housing and Planning Council, a powerful New
York group that lobbied hard for public housing, was warning that
East Harlem's new projects were re-creating a racial ghetto-within-
a-ghetto.[3] In the spring of 1958, as Jacobs was thinking about her
book proposal, Harrison Salisbury of the *New York Times* published
a long article documenting the "corrupt and rotten environment"
of a Brooklyn housing project, "a twenty million dollar slum."

Mumford, though, did not unconditionally condemn public
housing design. His *New Yorker* "Sky Line" column of May 5, 1950,
illustrates his ambivalence. First he says that high-rise projects represent some progress compared to the "dark, congested, insanitary,
rat-infested Manhattan slums they have replaced." But in some
ways, he then says, "it has gone backward." He faults the monotony
and grimness of the buildings and their design, with small windows
and large red bricks. They represent "the inflexible carrying out of a
system that has no regard for the site or the needs of its inhabitants."
He also faults the social segregation and the lack of facilities such as
movies, synagogues, or churches. "There is no architectural substitute for the variety, stir, and color of a real neighborhood," he writes.
And then he abruptly flip-flops, praising the empty superblock—it is
"not only economical . . . but provides pools of quiet in metropolitan areas. The people who live in the housing projects probably sleep
better than the inhabitants of most parts of the city."

Jacobs, though, knew exactly how she felt about housing projects,
and cities, too. Mumford, she would later claim publicly, did not.[4]
Mumford hadn't lived in the city since 1936, when he'd moved permanently with his family to his country home in upstate New York.
He rarely even came into the city anymore. "He no longer felt com-

fortable in crowded, crime-ridden New York, a city that in his youth had for him, as for the young F. Scott Fitzgerald, 'all the iridescence of the beginning of the world,'" writes Mumford's biographer Donald L. Miller.[5] Jacobs recalled once driving with Mumford in a car into Manhattan. The closer they got to the city, the more irritable he became. But Mumford—who had been born in and grew up in Manhattan, and spent his childhood walking the streets, observing the city—still saw himself as the quintessential urbanite.

Mumford's ambivalence about cities, a subject he had been studying all his life, came through in his books. His prose style was heavy-handed and academic. ("The city's active role in the future is to bring to the highest pitch of development the variety and individuality of regions, cultures, personalities," he wrote in his 1961 book *The City in History.*) In contrast, Jacobs's prose reads like a fresh breeze. She not only knew completely what she felt about cities, but instinctively knew how to say how she felt. Her prose has clarity, one of the virtues of eloquence. Through its simplicity, her language clearly gets across complicated ideas. You can reread her book over and over again; each time, another layer of thought will emerge.

The underlying theme of *Death and Life,* just as Jacobs had envisioned in her original proposal, is that the city is a complex organism that makes itself up as it goes along—that is, by its very nature it is messy. A city, she states flatly, cannot be a work of art. In other words, she implies, you cannot just stick a civic center or a housing project in a neighborhood and expect it to put down roots and grow, just like that—any more than you can plant a date palm in a northern climate. Cities are delicate, teeming ecosystems. You cannot, Jacobs says, impose a grand plan on the city, as planners keep trying to do. The city will refuse to bend to their will, and will stubbornly rebel and do what it wants to do, like Boston's North End, which despite being slated for destruction simply refused to roll over and die; instead, its streets were looking better and better. Or Jacobs's own neighborhood, Greenwich Village. Both places were constant irritants to city officials because they did as they liked.

Forcing plans upon a city flies in the face how cities behave: for all their chaotic appearance, she writes, a certain order reigns beneath the city's surface, "a marvelous order for maintaining the safety of the streets and the freedom of the city." And you can actually see that order in a daily dance that people perform on city sidewalks.

Jacobs poses questions such as: What makes for a successful park? What is a slum? How do you define the concept of a neighborhood? What makes a neighborhood stable? She carefully ponders these queries in a way reminiscent of ancient philosophers, often flipping her responses around to sometimes reveal a wholly different angle on the original question. This is precisely the genius of her book: she shows us a different way of asking. Often she can offer us no clear answers; it is enough to have simply asked the question. "The key link in a perpetual slum is that too many people move out of it too fast—and in the meantime dream of moving out," she writes. But the link, she assures us, can be broken, as happened in Greenwich Village, "the unslummed former slum in which I live." "A successful city neighborhood," she writes, "is a place that keeps sufficiently abreast of its problems so it is not destroyed by them." A factor in neighborhood stability is time; another is networks between people, "a city's irreplaceable social capital." A successful neighborhood must have "mixed primary uses."

In other words, businesses and residences should exist side by side—an idea that at the time amounted to heresy. Separating the two, then-current thinking went, was a matter of both health and aesthetics. This was the principle behind zoning, which was a key factor in New York's mind-set. In fact, the city had passed the first zoning code in the nation in 1916, which it had been updating since World War II. The new code would finally be implemented in 1961, the same year that *Death and Life* came out. It encouraged mega blocks and tower-in-the-park structures—the antithesis of diversity.[6]

"Social capital," "mixed primary uses," "eyes on the street": from Jacobs's book these terms would enter our lexicon and remain there, enriching the dialogue people were having about cities. The expressions represent ideas that today seem so obvious, and they badly needed to be expressed. She keeps returning to the subject of time as a function of the city. The ethos of the times was modernism, which demanded that the old must be torn down in the name of progress. But no, Jacobs writes, in contrast to current practice neighborhoods need old buildings in order to generate a city's economic growth.

The subject of time leads her back to diversity, another word that she was now interjecting into public dialogue. Diversity, she says, is one of the chief characteristics of any city, a point that Jacobs illustrates with a banal yet insightful image: "Classified telephone directories tell us the greatest single fact about cities: the immense numbers of parts that make up a city, and the immense diversity of those parts. Diversity is natural to big cities." Cities by nature incubate diversity and new enterprises because "of the various efficient economic pools of use that they form." Urban renewal, she says, kills economic diversity.

Diversity, moreover, is connected to time. The two entities, both tremendously complex and delicate, nourish each other. Neither diversity nor time can be artificially imposed on a city. She was furious when, after her 1956 Harvard speech about East Harlem, people started sticking a corner grocery store into their public project plans, what she calls in *Death and Life* "a thin, patronizing conception of city diversity." Time and diversity in a city must happen organically. And both are essential for a city's health.

Jacobs gives us a breathtakingly prescient and concrete example of her thesis: Lower Manhattan. She was writing at a time when Lower Manhattan, ever a challenge for New York City to solve, consisted mostly of urban rot surrounding the tall buildings of Wall Street. Small businesses could not make a go of it down there, and were leaving. After the chaotic exodus of the district's hundreds of thousands of workers each weekday, the entire area felt as dead as the inside of a mausoleum. Jacobs posed the question, what can be done to pump life into this neighborhood? Certainly not the vague plans that the Downtown-Lower Manhattan Association, in conjunction with David Rockefeller, was touting: "business centers including offices, banks, telephone and telegraph buildings," along with space to park all kinds of vehicles, not only cars but trucks and helicopters.[7] In other words, what would become the World Trade Center. The plans included a highway, one of Robert Moses's longtime dreams, that would stretch from east to west. The association's grand plans, Jacobs wrote, fail utterly to utilize what is special about Lower Manhattan. "It is the character of lower Manhattan to be intensive, to be exciting, to be dramatic, and this is one of its greatest assets."

"What is more dramatic, even romantic, than the tumbled towers of lower Manhattan, rising suddenly to the clouds like a magic castle girdled by water? Its very touch of jumbled jaggedness, its towering-sided canyons, are its magnificence. What vandalism it would represent . . . to dilute this magnificent city presence with the humdrum and the regimented!" Which is precisely what the present plans would do. They say "in the plainest terms . . . 'Go away! Leave me alone!'" Why, she asked, does Lower Manhattan turn its back on the waterfront? More leisure-time activities would encourage diversity. The area should be developed into "a great marine museum . . . an embarkation point for pleasure voyages in the harbor and around the island; these embarkation points should be as glamorous and salty as art can make them. If new sea-food restaurants and much else would not start up nearby, I will eat my lobster shell."

The 110-story World Trade Center project was unveiled in the mid-1960s. Jacobs publicly opposed it, as did Mumford and other well-known figures. The project was designed by Minoru Yamasaki, a faithful disciple of Le Corbusier and the same architect who had done the Pruitt-Igoe project in St. Louis. When the Twin Towers were completed in 1973, the timing couldn't have been worse. The United States was about to fall into a deep economic recession. New York City would be hit hard, and vacant office space would abound. Throughout the 1970s and 1980s Lower Manhattan remained a depressing place. But by the late 1980s, the area began to come alive. As if in reaction to the overwhelming presence of the steely Towers, the culmination of modernism, the old way of thinking, the South Street Seaport, with its historic old buildings restored, opened. At this time Battery Park City was built, along with its neighboring waterfront park, on top of landfill from the Trade Center dredging. Finally, with office space now at a premium, the Towers, after years of vacancies, filled up. People began to take them for granted. Then they embraced them. The Twin Towers became an integral part of New York City's skyline and its identity. When they were destroyed in the 9/11 attack, the city lost a part of itself.

Still, Jacobs's belief that building the ill-fated Trade Center by itself could not revitalize Lower Manhattan had been correct. And her instincts about Lower Manhattan's waterfront were right on target. Seeing the rotting piers next to the old Fulton Fish Market, she envisioned the bustling South Street Seaport with its museums and shops and, yes, seafood restaurants, now one of New York City's major tourist attractions, twenty-two years before it opened.

In *Death and Life* Jacobs unflinchingly tackles just about every aspect of then-current urban planning practices. Beware of "cataclysmic money," she warns us, at a time when federal money was pouring into city coffers. Such influxes "behave not like irrigation systems, bringing life-giving streams to feed steady, continual growth. Instead, they behave like manifestations of malevolent climates beyond the control of man—affording either searing droughts or torrential, eroding floods." She overturns longtime assumptions about high dwelling densities in cities, something policy makers were forever condemning. "The congestion of New York City's population in East Side and Harlem tenements . . . represents a density of urban population over large areas unequalled in any other American city," reads a 1944 study undertaken by New York City as part of the effort to rewrite the zoning code. The report recommends "spreading population more evenly throughout the city," because "the density of population in New York seriously affects the welfare and future development of the city . . . it is obvious that existing and proposed densities of central areas are too high." A possible solution is recommended: "More rigid zoning restrictions . . . that will prevent the over-intensive development of any large section of the city."[8]

But no, Jacobs writes, in fact just the opposite is true: high dwelling densities are a sign of a district's health. Just look around you, she says. The dwelling densities in Brooklyn Heights are twice those of the borough's slum neighborhoods. Boston's lively North End has nine times the dwelling densities as, say, Roxbury. The problem is that people confuse high densities with overcrowding. "High densities mean large numbers of dwellings per acre of land. Overcrowding means too many people in a dwelling for the number of rooms it contains."

Likewise the experts don't understand how highways affect cities. They assume that highways through and around the perimeters of cities relieve street congestion. That was the argument that Robert Moses always used to justify his massive highway projects. But, Jacobs contends, just the opposite is true. Highways, obviously, bring in more cars. They therefore increase congestion. All you have to do is look around—for example, right in Jacobs's own neighborhood. Villagers had recently defeated Moses's Washington Square high-speed roadway project, even closing the park completely to traffic. Moses, furious, told the Villagers that they would soon regret their intransigence. He predicted that traffic around the Square would now become so horrendous that they would come back to him, chastened, and tell him that they had changed their collective minds, that he should, please, build his highway through the park.

But the increased traffic never materialized. In fact, the doormen at the buildings around the Square reported that if anything, they were seeing fewer cars on the streets than before the road through the park was closed. And here's the reason, Jacobs wrote: with cars now banned completely from Washington Square, there is nowhere for them to go. Certainly not to the perimeter streets, which "narrow, beset with many lights, cluttered with parked cars, whimsically used by jaywalkers, replete with hard-to-negotiate corners, were already a most aggravating and slow route for automobiles." Closing the road, then, besides making the park safer and more attractive to the people who used it, had also, unintentionally, helped to eliminate traffic from streets. A much simpler and cheaper solution for unclogging New York's streets than Moses's roadway, which doubtless and ironically would have increased the traffic problem.

"Attrition of automobiles," Jacobs writes, "operates by making conditions *less* convenient for cars." She was stating something perfectly obvious yet elusive, and in the process overturning a widely accepted belief. Anybody with eyes and ears could see that what Jacobs was saying was true. All a person had to do was walk around the city and notice where the traffic buildups occurred: near the entrance to the Midtown Tunnel, or the FDR Drive on Manhattan's East Side, or the Henry Hudson Parkway on the West Side.

There were so many misconceptions that Americans had about cities that Jacobs was now setting forth to right. Americans do not, she states emphatically, hate cities, despite widespread belief to the contrary. And it is true that a hatred for cities seemed to run deep through the American psyche. Thomas Jefferson suggested that the state of Virginia send its raw materials overseas to Europe for manufacturing in cities there, rather than build cities here, which would only mar the pristine American landscape. "Those who labour in the earth are the chosen people of God," Jefferson wrote in his *Notes on the State of Virginia*. "The mobs of great cities add just so much to the support of pure government, as sores do to the strength of the human body."[9]

New York City disgusted Henry James. Frank Lloyd Wright, whose architecture idealized the prairie, saw cities as a cancer to be excised, to be replaced with "a continuous union of town and country."[10] Even Louis Sullivan, one of the creators of the modern skyscraper, the most urban of architectural forms, thought that cities were morally depraved. "Its many crooked streets, its filthy streets, lined with stupid houses crowded together shoulder-to-shoulder, like selfish hogs upon these trough-like lanes . . . the crowds of people, and wagons, hurrying here and there so aimlessly . . . aroused amazement, nausea, and dismay," Sullivan wrote about Boston in the 1860s.[11]

You could understand urban renewal practice, which was wiping out streets and putting up bleak high-rise projects, as the ultimate expression of Americans' hatred for the city. But no, Jacobs was now saying, it's the other way around. It's not the cities *per se* that people hate, *but what is now happening to them.* "I think it is probable that Americans hate city failure, but, from the evidence, we certainly do not hate successful and vital city areas," she writes in *Death and Life.* The evidence existed right outside her door, on lively Hudson Street in Greenwich Village. Villagers, having already learned how to organize against the combination of city bureaucracy and big money, were now digging in their heels further to save their precious neighborhood, which in the coming years would be constantly threatened by a combination of Robert Moses's plans and rising real estate values.

Death and Life never made the best-seller list, but as soon as the book came out, it hit a nerve. Everywhere, people were talking about it, in newspaper editorials and book reviews, in classrooms and boardrooms, and in public symposia. Jacobs had stated her case so forcefully that you couldn't ignore *Death and Life* even if you hated it, as, predictably, many did—especially politicians and developers, and anybody else whose interests she had attacked. Most reviewers praised it. "Her book has the brilliance of an ordinary sunny day," wrote a reviewer in England, where *Death and Life* was also published. "I wish everyone in Britain would read it."[12]

But among the accolades many had plenty of criticisms. As well they might, because Jacobs's arguments were far from airtight. Her breathtaking clarity of expression, used to articulate basic but elusive ideas, dazzled readers. But her talent did not translate into on-the-ground solutions for urban problems. Herbert Gans, who had shown her around Boston's North End, called her book "a path-breaking achievement" for its details and insights, and the forcefulness of expression. But, Gans said in his February 1962 review of *Death and Life* for *Commentary,* her analysis is much too simple. Take, for example, her demonizing of the high-rise design as the decisive factor in the pathology of poverty. Gans, who had studied urban poverty long and hard, was convinced that it was not the physical environment that caused the pathologies of poverty. The reality, he argued, was far more complex.

That was but one of his criticisms of Jacobs. Another was that her proposed alternative to large-scale urban renewal—that the government should subsidize private landlords to house needy tenants instead of building low-income housing—was unrealistic. Gans was one of many critics who would note that it was Jacobs's insights that made her book brilliant, but not her prescriptions. Also, wrote Gans, her point of view—Greenwich Village—was too limited and out of touch with how most Americans now wanted to live, in a house with a yard and a car in the driveway. Still, "the principles she has inferred from her observations can—and ought to be—adapted for use in planning cities and suburbs in the future." Because *Death and Life,* he wrote, "is so often right, I am all the more disappointed by the fact that it is also so often wrong."

"Some of her cherished reforms . . . are as romantic and 'utopian' as those she rejects," wrote Lloyd Rodwin, an MIT professor who reviewed the book for the *New York Times.*[13] He also noted her "transparent gaps and blind spots, such as her blasé misunderstandings of theory and her amiable preference for evidence congenial to her thesis." But "except to the miscellaneous victims and the academic purists, it won't matter that what this author has to say isn't always fair or right or 'scientific.' Few significant works ever are." He concluded: "A great book, like a great man, is a strategic point in the campaign of history, and part of its greatness consists in being there. For all its weakness, Jane Jacobs has written such a book. Readers will vehemently agree and disagree with the views; but few of them will go through the volume without looking at their streets and neighborhoods a little differently."

"This angry young woman attacks our contemporary conventional city planning wisdom and its obsession with cataclysmic urban renewal," wrote Wolf Von Eckardt in the June 1962 issue of *Scientific American.* "Her lengthy book is not a literary masterpiece. But it has already jolted the city planner and stands a good chance of having the same profound effect on the craft as the Garden City theory did more than sixty years ago."

The publication of *Death and Life,* Jacobs's editors at *Architectural Forum* wrote in a February 1962 editorial, "could not have come at a more opportune time," when everybody "is suddenly becoming aware of the crisis in our cities." Although her magazine did not agree with everything that she said, her editors—all men—were unabashedly proud of her. "Is it not wonderful," they wrote, "whenever long-accepted notions in *any* field are challenged, especially when that challenge is made with high intelligence and on humanistic grounds?" On the left margin of the page was a sidebar featuring interesting quotes relevant to the editorial. One came from architect Edward Durell Stone, a protégé of Frank Lloyd Wright: "Prohibition demonstrated that a few militant dames could put over anything."

Jane Jacobs had challenged long-entrenched ideas, tied to very powerful male interests through politics and money. She had also attacked an entire profession. "The pseudoscience of city planning... has not yet broken with the specious comfort of wishes, familiar superstitions, oversimplifications, and symbols, and has not yet embarked upon the adventure of probing the real world," she wrote, throwing one of her many darts at the profession. Another: "In orthodox city planning, neighborhood open spaces are venerated in an amazingly uncritical fashion, much as savages venerate magical fetishes." At the American Institute of Planning Officials meeting in Detroit in 1962, following the publication of *Death and Life,* nine hundred planners met to "well, as it turned out, to talk about Jane Jacobs's book. (Although it was not on the agenda and most hadn't read it.)," wrote the AIPO director, Dennis O'Harrow in his organization's newsletter:

Using a well-proven technique of demagogy, Mrs. Jacobs has selected the planner as the public whipping boy. . . . Mrs. Jacobs clearly knows so little about planning that she continually (or intentionally) confuses it with architecture and, especially, with public housing and site design. . . . It is also exasperating for planners to hear Mrs. Jacobs hailed as having discovered something new. Every valid criticism of urban development that she makes has been made by planners for years. If she had bothered to seek out real planners, she would have known this. . . . The Jane Jacobs book is going to do a lot of harm, throw a lot of monkey wrenches into the machinery. But we are going to have to live with it. So batten down the hatches, boys, we are in for a big blow![14]

"How have the planners reacted to the toppling of their dogma?" wrote planner Edward Chase in *Architectural Forum*'s April 1962 issue. "Rather badly, I would say. There is resort to ridicule; there is patronizing dismissal of Mrs. Jacobs as a crackpot anti-intellectual, anti-planner; and, there is . . . malicious misrepresentation of her book." Such reactions came as no surprise. Because who, after all, was this woman, this "militant dame," a rank amateur with no college degree who dared to challenge the entire planning profession, and virtually all of city officialdom besides?

Jacobs had even criticized Robert Moses in her book, a full thirteen years before the publication of Robert Caro's sensational *The Power Broker*. "Robert Moses . . . has made an art of using control of public money to get his way with those whom the voters elect and depend on to represent their frequently opposing interests," Jacobs writes in a discussion of how city districts function. What a nerve she had! Libelous, intemperate, and inaccurate, Robert Moses called *Death and Life* in an angry note he dashed off to Random House's Bennett Cerf after he received a complimentary copy from Cerf.[15]

As if her book weren't enough of a jab in the ribs of the policy makers, Jacobs was now traveling around the country giving speeches to professional groups and participating in official forums, as if she were an expert on urban affairs. Addressing the annual American Institute of Architects meeting in Dallas in 1962, she accused architects of becoming "more and more infatuated with pretentious and windy abstractions."[16]

Editors all over New York, from different sides of the political spectrum, were sending her letters. *Esquire,* the *Herald Tribune, Atlantic Monthly,* William F. Buckley's *National Review,* the anti-Stalinist left's *Partisan Review, The American Scholar,* the *New York Times Book Review*—these were some of the publications inviting her to contribute articles.

Jacobs had put herself in the limelight and now she was going to pay the price. The attacks upon her came quickly. Everywhere you looked, professionals and officials were denigrating her as a "housewife" who had no right to criticize experts because she lacked credentials. *American City* magazine in a scathing review sneered at Jacobs's description of the North End. "It is of no importance that planners classify it as a slum; that the professors at Harvard and MIT send their students there to practice preparing urban-development plans; or that bankers do not care to risk lending money on the property there. These people are, to be charitable, misguided and uninformed. And charity does not seem to be one of the book's strong points." Pittsburgh's housing commissioner Alfred Tronzo scioffed at her for her "seemingly limited experience in her chosen field," while the *Pittsburgh Post-Gazette* described her as "a housewife who likes her neighborhood as it is, diverse." [17] "New York Homemaker Fights Public Housing, Urban Renewal," read the headline in the *Dallas Morning News* (May 9, 1962) above a story on Jacobs's speech to the American Institute of Architects meeting. Baltimore's *Sunday American* trumpeted: "Mistakes in City Planning Get a Housewife's Panning" (October 12, 1961).

It is worth noting that Jacobs wasn't the only "housewife" now raising a distinctly female voice against the status quo. At a time when even women with college degrees were supposed to find happiness in their new suburban homes playing with all their new consumer products and raising their baby-boom children, Jacobs, Betty Friedan, and Rachel Carson each wrote a polemic that would change the world. Friedan's *Feminine Mystique,* also a Random House book, came out in 1962. It documented the despair and isolation of women's lives in the postwar period. Carson's 1963 book *Silent Spring* told about the malignant effects of DDT upon the environment. Both books would be published shortly after *Death and Life.* These three women were daring to take on big subjects in what was strictly a man's world. And they told their stories from a distinct woman's perspective.

Jacobs's discussion of sidewalks in *Death and Life*, for example, reveals a mother's concerns. Sidewalks, she observes, are invariably safer than playgrounds. "People with actual, not theoretical, responsibility for bringing up children in cities often know this well. 'You can go out,' say city mothers, 'but stay on the sidewalk.' I say it to my own children. And by this we mean more than 'Don't go into the street where the cars are.'" Many a male editor of that time would have edited out, or at least pared down, such expressions of maternal feeling. But not so Jacobs's editor, Jason Epstein, who clearly appreciated everything about this writer's voice and sensed that people would want to hear such expressions. And he was right; everybody was talking about *Death and Life*. So much so that the objects of Jacobs's darts could not just dismiss her. They felt they had to respond. So they did, and viciously.

"I still think the idea that America's cities should become one vast Greenwich Village is pretty ridiculous. Charm, you know, is something like chocolate ice cream. It has its limits," Donald M. Graham, planning administrator for the Boston Redevelopment Authority, told the *Boston Globe* (October 15, 1961). Roger Starr, head of New York City's powerful Citizens Housing and Planning Council, which since the 1930s had led the fight to build public housing, wrote that in Jacobs's version of reality,

people dance . . . the "ballet of the sidewalks," . . . she describes her folksy urban place on Hudson Street with such spirit and womanly verve that she has made a considerable number of readers believe it really exists. She has even set herself to wondering why the rest of the world isn't like Mooritania (i.e. the Village). . . . Mrs. Jacobs's Mooritania is distinguished by the diversity of its occupants, and their occupations. Factories nestle beside homes, and never give off smells or smoke. The streets are thronged day and night but the traffic is never bothersome or noisy. When a prankish child merrily falls through a plate-glass window, a quietly competent stranger appears from nowhere to save his arm with an expertly applied tourniquet.

Her solution to city problems, wrote Starr, is to

> bend the knee to no other gods before diversity, noise, and crowding, short blocks everywhere . . . the rest is easy, chum. You takes $20,000 out of your savings . . . and you buys a house in a part of the city that's known as a slum, but has potentialities. Then, says Mrs. Jacobs, you and your like-minded (and like-financed) neighbors "unslum" it. . . . . Mrs. Jacobs is an advanced thinker, and cannot keep herself from acknowledging, though briefly, that there are race and economic problems in the city. Race problems, she tells us, should be met by keeping lots of people on the streets, so that we needn't be *afraid* of members of another group. . . . Jane Jacobs has described Mooritania so well your mouth waters. [But] . . . she's just a teeny bit hazy about how we're all a-gwine to get there. (*Village Voice,* November 11, 1962)

Jacobs infuriated officials in Boston with her assertion in *Death and Life* that plans for "massive clearance" of the North End were at that very moment in the works. The offending passage, which was excerpted in the *Saturday Evening Post* several months before the book's publication, elicited a furious and immediate denial from Boston officials Donald Graham and his boss Ed Logue. "We couldn't agree with her more. I don't know where she got the idea that we feel any differently about the North End than she does," Graham told the *Boston Globe* (October 15, 1961), pointing to a passage in *Death and Life* in which Jacobs says that a clearance project for the North End "would be an outrage." Logue, Boston's equivalent to Robert Moses, had torn down and rebuilt New Haven, and now had big plans to clean up Boston's decidedly grimy infrastructure. In the mid-1960s he would replace the city's shabby center with the controversial Government Center complex. Later he would move to New York, where Governor Rockefeller would grant him sweeping powers that he would use to build Roosevelt Island. Afterward, as head of the South Bronx Development Organization, he would help to bring back to life the devastated neighborhood that had come to symbolize the failure of urban policy.

Logue called Jacobs's article "wildly inaccurate." Yes, he conceded, it was true that Boston was the recipient of ninety million federal urban renewal dollars earmarked specifically for an area that was much wider than the North End. Although it did include the North End, Logue claimed that the North End would be spared. "We have a new approach in Boston," Logue said. "It has been the basis of our program for more than a year, and I'm sorry the *Post* did not take the trouble to become acquainted with it. Just to keep the record straight, we have no plans whatsoever for clearance in the North End." The *Post*'s editor told Jacobs that Logue's reaction required a response from her. She agreed—and held her ground.

In order for the area to have gotten all that federal money for urban renewal, she replied pointedly in her response, the North End had to have been first condemned as a slum. Federal regulations on urban renewal, she demonstrated, cite as flaws everything that makes the North End a wonderful place to live. Things like mixed uses and small blocks. The aim of urban renewal, she wrote, is to "correct" these supposed "flaws." She quoted from the Boston housing agency's description of the North End: "a blighted area to be removed and replaced." Boston's housing officials, Jacobs wrote, don't understand federal regulations. Or the other possibility, she suggested slyly, was that they were not telling the truth.[18]

Jacobs had put Logue on the defensive. One year after *Death and Life* appeared, at a debate at New York's Museum of Modern Art with Ed Bacon of Philadelphia and Jacobs, Logue was saying publicly that the large-scale public housing program was "one of the greatest social failures of our time . . . but rehabilitation is the wave of the future. . . . The day of the bulldozer is over." Still, he was proposing to rip out and replace 5 percent of the North End. *Only* 5 percent. The real problem, he said, was that the residents wanted *more* complete renewal, not less, "because the suburbs are luring the younger generations away from the old Italian community."[19]

The North End, in fact, was saved, afterward going on to become one of Boston's favorite neighborhoods. The tragedy of the West End's destruction, which Herbert Gans had chronicled in *The Urban Villagers*, coupled with the publication of *Death and Life* the previous year made it politically impossible for Boston politicians to touch the North End.

Forty-three years later, on May 5, 2004, Jacobs delivered the first annual Lewis Mumford Lecture at City College in New York before a group that included fellow veterans who had fought with her to save their neighborhood. She explained one of the cardinal rules of fighting against big plans. "When we heard of something," she said, "we'd confront them publicly. They'd deny it. And then they could not do it." Jacobs was making life difficult for powerful men all over the country. In her home turf of New York City, Roger Starr, who subscribed to the Robert Moses dogma of slum clearance and public housing, wrote an entire book in response to the torrents of criticism now pouring forth against urban renewal practices.

"A Hundred Cities—A Hundred Critics," Starr titled the first chapter of *The Living End,* in which he vociferously defended the actions of officials like himself who were feeling more and more besieged by critics. Our thankless but noble efforts to solve the housing crisis, he said, are being met only with abuse by the likes of Jane Jacobs. Jacobs, "whose D&L has been quoted as the final word on their plight by citizens suffering from an angry variety of afflictions, talks to the city on their behalf as though it were an erring husband brought to grief by bad company." Starr mentions Jacobs frequently, often in connection with the adjective "irritating." "Mrs. Jacobs's writing on this subject is irritating not only because in these respects she is misunderstood by her readers, who, if they bothered to understand her, would call her wrong," writes Starr. He then adds, "It is far more irritating that, in some respects, she is right. The eye does require diversity and refreshment; the mind does choke on bland repetition; and Mrs. Jacobs tells us this with rare poignancy." Even he was seduced by the power of her prose.

Starr would go on to be an advisor to three successive mayors and an editorial writer for the *New York Times,* and he would become disillusioned with the results of large-scale planning. In his obituary (*New York Times,* September 11, 2001), his son Adam was quoted as saying, "Sometimes we would drive past a Mitchell-Lama project, and he [Starr] would say, 'Mea culpa, mea culpa.'"

Of all the barbs thrown at Jacobs and her book, Lewis Mumford's had to have cut her the deepest. Likewise, what she said about him in *Death and Life,* calling his much-praised book *The Culture of Cities* a "morbid and biased catalog of ills," must have hurt him badly—especially since he'd been so kind to her, beginning with the time of their very first meeting at Harvard in 1956 when she had given her speech about the evils of public high-rises. He had been so impressed with her. The two began a correspondence, exchanging ideas in a most collegial fashion. The fact was, on many issues he and Jacobs were in agreement.

After hearing her speak in 1958 at the New School for Social Research, where she called the proposed Lincoln Center "a built-in piece of rigor mortis," he wrote her what could be called a polite mash note. "Your analysis of the vast bungle called Lincoln Center is devastatingly just: I myself had held off attacking it in the *New Yorker* because I mistakenly felt that, even in an age as irrational as ours, a plan as massively inept as that one would never get beyond the stage of advance publicity. But I did not reckon with our present American capacity for organizing and capitalizing emptiness."

In her response, she praised a recent article by him in which he warned passionately of the price that not only Americans but the whole world would pay for their uncritical embrace of "insolent chariots," as he called automobiles. Since the 1940s, Mumford had been warning about cars' pernicious effects upon cities. Incensed at Robert Moses and his determination to keep building highways around and through New York City, he attacked the planning czar in a series of *New Yorker* columns. "Instead of maximizing facilities for motorcars, we should maximize the advantages of urban life. Parks, playgrounds, and schools, theaters, universities, and concert halls, to say nothing of a quiet night's sleep and a sunny outlook when one wakes up, are more important than any benefits to be derived from the constant use of the automobile," Mumford wrote presciently in 1955. Cities, he believed with all his heart, existed for pedestrians, not cars.

Mumford and Jacobs shared the same sensibilities and wanted much the same things for cities. Or so it seemed. Her ideas, he suggested in a 1958 letter to her, ought to reach a wider audience; had she thought of writing an article for the *Saturday Evening Post?* By then *Death and Life* was clearly already taking shape in Jacobs's mind: in her reply to Mumford she wrote that she would like, instead, to write a book. She asked him what he thought. Mumford answered her letter the very next day: "There are half a dozen publishers who'd snap up a ms. of yours on the city: and though I can't guess how the public would take to it you have a duty to produce the book! There's no one else who's had so many fresh and sensible things to say about the city—and it is high time these things were said and discussed. . . . I'm now finishing the first draft of volume I of my new book on cities. . . . I shan't finish the second volume on what to do about it till your work is done! Faithfully, LM."

But now, four years later, what Mumford was reading about himself in *Death and Life* wasn't exactly what he had expected of Jacobs. Moreover, her book was published the same year as his *The City in History,* the book he referred to in his letter to her. Both were nominated for a National Book Award. Mumford won, but even that honor did not assuage his wounded pride. More than one critic who reviewed *Death and Life* compared him unfavorably with Jacobs. "*Death and Life* is lively and gossipy, whereas Mumford is involved, turgid, impossibly heavy going. . . . She appeals to the reader through his emotion and she is very good at this technique," wrote Dennis O'Harrow in the AIPO bulletin. "It might well become the most influential work on cities since Lewis Mumford's classic, *The Culture of Cities* . . . it is wittier, more optimistic, less scholarly and even more pontifical," wrote Lloyd Rodwin in the *New York Times*.

Mumford was so livid that it took almost a year before he could sit down and write a response in the form of a long piece for the

New Yorker. "I have done something no one else has seriously attempted," he wrote to a friend soon after completing his diatribe. "I have grappled with Jane Jacobs's stimulating and awful book. . . . But I can't pretend that I didn't enjoy giving her an awful walloping on the soft part of her carcass that she had so carelessly exposed." Even after the passage of so much time, he wrote to a friend, "the paper burned, in spite of the long cooling period." Titled "Mother Jacobs's Home Remedies," Mumford launched a many-pronged attack on her book. He accused her of vastly oversimplifying the ideas of Ebenezer Howard—"I shall say no more of Mrs. Jacobs's lack of historical knowledge and scholarly scruple except that her disregard of easily ascertainable facts is all too frequent"—and deliberately ignoring the everyday, gritty reality of city life with its roaring traffic and sordid tenement houses from her starry-eyed Greenwich Village vantage point. He was furious at her assertion that "a city cannot be a work of art." Above all, Mumford reminds readers that he is "a born and bred New Yorker, who in his time has walked over almost every street in Manhattan, and lived in every kind of neighborhood," who has spent more than fifty years in New York. In contrast, "Mrs. Jacobs," as he calls her, is "a native of Scranton, who has not." Her book, he said, is replete with "schoolgirl howlers."

Notwithstanding his condescension and outrageous expressions of what would later be called sexism, to be fair, much of Mumford's criticism of Jacobs's book was justified. It was true, for example, that Jacobs had vastly oversimplified Ebenezer Howard's ideas. And Mumford was but one of many critics who faulted her for her dearth of practical solutions to the city problems that she described. He rightly criticizes her insistence on purely physical causes for all that ails or benefits the city. New York parks, such as Central and Riverside parks, now unusable because of crime, he points out, were in recent memory perfectly safe for walking at all hours of the day and night. As for her now famous and oft-quoted statement, "A city cannot be a work of art," Mumford, who deemed architecture "a home for man," retorted: "The citizens of Florence, Siena, Venice, and Turin will please take note!"

But for all his venom, Mumford still recognized Jacobs's genius. *Death and Life* mattered, and he said so despite the affront that his huge—and therefore fragile—ego had suffered. He noted that her sharp, articulate criticism of urban renewal practices came at just the right time, when people were beginning to feel that something was going terribly wrong. Her mind, he wrote, was "big with fresh insights and pertinent ideas." So more was the pity, he wrote, that her research was so sloppy.[20]

Jacobs has often claimed that Mumford's attacks upon her didn't bother her. "I thought his reaction to the book was not quite rational," Jacobs said in her May 2004 lecture at City College in New York. "I believe now that he felt hurt and betrayed that I didn't position myself as a disciple of his. I didn't take this personally. I think it had to do with his time. . . . Maybe if he'd lived at a different time he would have understood that women didn't necessarily aspire to be patronized. He believed that women were sort of a ladies' auxiliary of the human race." But Jacobs's professed astonishment over Mumford's reaction to what she says about him in *Death and Life* sounds disingenuous—especially in view of the fact that she often does not take criticism well. She was, for example, very angry with Herbert Gans for his review of *Death and Life,* who, for all his criticisms, nevertheless praises the book for its originality.[21]

Mumford never wrote his planned second volume of *The City in History.* Perhaps the critics' unfavorable comparison of his style to Jacobs's—boring, they called him, compared to her sharp way with words—made him lose heart. Even beating Jacobs out for the National Book Award, it seems, couldn't make up for the slight.

But however much these two huge egos rubbed each other the wrong way, Jacobs and Mumford would soon put aside their differences to fight against a common enemy: Robert Moses.

CHAPTER SIX

The West Village
and Lomex Battles

T he battle that Villagers had fought and won during the 1950s over Robert Moses's road-way through Washington Square Park, Jacobs wrote in *Death and Life,* had made her into "a public character," somebody who "is in frequent contact with a wide circle of people and who is sufficiently interested to make himself a public character." From then on, Villagers would look to Jacobs whenever their neighborhood was threatened by the city's plans for "improvement." Jane, say old friends from her Village days, remembering events from forty years earlier, always knew what to do. She had a way of thinking, a way of seeing things.

And ever since the roadway battle, Jacobs and her neighbors hadn't had a moment to let down their guard. Urban renewal in New York was continuing at a feverish pace, and real estate was going up in value. Hungry developers were eyeing the Village. New York University was another constant threat. You had to be vigilant. Otherwise, you would wake up one morning and find the windows on the building across the street from you marked with a big white X, a sign that the property had been condemned. Which, one way or another, meant it was doomed. Either it was going to be bulldozed away or it might sit there for years, neglected by a

95

Hudson Street, Greenwich Village, 2005. Photo by Alice Sparberg Alexiou.

landlord understandably unwilling to invest in a property that would sooner or later be destroyed.

And there were other ways in which the city might wreck your neighborhood in the name of making things better unless you nipped it in the bud. This is what happened in the spring of 1960, as Jacobs was working on *Death and Life*. A team of surveyors arrived one morning right at her doorstep on Hudson Street, where they spent a few days marking up the sidewalks between Fourteenth and Houston streets. When passersby, including Jacobs, asked them why, the surveyors were evasive. But when her younger son, Ned, age ten, asked them what they were doing, they told him the truth: they were taking measurements because Hudson Street was going to be widened by ten feet. In exchange, five feet would be cut off the sidewalks. As Jacobs was putting Ned to bed that night, he told his mother that they were going to lose their tree, which the Jacobs family had planted in front of their house in 1956. When

Jacobs asked her son what he meant, he told his mother what the surveyors had told him.

The next morning Jacobs and her children had a local printer—"it is very convenient to live in a mixed neighborhood," she commented happily many years later while reminiscing over this particular incident—print out petitions against the street widening. Ten-year-old Ned and five-year-old Mary sat at a table set up in front of the Jacobs house on a cold day in early spring, bundled up in their coats. Behind them they had hung a sign: "Save the Sidewalks on Hudson Street." As people walked by, they asked them, please, to sign the petition. And people did. The petitions of course were not enough—"We needed power to back up our pipsqueak protest," writes Jacobs in *Death and Life*. She immediately activated the local networks already in place from the last battle, over the Washington Square Park roadway. Immediately a new ad hoc committee, Save the Sidewalks, was formed with Jacobs as chairman.

Power, Jacobs goes on to say in her book, comes from the district, which she defines in typical Jacobs fashion—that is, by describing it as part of something larger: "The chief function of a successful district is to mediate between the indispensable, but inherently politically powerless, street neighborhoods, and the inherently powerful city as a whole." And a sine qua non of a district is public characters. Like Jacobs, another of her fellow grassroots activists, Anthony Dapolito, was a member of the community board. Dapolito had lots of friends in city government. His neighbors affectionately called him "the mayor of Greenwich Village." His Vesuvio Bakery on Prince Street, founded by his Neapolitan immigrant parents in 1920, survives and is still fabulous. (Dapolito died in 2003.) The crucial thing about Dapolito, Jacobs writes, is that he came all the way from the other side of the Village. He went right to the borough president's office, where he learned that the city had the right to widen the streets at its discretion. The affected citizens didn't have to be told first, and there was nothing they could do legally to stop it.

So it all came down to power. And the power, Jacobs writes in her book, "came from our district—Greenwich Village." Not just on one street, but throughout the district. If only the street that was going to be widened had complained, she writes, nobody would have listened. But because the protests came from throughout the district, elected officials, fearing for their political lives, were forced to pay attention. Save the Sidewalks put the pressure on the right people in the borough president's office, who were responsive to their concerns. In the end, the city backed down. The plans to widen Hudson Street were dropped.

Once again, Villagers saw that they could wage a tough battle— and win. But their problems were far from over. Within a few months, they would take on a much larger battle to save their neighborhood.

Save the West Village

In February 1961, just after she had completed *Death and Life,* Jacobs opened the *New York Times* one morning and discovered that a fourteen-block area of the West Village that included her address was going to be the subject of a study that would cost $350,000 and determine whether the neighborhood was eligible for urban renewal. The area, filled with early nineteenth-century houses, was bounded by Eleventh Street on the north, Hudson, Christopher, and Washington streets on the east, Morton Street on the south, and West Street on the west. Besides the Jacobs residence, the "slum" included the historic White Horse Tavern and St. Luke's Church, both on Hudson Street.

Being the subject of a study sounded benign enough, but Jacobs knew, after all the reporting she had done on urban renewal, what the real agenda was. For one, the West Village study would be only one among eighteen others, a "package" that included Cobble Hill and Brooklyn Heights, as well as areas of the Bronx and Manhattan. The plan, James Felt, the head of the City Planning Commission, told the *New York Times* (June 15, 1961), was to build middle-income housing.

"We were going to be designated to be wiped out," Jacobs would late recall. "The study always showed that yes, this area was susceptible to urban renewal. Furthermore, I had an idea about the scope of the thing because the study money that was asked for and granted was always a given percentage of the cost of the whole urban renewal program." And the cost of this proposed study was, in Jacobs's words, "just what you would expect for wiping out completely these fourteen blocks and putting in, probably, high rent apartments."

Greenwich Village, beloved by its residents, was little by little getting eaten up by outside forces that by all accounts seemed just too powerful to defeat. Still, in the 1950s Village activists had stopped Moses from building his road through Washington Square Park. And the previous year they had prevented the city from widening Hudson Street. So now, despite this latest bad news, they refused to feel hopeless. They had learned the hard way how to defend their turf. You had to come to the battle prepared. Information was your best weapon. And you had better act quickly, and on all fronts. Otherwise the city could sneak its agenda through in the middle of the night when nobody was looking. And New York City's multilayered, byzantine bureaucracy would make it impossible for you stop them. The decision making was so far removed from the voting public as to make them virtually voiceless. There were so many agencies and individuals involved in an urban renewal project: the Board of Estimate, the Housing and Redevelopment Board, the mayor. None of them were answerable to the people living in the affected neighborhood, who could wake up one morning and find the wrecking balls poised over their buildings.

And in fact, the city, quite correctly fearing that there would be opposition to such a project for the Village, had not held any public hearing about it before the February 1961 announcement in the newspaper. Obviously the Board of Estimate was trying to push it through before anybody knew what was happening. What is more, the City Planning Commission, Jacobs would later recall, "had gotten all their ducks in a row before this was announced." They had contacted all kinds of people in the Village, from different churches and organizations, and were sweet-talking them into believing how much urban renewal would benefit them. Especially a group called Micove, Middle Income Cooperators of Greenwich Village, led by Charlotte Schwab, a self-described "young housewife from Maine."

Micove had called for a middle-income coop to be built within twelve square blocks in the area south of Houston Street known as "Hell's Hundred Acres," so-called because of the frequent fires started by the combustible paints and other materials used by many artists now living illegally in this once-manufacturing district's deteriorating loft buildings. Later, Hell's Hundred Acres would acquire a new name, SoHo, and become one of New York's jazziest neighborhoods. But at the time it was thought of as nothing more than a slum.

But nothing had happened with Micove's plans, and now all of a sudden Mayor Robert Wagner was interested in this dormant organization, suggesting that their coop could instead be built in the West Village, within the proposed renewal area. (According to Jacobs, Schwab had been coached by city planning employees and promised an apartment).[1] Micove was the most visible example of what amounted to puppet organizations that the city was now setting up to give the impression that Villagers supported the city's plans—plans that might seem, on the surface, unassailable.[2] Housing was still in desperately short supply, and a lot of people sincerely thought that what the city had in mind would benefit them.

Others felt that resistance was useless. Indeed, local opposition to urban renewal projects almost always proved futile. When faced with the imminent demolition of their homes, people were usually resigned. You can't fight city hall, they'd sigh. Look what had happened to the poor denizens of East Tremont in the Bronx when Robert Moses built the Cross Bronx Expressway in the mid-1950s. In *The Power Broker,* Robert Caro relates the poignant story of how a group of more than two hundred East Tremont housewives about to lose their homes attended a Board of Estimate meeting where their fate was being decided. As the women were presenting their case, Robert Moses looked at them with contempt. Then, turning his eyes away, he began whispering to each of the borough presidents, who, in the meantime were talking, even laughing, among themselves. City officials were ignoring and ridiculing these citizens because they could.[3]

But the fight that Jane Jacobs was now going to lead would turn out differently.

Within two or three days after the *New York Times* announcement, Jacobs along with other Village activists—among them was Rachelle Wall—held a meeting at St. Luke's Church. They immediately formed an ad hoc committee, the Committee to Save the West Village, and set to work. Rachelle Wall had a friend, Lester Eisner, who headed the office that oversaw all the federal urban renewal programs in New York and New England.[4] Eisner was their man. The Committee to Save the West Village took him on a tour to show him that not only was their neighborhood no slum, but a wonderful place to live. Eisner, Jacobs recalled years later, could not understand why the city was claiming that it was a slum.

He then explained to the group how urban renewal law worked. For an area to be considered a slum, it had to meet specific physical criteria regarding, for example, hygiene, crowding, and the amount of abandoned property. Those regulations were a matter of public record. You just had to find them. Also, the law required that people living in an area being considered for urban renewal had to participate in any decision making. But the law was vague about what "participate" actually meant.

Eisner told Jacobs and her colleagues how to beat the system. First off, he said, you must document the physical conditions in the fourteen-block area that the city wants to condemn. That way, you'll prove that officials are dead wrong, that your neighborhood is no slum. And second, he said, never, never tell anybody in city or state government what you want. Even something as small as planting a tree. Because once you do that, you have become "participating citizens," and have in effect given officials the green light to do whatever they want to your neighborhood.

Armed with Lester Eisner's advice, people hit the streets. During the next month, the children, including Jacobs's, who were already experienced in defending their turf, distributed petitions and made posters. Their parents went door-to-door with questionnaires to record such facts as each apartment's size, number of occupants, and rent paid. It was all part of a survey they were doing about conditions in the so-called "urban renewal" area, to prove that the city had no case. Volunteers were first instructed in how to conduct the survey by some of the many professionals who lived in the Village, whose homes were also threatened with demolition and therefore offered their services free of charge.

People worked hard, often at night, the only time they had free. They met almost every night, either at Leon Seidel's Lion's Head Coffee House, the ground floor of a sagging old three-story building dating from 1810 on the corner of Charles and Hudson, or in the Jacobs's living room at 555 Hudson Street, to strategize over martinis and cigarettes. Seidel, Jacobs recalled years later, "got information almost sooner than anyone else and then spread it almost sooner than anyone else. You just dropped in at Leon's to get the news even if you weren't getting a coffee or dinner or anything." Seidel, like Jacobs, was a "public character." And he had a friend who was a printer, who did all of the committee's leaflets and posters; if you dropped off your order at the Lion's Head before one in the morning, it would be ready by eight or nine. Everybody, Jacobs would later recall, must have been suffering from sleep deprivation. "But we were, everybody was, in on this," Jacobs said. "Either their second, or their third job, was saving the neighborhood."

Based on their findings, the Committee to Save the West Village produced a document that Eisner pronounced the best survey he had ever seen. If the government had paid for such a survey, he told them, it would have cost them fifty thousand dollars. And the document proved beyond a doubt that legally the West Village did not meet the criteria for slum designation. But the Board of Estimate paid no attention to the report when Villagers proudly presented it to them in March.

Never mind. The committee dug in their heels and kept on going.[5] They went to court and won some time, but this cost them money. They ran book sales, Christmas wreath sales, and book signings of *Death and Life*. People were exhausted, and also worried about their public image; the press was portraying Jacobs and her colleagues as negative because whenever officials asked Villagers what they would like instead of what they were being offered, the only answer they got was "remove the slum designation." The press, especially the *New York Times,* just didn't get what Save the West Village was doing. And this was, Jacobs said, terribly frustrating. At every strategy meeting, people kept reminding one another not to mind being called negative. They had to keep fighting. They had to remain on the radar screen.

And they did. They would stage demonstrations in their neighborhood streets, carrying torches and signs reading "Save the West Village." They would call public meetings in places on their turf, to which they would invite officials to explain exactly why the neighborhood needed fixing. The unhappy officials had to oblige. Sometimes they had to face the wrath of other New Yorkers as well, for example Brooklynites and Upper West Siders who came to these meetings at the suggestion of their friends in the Village to bear witness to the havoc that Title I had wreaked in their own neighborhoods. Save the West Village made it a point to attend and stir up Board of Estimate meetings at City Hall. Once Jacobs and her colleagues, a total of some several hundred people, all turned up wearing identical pairs of cheap eyeglasses with big Xs taped across the lenses. It was a not-so-subtle allusion to the whitewashed Xs that marked buildings condemned by the city, and it made for a great photo op—the Associated Press wire service distributed the picture to newspapers around the country and the world (March 27, 1961).

For this story was turning out to have legs. People all over were reading about Mrs. Jacobs, the author of a just-published book on cities who was leading a neighborhood fight against urban renewal and taking no prisoners. It all made for great copy. Jacobs gave reporters terrific quotes. "An irresponsible boondoggle which will gratuitously jeopardize a sound and healthy community composed of people with a great love and pride of neighborhood," she told the

New York Times when asked to comment on the redevelopment project. City authorities, she charged, were practicing "vast deception." The struggle of this little grassroots group against the Goliath New York City had wide appeal, especially at a time when people were starting to question the wisdom of large-scale bulldozing. Jacobs was now getting letters from citizens around the city and the country as well, telling of their struggles to get their voices heard. Her story, they were saying, gave them encouragement.

She was backing New York's officials into a corner. They had to respond. Jane Jacobs, they were saying, doesn't speak for everybody. Look, there are plenty of Villagers who are eager to see their neighborhood redeveloped. Look at the good people of Micove. (Micove, Jacobs bluntly told the *New York Times,* was nothing but "a puppet organization.") The city also got the support of the powerful Citizens Housing and Planning Council. But clearly officials were feeling defensive. The wealthy real estate developer and Robert Moses's protégé James Felt, chairman of the City Planning Commission, was now telling the *New York Times* that "the backbone of renewal is in conserving and improving our existing structures and relating new development to the character and needs of the community." But, he added patronizingly, "this approach also calls for responsible citizenship as well. Urban renewal—which represents New York's golden opportunity to overcome immediate urban problems—has found itself the subject of some misguided criticism of late." The following night, in front of an angry audience in Greenwich Village, he declared: "I say categorically that this is not a clearance area and I say categorically that it's not a blighted area. It's a renewal area." Jacobs, in her own words, despised Felt, and the feeling was certainly mutual.

As for Mayor Wagner, he was retreating, a little at a time, from his initial support for the study. He began talking vaguely about urban renewal without any bulldozing. "Any new improvements," he told the *Villager,* "must conform to 'Village tradition.'" Jacobs's response was to blow off Wagner for "his pious platitudes." "If the Mayor," she told the *New York Times* on August 18, 1961, "cares about the wishes, character and well-being of Greenwich Village and its citizens, he will have the urban renewal proposal killed outright."

By the fall, Wagner had asked the City Planning Commission to shelve the project. The 1961 mayoral election was approaching, and Wagner was feeling vulnerable. But the commission disregarded the mayor, approving the study request in October—secretly, in a closed meeting. It waited two weeks before announcing its decision at a public meeting in City Hall, in the presence of James Felt. Also present were twenty-five Villagers, who now, the *New York Times* reported on the next day's front page, jumped up from their seats, shouting that a "deal" had been made between Felt and Rose Associates, a builder, and that the mayor had been "double-crossed." "Down with Felt," the Villagers shouted.

One by one, they would get up and try to speak, but the police would drag them out. Stephen Zoll, an editor at Macmillan, was carried out feet first as he shouted, "You have made a deal. Your name will be remembered with horror." They were trying to explain evidence showing that Felt had made a deal with a developer. "How dare you assume such authority?" one woman said to Felt. "Who the hell do you think you are making decisions in the interest of builders?"

"It's the same old story," Jacobs told the *New York Herald Tribune*. "First the builder picks the property, then he gets the Planning Commission to designate it, and then the people get bulldozed out of their homes." In the following weeks, disapproving officials and individuals wagged their fingers at what the papers called the Villagers' "near-riot."[6] "This is the most disgraceful demonstration I have ever seen," Felt said, before beating a hasty retreat from the room. Ira S. Robbins, City Housing Authority commissioner, called the Villagers "ignorant, neurotic, dishonest, slanderous, disorderly and disgusting." The Citizens Housing and Planning Council called the demonstration "riot tactics" and "an attack on the democratic processes."

But Jacobs and her allies didn't care what authorities, or anybody else, were saying about them. Anyway, by now the city had lost its case in the court of public opinion.

The following week, the commission reversed itself and abandoned the plans for the study. James Felt, furious, asked Wagner for one more chance to try to convince Villagers of the wisdom of urban renewal. Wagner agreed. Twelve people met with Felt. After remarking on how intelligent they were, he asked each of them, what would you like? Flush with their victory, the group nevertheless knew not to let down their guard. The answer he got from every one was the same: "Drop the slum designation." A few months later, on January 31, 1962, almost a year from when Jacobs had first read in the newspaper the alarming news about the city's plans for her neighborhood, the City Planning Commission removed the slum designation by unanimous vote.

The full story of the Committee to Save the West Village's tactics is far more complicated than this account. Suffice it to say that during this year-long fight, which historian and architect Richard Plunz, an expert on New York City's housing history, called "the longest and hardest-fought battle for community self-control over development ever waged in New York City," Jacobs and her colleagues could not afford to avert their eyes for one second. Despite their determination, and the attention that Jacobs was getting from the press, officials behind the scenes were trying to sneak through the urban renewal project up to the very last minute. But they kept getting caught.

Unbeknownst to them, there were, by chance, a few Villagers working in city government. Moles, Jacobs called them. They would overhear conversations between, say, Felt and David Rockefeller, and then report what they had heard to committee members. The committee members would then promptly call Felt and ask him about it. Is it really true? they'd ask him. Are you really planning to do such-and-such? It was the tactic that Robert Jacobs had devised: accusing somebody of intending to do something before they actually do it. Because then they'll have to deny it. And then they won't be able to do it.

In the summer of 1962, six months after the urban renewal plan for the West Village had been killed for good, Felt resigned as chairman of the City Planning Commission.

The Lower Manhattan Expressway

Jane Jacobs, having finished her book, gone on speaking tours, and prevented the West Village from being bulldozed into the ground, was exhausted. She returned to her job at *Architectural Forum,* and "breathed a sign of relief. Now I could get along only with my job and with my domestic duties and interests as a wife and mother. My, wasn't life calming down?"[7]

But not for long. Father La Mountain, pastor of the Church of the Most Sacred Heart on Broome Street, dropped in to see her one summer day in 1962. He wanted Jacobs's advice because the city was planning to build an expressway across lower Manhattan that was going to destroy his church, along with the lives of his parishioners.

This was hardly a new idea: since before World War II, Robert Moses had been talking about building at least three elevated expressways across Manhattan, yet more arteries in his sprawling road system that would make it possible to travel through and around New York City's boroughs without ever getting out of your car. The Lower Manhattan Expressway—Lomex—that the Board of Estimate, the City Planning Commission, and Mayor Wagner were now in the midst of planning would, as part of the federal interstate highway system, be 90 percent federally funded. It would be an elevated monstrosity of ten lanes, stretching for two and a half miles from east to west, along the entire length of Broome Street from the two-lane Holland Tunnel all the way to the two-lane Manhattan and Williamsburg bridges. It would cost $100 million.

Lomex, Moses claimed, was an absolute necessity to relieve traffic congestion in lower Manhattan. True, Broome and Canal streets were clogged with trucks, the only means for transporting freight in and out of New York. But you could look at the traffic situation in a Jane Jacobs way: Lomex, part of the interstate system, proposed with an intricate system of exits and ramps, could only increase the number of vehicles in the city.

Starting at the Holland Tunnel, Lomex, following the route of Broome Street, would cut right through SoHo, then "Hell's Hundred Acres," and continue across Mulberry and Mott streets, slicing up Little Italy and Chinatown, and then cross the Bowery into the Lower East Side. The roadway would push out two thousand families, including Father La Mountain's parishioners, and eight hundred small businesses that employed some ten thousand people. It would have destroyed SoHo just as this neighborhood, with its wonderful cast-iron structures that once housed textile factories, was spontaneously becoming an artists' colony. Nobody could have planned SoHo; it was an urban ecosystem in the truest Jane Jacobs sense.

Lomex would have doomed the gargantuan domed Italianate Police Department headquarters on Cleveland Place off Broome (which was later turned into a deluxe residential building, where, it so happens, Jason Epstein lives today), eight churches, including the beautiful little rococo Church of San Salvatore, and Engine Company Number Fifty-five, a little gem of a firehouse built in Renaissance Revival style. Lomex would have wiped out the pastry shops and restaurants of Little Italy, and then eaten up the lighting and restaurant supply stores clustered in and around the Bowery. Finally, it would cut across Chrystie Street, wiping out the shady park in the street's center, then continue east until finally it would hook up to the bridges leading to Brooklyn.

Father La Mountain told Jacobs that his flock felt fatalistic about losing their homes. But he was not willing to give up. Would Jacobs, he asked, be willing to help?

Jacobs hesitated. "I felt very resistant to getting into another fight. I wanted to work on my work." But soon she found herself at the helm, leading a savvy and tenacious bunch of New Yorkers that cut right across the political spectrum. United, they formed the Joint Committee to Stop the Lower Manhattan Expressway. They included Villagers and Lower East Siders, "loft-dwelling artists joining hands with elderly Italy housewives, a multi-partisan group which embraces not only regular Republicans, Tammany and reform Democrats, right wing Young Americans for Freedom and anarcho-pacifists of the Catholic Worker group." Also Hy Harmatz, the owner of the famous Ratner's on Delancey Street, which would have been another casualty of the expressway. Jacobs and many other good citizens would fight Lomex with an arsenal of weapons they had acquired through years of local battles, which now linked them together into a loop that interconnected with other loops, all of which together, Villagers had seen, wielded power.

So now here was Jane Jacobs, along with another Village activist, Joan Stoliar, at a Board of Estimate meeting with gas masks over their faces, an allusion to the pollution that an interstate highway would bring to Manhattan. Leading a demonstration at another meeting, Jacobs yelled "The expressway would Los Angelize New York!" into high-profile television reporter Gabe Pressman's microphone. It was, she told the *New York Times,* "a monstrous and useless folly." Lomex, she told the *Village Voice,* was all part of an interstate system that was getting approved "a piece at a time, so people won't be able to grasp the whole picture." If Lomex isn't stopped, she said, "we'll be fighting the tentacles of that stupid octopus forever." She referred to Moses's arguments for expressways in lower Manhattan as "piffle."

Jacobs and La Mountain had plenty of support from their local elected officials from both parties, including then-congressman John V. Lindsay, who joined their constituents at a rally and parade along the expressway's proposed route on Broome Street, accompanied by a live band playing Dixieland music. The politicians knew they'd better show their faces if they wanted to get reelected—two hundred community groups had joined the fight.

Besieged city officials were now looking for ways to discredit Jacobs. So when Lewis Mumford's scathing *New Yorker* review of *Death and Life* appeared on December 1, 1962, they used it as ammunition. Jacobs, knowing that Mumford, for all his anger at her, was 100 percent behind the anti-expressway cause, called him up. "This isn't about the *New Yorker,*" she said. "Of course, I don't agree with you, but that doesn't matter. We're having this fight and would you send a letter of opposition to the expressway that could be read at a hearing coming up and that we could publish too?"[8] He wrote "a wonderfully effective letter," Jacobs would recall during her May 2004 speech for the first annual Lewis Mumford lecture at the City College of New York. "Nobody," she would say, "could have exerted the influence that he did. . . . So I hereby say a loud public thank you to Lewis Mumford."

Mumford's letter was read out loud at a public hearing at the Board of Estimate in December 1962. The expressway, Mumford had written, "would be the first serious step in turning New York into Los Angeles. Since Los Angeles has already discovered the futility of sacrificing its living space to expressways and parking lots," he said, "why should New York follow that backward example?"[9] At the same meeting thirty-nine people spoke out against the expressway plan, including seven Democratic and Republican elected officials. State Assemblyman Louis DeSalvio called Robert Moses "a cantankerous, stubborn old man. . . . I, and the peoples of New York City, think that the time has come for the stubborn old man to realize that too many of his technicians' dreams turn out to be a nightmare for the City. . . . This Board must realize, that if he does not, now, once and for all, kill this stupid example of bad city planning that the stench of it will haunt them and this great City of New York for many years to come."

Five days later, the Board of Estimate by unanimous vote shelved the expressway plan. Jacobs sent Mumford a gracious note, thanking him for his help. The *New York Times* called the victory "the most spectacular demonstration of the new-found powers of local citizens' groups." Indeed, the expressway battle had lasted only a few months. Robert Moses, of course, was furious. "Nothing is easier than to drum up opposition to any major public work where the press leans to sensation, libel goes unpunished and officialdom worries about block votes and reprisals," Moses said in a speech he gave at the opening of a new Port Authority facility a month after Lomex's defeat. December 1962 had been an especially bad month for the seventy-four-year-old Moses. In addition to the Lomex defeat, he had finally come head-to-head with an elected official who was willing to take him on. Governor Nelson Rockefeller hated Moses, and piece by piece, he was divesting Moses of his power.[10]

Nevertheless, Lomex remained on the official city map, which meant that the Board of Estimate could try again to revive it at any time. And other powerful interests besides Moses—the New York

State government, the Automobile Club of New York, along with a consortium of downtown businesses—remained behind Lomex. An editorial in the *Villager* blasted Jacobs and her "cohorts" for

> attempting to impose their will on the City. . . . They have kept up a steady barrage of propaganda and won the support of certain politicians. . . . There are some sound, experienced and accomplished people who favor the Lower Manhattan Expressway, and their reasons are hardly "piffle." . . . So let's throw out all of the emotionalized, inherently selfish buncombe, the politically inspired hokum and other irrelevant considerations, face up to the real problems involved, and come up with some sensible solutions. Because after all the hysteria dies down, the traffic congestion and the disease-breeding and delinquency-breeding slums will still remain to be coped with.

The following year, 1963, Robert Moses presented a new plan for Lomex at the suggestion of Mayor Wagner. Despite the public's antipathy, the possibility of Lomex remained.

"The rule of thumb," Jacobs would say many years later, "is that you have to kill expressways three times before they die."

CHAPTER SEVEN

More Battles

Jane Jacobs, author and now maven of bringing the New York City government to its knees, became the subject of editorials in such national publications as *Newsweek* and the *Saturday Evening Post,* and was sought out for interviews. During the summer of 1962, as she was leading the battle against Lomex, her name was everywhere. Discussing grassroots strategies with a reporter for *Mademoiselle* magazine, Jacobs said, "Go to public documents, you have access! You go down and photograph and they have a fit and then you make them sign something that they've shown you every document. And then they get worried if they've been hiding anything. In fact it's war. . . . Too many people are afraid of antagonizing bureaucrats. . . . You just make up your mind to win, and if you antagonize a lot of people, well, you do. But in the end they fawn on you" (August 1962).

"Queen Jane," Susan Brownmiller called her in a story for *Vogue* magazine. Jacobs was photographed by Diane Arbus; she had more enemies "than any American woman since Margaret Sanger," wrote the *Village Voice*'s Jane Kramer (December 20, 1962). "If the lawyer's idea of aroused civic conscience is a runaway jury, then Jane Jacobs is the amateur's equivalent, a one-woman, runaway PTA meeting," wrote Eric Larrabee in the July 1962 issue of *Horizon,* a highbrow

Drawing of the proposed Lower Manhattan Expressway linking the Holland Tunnel to the Manhattan Bridge through what is now SoHo, 1950. Metropolitan Transit Authority, Bridges and Tunnels.

arts-and-letters monthly. Jane Jacobs, wrote Kramer in the *Voice,* "looks like a prophet. People who have seen her in action at the Board of Estimate or down on Broome Street rarely forget that clomping, sandaled stride and that straight gray hair flying every which way around a sharp, quizzical face. . . . In the past year and a half she had led the people of lower Manhattan into innumerable battles. . . . She has turned her causes into hot-potato issues and is lately the terror of every politico in town. She has mustered public support and sympathy to the extent that now even the Mayor bends to a Jacobs decree or completely loses face."

All over the country people were reading *Death and Life,* even using it like a textbook, as they fought plans to tear down and rebuild their neighborhoods. "What really pleases me," Jacobs told the

Milwaukee Journal (July 8, 1962), "is the mail from alert, concerned citizens who have much love for their cities." Her book was opening up dialogues where none had existed but were badly needed. Basic assumptions about fixing cities were now being openly questioned. Sometimes citizen groups were succeeding in saving their neighborhoods from the bulldozers, like Cobble Hill in Brooklyn, which had been designated along with the West Village for urban renewal, and Boston's North End.

And it was not only the sons and daughters of European immigrants who were questioning the status quo, but now the newest arrivals, African-Americans from the South who, in the hundreds of thousands, had come up north during the last twenty years. They, like immigrants, had arrived in the cities—Detroit and Chicago, Buffalo and Cleveland, New York and Boston, Newark and Philadelphia—in search of jobs and a better life. The white people already living in the poor neighborhoods where the black newcomers settled fled whenever they could. Banks were now engaging in "blockbusting," that is, they refused to lend money to these so-called "changing" neighborhoods, which then deteriorated further.

And now, the trajectory to poverty and isolation was gaining further momentum as blacks were being evicted from their homes and pushed into new high-rise housing projects, which fast turned into incubators of all the pathologies that accompany poverty. All in the name of "urban renewal," a term now hateful to black people. In the words of James Baldwin, urban renewal meant Negro removal.[1] Indeed, the real aim of urban renewal, some perceptive critics were saying, was to get rid of black ghettos, the existence of which offended white people and also occupied land that was potentially valuable.[2] Bulldozing the ghettos on, say, Manhattan's West Side, and rebuilding them as Lincoln Center and Fordham University amounted to a land grab, according to the critics.

The people of color who lost their homes to Lincoln Center ended up in housing projects in Harlem or Brownsville—that is, the lucky ones. Others fell through the cracks; Title I, we have seen, did not require localities to provide replacement housing for displaced people. Urban renewal was increasing ghettoization, perniciously separating people by income and color not only from the white world but even from their own familiar streets, which were now being obliterated.

At first some black leaders had supported, albeit warily, urban renewal on the grounds that it would provide desperately needed housing.[3] But by now, "the projects," as people called them, were hated and people were saying it so openly that New York housing expert Charles Abrams told the *New York Times* (January 6, 1966) that the term "projects" had become so toxic that it should no longer be used. Another word, he said, should be found to designate public housing. "They are hated almost as much as policemen, and this is saying a great deal," wrote James Baldwin in his 1961 book *Nobody Knows My Name*. They are, he wrote, "colorless, bleak, high, and revolting." The administration of them, Baldwin wrote, is "insanely humiliating." You had to tell the management when you got a raise and who was living with you.

Roger Starr, then director of New York's powerful Citizens Housing and Planning Council, told the following anecdote about a Board of Estimate meeting he attended in the early 1960s: "I watched a stout Negro lady, her black coat held together with a big blanket pin, as she arrived at City Hall to protest against a city proposal to demolish [her block]. She carried under her arm, as the rationale for her opposition, a copy of Mrs. Jacobs's book. 'We don't live in no slum,' she said, 'and we don't want to live in no project. We want to stay where we is, but we want it fixed up the way she says.'"[4]

But how? Starr asks angrily, feeling besieged by all the critics of urban housing policy, and especially by Jane Jacobs. Where will the woman carrying her copy of *Death and Life* get the means to rehabilitate the old building where she lives, as Jacobs and her Village neighbors have done? They, Starr and others pointed out, lived in a comfortable world, one far different from the woman Starr was quoting. They could afford to buy and renovate old buildings. Starr, Jacobs's bitter enemy, was asking a perfectly valid question. Without saying so directly, he had put his finger on the most serious shortcoming in Jacobs's otherwise brilliant book: her failure to include any meaningful discussion of race. And there were, Starr and others thought, other weaknesses in her arguments. The possible alternatives to building large projects that Jacobs had offered, such as housing the poor in existing buildings through direct subsidies to landlords, seemed to her many critics ridiculously inadequate to the urgency and sheer magnitude of New York's housing problem.

Still, as far out as Jacobs's subsidy idea seemed at the time, the fact is that she was prescient. In 1974 Congress passed the Federal Housing and Community Development Act, and buried the urban renewal program. There would be no more huge-scale government-built public housing for the poor. Instead, the federal government would now provide grants to state and local authorities, thereby shifting the responsibility for providing people with shelter to the local level. In keeping with this new post–Great Society philosophy, Section 8 of the 1974 housing law provided for subsidies to place needy families in already-existing apartments—an idea that Jacobs had first suggested in her book thirteen years earlier. Today, thirty-plus years later, Section 8 is still with us and seems to be here to stay, at least until somebody figures out a better way to solve the housing problem.

What Jacobs did and would continue to do best was to observe and then describe what existed, things that others either couldn't or didn't want to see. Whether you liked the facts she presented to you wasn't her concern. The important thing was that she was putting it all out there in a way that nobody else did, and so powerfully that you could see the city through her eyes. Her power to change people's perceptions came from her ability to tell the story. What she said, and, most of all, how she said it, touched your emotions, went beyond logic. Her words moved you, like music or poetry. And her language was equal to the gravity of her subject, cities: "Now we must dig a little deeper into the bog of intellectual misconceptions about cities in which orthodox reformers and planners have mired themselves (and the rest of us). Underlying the city planners' deep disrespect for their subject matter, underlying the jejune belief in the 'dark and foreboding' irrationality or chaos of cities, lies a long-established misconception about the relationship of cities—and indeed of men—with the rest of nature."

And it wasn't only her written words that got people all riled up, but also her on-the-ground, in-your-face Village activism. Her readiness to stand up and mouth off to anybody, even Robert Moses, delighted thousands. After some thirty years of being bullied by Moses's huge urban renewal and roadway projects, unilaterally imposed upon the people of New York seemingly without his having one instant's thought about the lives he was ruining in the process, they had had enough. And now, here was a woman fighting everybody's fight, an antidote to Moses.

Jacobs was often thought of as a Village lefty-radical, although her criticism of government-as-caretaker inspired people on the right of the political spectrum, including libertarians, to sometimes claim her as theirs. In an editorial the *Wall Street Journal* (June 19, 1961) praised *Death and Life* because, the newspaper said, Jacobs opposed "centralized Federal planning." William F. Buckley, a great Jacobs admirer, included a passage from *Death and Life* in *Did You Ever See a Dream Walking,* a 1970 anthology he edited that showcased American conservative thinking.

Others criticized Jacobs for being evasive about her political stance. Academics questioned which side of the urban renewal debate she was on, the left or the right. These were perfectly valid questions—all of which Jacobs refused to address. She simply rejected political labels. She did not like ideologies, she said, a point she continues to make in the present. Ideologies, she told an interviewer in 2002, are "one of the greatest afflictions, because they blind us to seeing what is going on or to what is being done."[5] The truth is that it was impossible to locate Jacobs's precise place on the political spectrum.

Some compare her to William James, who introduced the term "pragmatism," a philosophy that insists above all on the practical, not the metaphysical. Whatever thinking a pragmatist doesn't like, she may simply discard and then continue on to perform those actions she deems correct. With its emphasis on individuality, pragmatism underlies much of what we think of as American. All of which seems to perfectly describe Jacobs, who took ideas from wherever she liked on the political spectrum, basing her choice only on whether they worked in the real world. When fighting her civic battles, Jacobs accepted support from all places on the political spectrum.

The tough image of Jacobs the street fighter blended with another, cozier one: Mrs. Jacobs, as the papers called her, the mother of three. Occasionally the press snapped a picture of one of the Jacobs children, such as one the *New York Times* ran in 1961, a wonderful candid shot of Jacobs with her gray bangs and usual dowdy attire standing on Hudson Street talking to two women with her arm tightly around her eight-year-old daughter, who is snuggling into her mother's embrace. The maternal side of Jane Jacobs was obvious and softened her impact, making her a safe guest for the Johnson White House, where Lady Bird was holding small ladies' luncheons for "women doers," as the First Lady called them, in the blue-and-white Presidential family dining room. The invitation was addressed to "Mrs. Robert Jacobs," a usual form of address in those days even for a famous writer. (Afterward, Jacobs dutifully sent her mother, to whom she wrote regularly, a copy of the menu.)

Jacobs did not exactly fit the idealized image of the post–World War II American mother raising her brood in her new suburban house. We know now that there was something seriously amiss with that image, a fact that Betty Friedan trenchantly exposed in *The Feminine Mystique,* which, concurrently with *Death and Life,* was unexpectedly hitting a nerve. It turned out that women who were supposedly finding contentment staying home with their babies and using their brand-new appliances were actually dying a slow spiritual death from boredom and isolation. At least many of them, to judge by how well Friedan's book sold. "Some women love the suburbs, kaffeeklatch life and running around to the neighbors. I think it's deadly myself, but it's a matter of personal taste. Seeing nobody but people very much like yourself or being isolated all day with the children are two of the most dulling things for human beings," Jane Jacobs told a reporter for the Long Island newspaper *Newsday* in 1961.

Besides fighting to save their neighborhood, Jane and Robert Jacobs were becoming active in the burgeoning anti–Vietnam War movement. Still, for all her public persona, Jacobs was essentially a private person. She hated, she said, being in the limelight. She hated having to fight all those battles. But, she said, what choice did she have in the face of all the stupid, destructive things that New York's bureaucrats inflicted upon the people they were ostensibly serving? Jacobs resented the imposition upon her time, which she would rather spend writing at her desk. She was first and foremost a writer.

After returning briefly to her magazine job following the publication of *Death and Life*, she left *Architectural Forum* for good in 1962 to begin work on a new book. It was also about cities, but this time her take focused on cities as the basis of economies. She wrote every day; during her working hours, nobody was allowed to disturb her. Once, Mayor John Lindsay, with whom Jacobs had a close relationship dating from his days as a congressional representative from Greenwich Village, called her at home. Jacobs's daughter Mary politely told the mayor that her mother could not be disturbed.

And she loved her home. She gardened in her small Greenwich Village backyard, baked pies and Christmas cookies, and gave her children birthday parties. In the frequent letters she wrote to her mother, Bess Butzner, descriptions of her political battles and her latest writing project were interspersed with cozy domestic details: the wonderful turkey-shaped bread that her husband and son had baked one Thanksgiving, the project her son had displayed at his school's science fair. Her date books from the period of her life when her children were young look like any busy mother's: a note to herself to boil the ham and soak the peas in preparation for Christmas, reminders about her children's dentist and eye doctor appointments, dancing lessons, and Brownie meetings. But scattered among her maternal duties she had jotted down other reminders: meetings with Village groups, the Expressway committee, and the Union Settlement board; to call John Lindsay; and a luncheon at the East Wing of the White House.

You could reasonably argue that working out the logical solutions to all the problems Jacobs articulated was somebody else's problem, not hers. The job of Jane Jacobs, the critic and prose-poet, was to criticize, something she did so well that changes immediately followed the publication of *Death and Life*.

Those first changes were metaphysical—that is, they were changes in how people thought about cities, an example of what the scientist Thomas Kuhn famously called a paradigm shift, a term that he coined in his book *The Structure of Scientific Revolutions*. Overturning a previously accepted paradigm, Kuhn argued, does not come about simply from gathering new facts that call the paradigm into question. Mere logic does not suffice to change people's minds. Against logic, scientists often cling to old models until their grasps are finally loosened by something other than logic, something far deeper and more difficult to articulate that we call by various names: emotion, the irrational, the metaphysical. Or faith.

Kuhn's book, like Jacobs's, changed perceptions. It became a classic, wielding an influence far beyond its intended audience. Kuhn's brilliant insights on how and why people reject long-held assumptions and accept the new paradigm apply not only to science but to just about any discipline. His book is cited by scholars and professionals, feminists and postmodernists, sociologists and psychotherapists. And Kuhn's name sometimes comes up during discussions of Jacobs's ideas. She was not by any means the first or only critic of urban renewal, but her criticism rattled people's emotions so thoroughly that they began to view cities differently.

Kuhn's book came out in 1962, a year after *Death and Life,* and their concurrence was no coincidence. This was a time when violent upheavals were shaking up America, causing the beginnings of a dazzling array of changes so profound and so complex that they are today still unfolding, and at intervals are still meeting with resistance and therefore not yet completed.

Within the space of a few years, Kennedy was assassinated, Betty Friedan's book was inspiring a women's revolution with demands for equal pay and legal and accessible abortion, the birth control pill helped propel a sexual revolution and New York comedian and social critic Lenny Bruce was standing trial for obscenity. The Stonewall rebellion in New York City in 1969 was starting what would become a revolution for gay and lesbian rights. Meanwhile, in the South state troopers were beating and firing tear gas at African-Americans marching for voting rights in Selma, Alabama, as Freedom Riders, both black and white, were boarding Greyhound buses. "Freedom Summer" in Mississippi resulted in the Klan's murder of James Chaney, Andrew Goodman, and Michael Schwerner. Up North, the epic struggle for civil rights was playing out in the form of despair-driven riots that were burning black ghettos into the ground. Simultaneously, the United States began bombing North Vietnam and the antiwar movement began to gain steam, breaking open a wound that to this day remains unhealed.

As all these traumas were happening around them, Americans were reading Jacobs's book. It was framing the national debate about urban renewal, although it was too soon for her ideas to have a concrete impact. Speaking at the National Housing Council conference on cities in 1962, Jacobs complained that officials were always giving lip service to good ideas but in the meantime were continuing to do things the same, bad old way. For example, with all their talk about how they ought now to build smaller public housing projects, the ones then under construction in New York and Chicago and Pittsburgh were more of the same monstrous high-rise varieties. Chicago's Robert Taylor Homes, in fact, would be the largest in the world, covering ninety-seven acres.

Another conference participant, Charles Abrams, a Jacobs supporter, also expressed frustration:

One of the things we ought to study is the whole psychology of social reform. When you talk about these things for ten or fifteen years and they seem perfectly sensible, why aren't changes made? If we are going to analyze what the trouble is with housing, and why we are not getting some of these reforms which everybody seems to accept, we have to study the American system and how it works here and on the Hill. There is a kind of a Newton's law in politics—a reform in motion continues in motion unless it is interrupted by some force and the force is not necessarily common sense. A public official, both in Washington and the locality, sells a program to the public. In the case of public housing we convinced even the courts that slums are responsible for a great many distortions in human civilization. After you sell it to the public, you get the law passed. After you get the law passed, you have to fight for its constitutionality. That is quite a problem. Then you get the funds and they are not spent so quickly. . . . By the time you get through all of this, it is too hard to start things all over again with a program that makes common sense. You are stuck with what you have. I have talked to a Senator who is very much interested in the housing problem and I put forth a very simple thesis: What the poor people want is to own homes, I said. "Why do you put them in public housing projects? Why don't you make it possible for the builder to build a simple home for them by giving them zero percent interest, if necessary?" The Senator said I was right but Congress is not yet ready for it.[6]

But Jacobs and Abrams were wrong to think that nothing was changing. Scientific revolutions happen, Kuhn argued, in response to a crisis. Then follows the "crisis-state"—something that "demands the competence of the psychologist even more than that of the historian" to explain adequately.[7] The eloquence of Jane Jacobs, in combination with her nervy actions, affected our souls so viscerally that decision makers could not for long ignore the passions she had stirred up. Within a year of the publication of *Death and Life,* architects were already submitting designs for low-rise housing projects for the first time since the Depression.[8] Six years later in 1968 Congress banned altogether the construction of any more high-rise public housing. That the Le Corbusier–inspired housing project was unequivocally dead was spectacularly demonstrated in 1972, when the St. Louis Housing Authority dynamited three of the Pruitt-Igoe project buildings, and razed the rest the following year. The image of this project being blown up got wide play in the media, and became the icon of a failed national policy that was formally ended two years later in 1974 when Congress passed the new housing law that included the Section 8 provision. This provision, along with subsidizing the rents of needy people to enable them to live in private housing, provided for incentives for private developers to build low-income housing.

The West Village Houses

From now on, all new public housing would be low-rise. The prototype had been created by Jacobs and her fellow Greenwich Village activists in the early 1960s after they had won their battle to save their neighborhood from urban renewal. Now they were finally able to tell the city exactly what kind of new housing they wanted in that fourteen-block area that had originally been slated to be wrecked and rebuilt into high-rises. They wanted low-rise structures in keeping with the scale of the neighborhood. The project would be built on a piece of vacant land on Washington Street, which ran along the Hudson River and was still primarily light industrial in character. No existing buildings were to be demolished for building the new housing—"infill," they called it, thereby introducing a new term into the housing lexicon. In keeping with the spirit of Jacobs's doctrine of mixed land use, the Village housing was to be shoehorned in right next to the warehouses and lofts without knocking down any existing structures. "Not a sparrow shall be moved" was the slogan of the West Village Committee, the new name for the former Committee to Save the West Village. The project would be a cooperative for middle-income owners, financed through New York State's Mitchell-Lama program.

From their inception, the West Village Houses, as the project was officially called, were angrily opposed by the supporters of the status quo, including real estate developers who, in an atmosphere of rising land values, were angry that residents of Greenwich Village were getting their hands on a valuable piece of property. Megabuilder William Zeckendorf was now looking to acquire an adjacent ten-block area where he would build a high-rise luxury residential complex, the highest building being 104 stories, all set atop a platform over a cloverleaf interchange. "A triumph of eggheadedness" was how he described the Village group's plans. He considered his project a noble cause: "It's not the money, it's the pleasure of wiping out an industrial slum," Zeckendorf told the *Village Voice* (January 18, 1968).

New York officials hated Zeckendorf, a real bully, but they didn't like Jacobs either, and now were enraged that the citizens of Greenwich Village had the audacity to dictate to the city what should be built in their neighborhood using taxpayers' money. They accused Villagers of being selfish, of not thinking of the public good. One City Planning Commission official was overheard saying that the Village project worried him because if the city let the West Village neighborhood plan for itself, then every neighborhood would want to plan for itself.[9] Other critics assailed the notion of walk-ups as a throwback to tenement days. Because of the city's opposition, the West Village Committee spent nine frustrating years bushwacking their way through the red tape that the city threw in the way before securing the necessary permits.

When the West Village Houses were finally completed in 1975 — forty-two five- and six-story walk-ups along seven blocks of Washington Street — it seemed like a Pyrrhic victory. The long construction delays, coupled with the economic woes of the time — inflation-cum-recession and New York City teetering toward bankruptcy — had turned the project into a financial nightmare that in the end had to be bailed out by the city. And as if that weren't bad enough, critics had scant praise for the design. The *New York Times*'s Paul Goldberger spoke of the "unrelieved plainness" of their exteriors. Still, Goldberger said, the houses represented "a curious mix of urbanistic success — their good scale and insistence on neighborhood preservation—and urbanistic disaster—their basic dreariness" (September 28, 1974).

Still, for all the angst associated with West Village Houses, they represented a real turning point in the new, post–urban renewal world. Low-rise infill housing, funded by a combination of private and public sources, now began to pop up in city neighborhoods across the country. Today, the notion of rebuilding a neighborhood without disturbing the buildings that are still viable seems so obvious. It is hard to imagine that the word "infill" only entered the vocabulary forty years ago.

Building Preservation

A sense of time is something crucial to the health of all cities, Jacobs argued both directly and indirectly throughout *Death and Life*. This is something people seem to realize instinctively when they visit Europe for the first time. Gazing upon the Roman Coliseum or Notre Dame de Paris, they realize that American cities just can't compare. Jacobs had been thinking about the relationship between time and cities for years, at least since the 1950s when William Kirk had first walked her through East Harlem and showed her how urban renewal was destroying viable buildings, along with the neighborhood's very soul. In *Death and Life* Jacobs took that insight further. A city, she argued, needed "aged buildings." The reasons were practical—shabby old structures rent for cheap and therefore serve as incubators for new businesses. And beyond that, they give us something deeper, a kind of spiritual nourishment. "Among the most admirable and enjoyable sights to be found along the sidewalks of big cities are the ingenious adaptions of old quarters to new uses. The town-house parlor that becomes a craftsman's showroom, the stable that becomes a house, the basement that becomes an immigrant's club."

How it jars us to think that not too long ago, old factory buildings now housing expensive lofts or chic malls were considered expendable. And that was the least of it. As Jacobs was penning *Death and Life,* Pennsylvania Railroad was making plans to tear down its magnificent New York City station. Penn Station, with its vaulted ceilings and sweeping marble staircase, was designed after the Baths of Caracalla in Rome, and built by the architectural firm of McKim, Meade and White. "This city's got the right name—New York. Nothing ever gets old around here," a counterman at the station's Savarin coffee shop told a reporter one morning as the first crews were arriving with their jackhammers to begin pulverizing the grand neo-classical structure.[10]

Nobody today questions that Penn Station's demise constituted an outrageous wrong. But at the time nobody seemed to care much, even after two hundred or so famous architects and other intelligentsia staged a demonstration in front of the doomed station during afternoon rush hour in August 1962, marching up and down for two hours carrying placards with messages like "Shame" and "Renovate, Don't Desecrate." The group, led by the architect Norval White, included Jane Jacobs, suitably dressed for the muggy August weather in her usual cotton dress and sandals.

But even some architects were shrugging their shoulders over the planned demolition, saying that it was high time for the station to go anyway. It was now a grimy white elephant that was bleeding its owner, Pennsylvania Railroad, of over $3 million a year. To boot, it was sitting on a piece of valuable real estate. The actual demolition started a little over a year later. It was performed piecemeal, which allowed the trains to operate and give the public time to absorb the loss. As Penn Station was being reduced to piles of marble and granite debris, most of which was carted off and dumped into a Secaucus, New Jersey, swamp, something finally began clicking in the public's mind. In 1965 New York finally passed its landmarks law. By then, a historic preservation movement was under way all over the country.

Jacobs was not directly involved with building preservation, but her very vocal and visible activism, in combination with the enormous wallop that her book delivered to the public consciousness, helped empower preservationists. The effects of *Death and Life* were immediate: in 1962, one year after the book's publication, the

New York City Planning Commission recommended that "Hell's Hundred Acres," one of the neighborhoods being considered for urban renewal, be preserved for the 651 businesses that, it said in its report, were flourishing there.[11] But the recommendation carried little clout, as New York City did not yet have a landmarks law. So while Jacobs was fighting her civic battles in the Village during the 1960s, other women were working simultaneously to save historic buildings, including those in Hell's Hundred Acres, whose section south of Houston Street would soon be renamed SoHo.

One of them was Margot Gayle, who during the 1950s had put together the lengthily named Committee of Neighbors to Get the Clock on the Jefferson Market Courthouse Started. After their mission was accomplished in 1960, the committee reinvented itself as the Committee for a Library in the Jefferson Courthouse. Seven years later, a branch of New York Public Library opened in the building. All the while, Gayle was discovering the charms of SoHo's gritty old industrial buildings with their cast-iron facades, where artists were now living for cheap.

So Gayle began another crusade, another of many that she would lead, this one to preserve the old cast-iron buildings, a uniquely American nineteenth-century architectural form that cunningly fused beloved classical motifs like Ionic and Doric columns with America's exuberant entrepreneurial spirit. People thought Gayle was out of her mind. "Commercial junk" was how a *Villager* columnist characterized the now gorgeously restored cast-iron buildings that are the pride of SoHo. These buildings, the *Villager* columnist wrote, "have outlived their usefulness; they are not only not quaint but are ugly eyesores, and should be torn down and replaced by publicly sponsored middle-income housing, or co-operatives" (January 31, 1963).

Gayle, however, wouldn't let up. She was a terrific grassroots organizer; once she got her teeth into something, she wouldn't let it go. She and Jacobs had a lot in common. "She wasn't a chit-chatty woman," Gayle recalled of Jacobs, "but I admired her nerve."[12] The two women weren't friends, but they knew the same people and went to the same meetings. And they had a common enemy in

Robert Moses. Their activism-cum-chutzpah, each one's running parallel with the other's, saved SoHo.

One of the first actions of the new Landmarks Preservation Commission in 1965 was to confer landmark designation on SoHo's Haughwout Building, which architect Peter Blake called the best example of cast-iron architecture in the country. Robert Moses objected vehemently; the building, he wrote in a letter to the Board of Estimate, stands "directly in the right of way of the Lower Manhattan Expressway."[13]

In 1973 SoHo officially received historical designation as the "Cast Iron District." By then, what writer and preservation activist Roberta Brandes Gratz calls the "SoHo syndrome" in her 1998 book *Cities Back from the Edge* was spreading all over New York. Starting at Lower Manhattan, the syndrome crossed the East River to Brooklyn, then moved across the Hudson to Hoboken, New Jersey, and clear across the country. Every city, Gratz writes, wants its own SoHo.[14]

But if Robert Moses had gotten his way and built the Lower Manhattan Expressway, we would not have SoHo, nor, perhaps, the SoHo-inspired loft districts in other cities.

Lomex Rises Again

After the defeat of the Lower Manhattan Expressway (Lomex) in 1962, it came back to life in 1965 when Mayor Wagner announced that construction on the expressway would begin as quickly as possible. "Most gratifying," Robert Moses told the *New York Times* (May 26, 1965) when he learned of Wagner's decision. But downtown residents vowed that the mayor would regret his decision come election day. And he surely did when he lost to John Lindsay, who had opposed the project as a congressman and now, as mayor, put it on hold.

But in 1968, talk of building Lomex began yet again. And this time, its completion looked inevitable. Lindsay, now mayor, had done a complete turnabout. He was now saying that he favored

Lomex, although not, mind you, the elevated highway that everybody was objecting to. Instead, he was proposing a compromise,
that Lomex be built below street level as "a cut-and-cover" tunnel.
"The in-and-out, over-and-under proposal that has come out of this
attempt to defang the monster makes no one very happy," wrote
Ada Louise Huxtable in the *New York Times* (February 2, 1969).
"Ducking subways, utilities and the water table, it struggles above
and below ground in a series of curious compromises of tortuous
complexity, complete with enough entrances, exits and connections
to turn Lower Manhattan into a concrete no man's land. Displaced
people will now number in the low thousands rather than the high
thousands. It is a question of degree: do you kill a city or maim it?"
Because Lomex was to be part of the federal highway system, the
federal government would pick up 90 percent of the $150 million
price tag and New York State the remaining 10 percent. With so
much money at stake, Lindsay was surely feeling the heat.

On April 10, 1968, officials from the State Department of Transportation held a public hearing at Seward Park High School, which
sat right beside Lomex's planned path through the Lower East
Side.[15] Turnout was high; people from the affected areas had urged
their neighbors to attend. The mood was tense and angry, but
Lomex wasn't the only reason. Just six days earlier, Martin Luther
King had been assassinated in Memphis. And the number of American troops in Vietnam was reaching its highest level ever, causing
the antiwar movement to grow ever more vocal and desperate. This
was the state of the world as New York's officials were telling the
press that traffic congestion in the city absolutely necessitated
building an expressway, to say nothing of the construction jobs it
would create. How could all these people not see that the expressway was for everybody's own good?

"It was patently a phony, the whole thing." Thus Jacobs described the hearing during her 1997 interview with Leticia Kent. "A
hearing is supposed to be held before a decision is made, of course,
and the decision itself is supposed to be based on what comes out
in the hearing, the information. This decision had been made. This
hearing was just to go through the motions."

The meeting was packed—residents, reporters, politicians, and police. Glossy fifteen-page booklets prepared by the same engineering firm that Robert Moses had used to justify a similar scheme twenty years earlier were distributed to the crowd. Officials sat on the stage behind tables. The microphone had been placed down below, on the floor, so the speaker would stand below the stage facing the audience, instead of addressing the officials.

Speaker after speaker was now walking up to the microphone, describing how much the expressway was going to hurt them. They would lose their homes. Their businesses would be destroyed. For some twenty years the threat of Lomex had loomed; for that long, their elected leaders had been jerking them around. And now residents realized bitterly that they were just talking to themselves, not to the officials sitting behind them on the stage who were spared the embarrassment of having to look each speaker in the eye because they faced the speakers' backs. "The whole thing was just to let off steam and to go through the motions," Jacobs recalled later.

But the tactic wasn't working.

The audience, knowing that they were being ignored, began getting restless. They were yelling, "We want Jane. We want Jane." She got up and, as people cheered, walked up to the stage. "We were all very angry . . . And I pointed out, how ridiculous it was that we were talking to ourselves the way the microphone had been set up, instead of to the officials who were supposed to be listening to us and making their decision on the basis of what they heard." So James Toth, the official chairing the meeting, ran down and turned the microphone around. "That was rank hypocrisy, and so I turned it around again and said we had been talking to ourselves so far and so we might as well continue. That they weren't listening to us. That nothing would make them listen to us. They had made their decision. That was clear. And that they were really only errand boys . . . who had no power to make decisions. They had been sent by their betters from Albany and they had no autonomy. So we had better let them take back a message . . . that we would never stand for this expressway."

Jacobs, the *Voice* afterwards reported, warned that if the expressway were approved, "there will be anarchy." But obviously, Jacobs then continued, according to a sworn statement that she gave on April 30, their message obviously would go nowhere if it were given only in words.[16] She then proposed that the residents join her right there in a peaceful demonstration. She and another community activist, Frances Goldin, climbed the stairs to the stage and began to march across. People in the audience, taking their cue, began getting up from their seats, walking down the center aisle and up the stairs to the stage to join the two women. "Elderly couples marched. Catholics and Jews. Italians and Russians. Businessmen and artists," wrote Leticia Kent in the *Voice,* all followed the two women across the stage. The officials on the stage began to panic, pushing their chairs backward from the table. During this era of political unrest in America, demonstrations, even peaceful ones like this, made people skittish.

James Toth got up and blocked Jacobs's path, telling her to get down off the stage. Jacobs told him that she wouldn't, that instead they were going to march across the stage and down the stairs on the other side. "Arrest this woman!" Toth yelled to the two policemen standing on the stage. "Arrest this woman!" But the policemen didn't. There are two versions of what happened next. According to Jacobs, amidst the confusion a stenotypist who had set up her machine on the stage to take the minutes of the meeting became frightened. Standing up, she clutched her machine to her chest, shouting "This is a new machine! This is a new machine!" The tape, yards and yards of it, fell out onto the stage floor. The marchers began to pick it up, tearing it, throwing it up and down in the air like confetti, trampling on it. There were piles of paper tape all over the stage. And suddenly the room, except for the stenotypist's mantra and Toth's as well—"Arrest this woman!"— grew quiet.

The other version of this event, the one that appeared in Toth's affidavit, is that Jacobs herself pulled the tape out of the stenotype machine and tore it up. Two other people who were present at the meeting, both Jacobs supporters, also remember that she tore up the tape. She presumably realized that with no tape, there would be no record and therefore the required public hearing never happened. The marchers then followed her lead. Jacobs, one woman recalled, then announced to the audience, Look! There's no tape, so there's been no meeting.

Jacobs's version, however, does not mention her touching the tape. As Jacobs tells it, she stood on the stage in the middle of the piles of paper tape that the marchers had torn up. She now realized that the meeting had to end, somehow. And obviously the people in charge didn't know how. She also realized that because the tape of the meeting had been destroyed, there was no record. So she went to the microphone and said, "Listen to this! There is no record. There is no hearing. We are through with this phony, fink hearing." Go home, she urged everyone.

As for what happened next, there is no disagreement. As people were getting up and leaving, a policeman tapped Jacobs on the shoulder and said that she, at Toth's insistence, had been arrested. "Well, that's not very bright of him," Jacobs remarked, and the policeman agreed. But, he told Jacobs, he had no choice. He and the rest of the policeman at the hearing were clearly sympathetic. Jacobs was taken by squad car to the police station a few blocks away. About a hundred supporters traipsed behind her, "like the Pied Piper," wrote the reporter for the *Villager*. Jacobs was fingerprinted, photographed for mug shots, then charged with disorderly conduct. A group of about twenty supporters remained outside the precinct house. For two hours they shouted "We want Jane! We want Jane!" The police asked them to quiet down, but they didn't until she was released. "I couldn't be arrested in a better cause," she told a *New York Post* reporter as she was exiting the building.

"Well, here I have been arrested again!" Jacobs wrote cheerfully to her mother the day after the protest. Better than "just lying down and dying and taking this crookedness."[17] She had been arrested once before, four months earlier, at an anti-draft demonstration by more than 2,500 protestors at an army induction center in Lower Manhattan. Jacobs was arrested along with 263 others, whose ranks included

Susan Sontag, Benjamin Spock, and Allen Ginsberg. Charged with disorderly conduct, Jacobs pleaded guilty and was released.

But this time her arrest would cause her major headaches. In an affidavit Toth was stating that Jacobs had urged people to engage in violence, torn up the minutes of the meeting, and damaged the stenotype machine.[18] At Jacobs's arraignment a week after the hearing, the D.A. upped the charges against Jacobs to misdemeanors, which included rioting, inciting to riot, and "criminal mischief." All of which, if she were found guilty, could mean up to four years in jail. The D.A. even asked for an injunction to keep Jacobs from participating in any more anti-expressway demonstrations. The judge refused.

"The inference seems to be that anybody who criticizes a state program is going to get it in the neck," Jacobs told the *New York Times* (April 18, 1968). And the charges, she added, "bear no relation to what happened."

"Stenocide," Jacobs's former editor, Peter Blake, called Jacobs's supposed crime. As for the charge of disorderly conduct, Blake remarked, "Of course Jane Jacobs is disorderly—that's her job!"[19]

Recounting the Lomex hearing in May 2004 during her talk in Greenwich Village, Jacobs giggled wickedly at the memory. Given her lifelong disrespect for authority, tearing up the tape would have seemed right in sync with her character. In any event, what actually happened to the tape during the demonstration on the stage does not matter. What did matter was that the Lomex hearing and Jane Jacobs's arrest got wide play in the New York press. Jacobs's Village friends immediately set up a defense fund for her and hosted a benefit at the venerable Village Gate club to cover her legal expenses. Her case dragged on for several years. On the advice of her lawyer, in the end she reluctantly pleaded guilty to disorderly conduct. In exchange, the D.A. agreed to drop the criminal charges. The matter finally ended with the payment of a fine.

As for Lomex, it limped along for a little while longer. But all the publicity surrounding Jacobs's arrest had served to increase the public's already-widespread antipathy to the project. No politician wanted to touch it anymore, and even less so after a much-publicized study warned that dangerously high carbon monoxide levels would accompany a new expressway across Lower Manhattan. In July 1969 Lindsay, who was running for his second term, announced the expressway "dead for all time." "Imperiously," wrote a disgruntled Robert Moses in his self-aggrandizing book, *Public Works,* commenting on Lindsay's pronouncement with positively breathtaking self-unawareness. "This edict has a note of finality not unfamiliar to those who cherish Roman and Napoleonic pronouncements and the vicissitudes of American municipal politics and public opinion."

In August 1969 the Board of Estimate officially removed the expressway from the city map, even as Robert Moses was still insisting that a Lower Manhattan Expressway was inevitable. But Moses's reign in New York was now finally coming to an end.[20]

CHAPTER EIGHT

Race, Gentrification, and the South Bronx

For all the praise that Jacobs received when *Death and Life* came out, there were those who objected that her vision was too narrow, that it applied only to places like her own Greenwich Village or Boston's North End. The West Village, wrote *The Nation* architecture critic Walter McQuade, "is not even a semi-solution to the main problem of the city: saturation by low-income non-whites" (March 17, 1962). "Solutions to the basic social problems caused by minority groups and low-income families have been ignored in the book," wrote reporter Lucille Preuss in the *Milwaukee Journal* (July 8, 1962). "After all, the planners and public officials cannot be blamed for the tremendous influx of underprivileged people to our nation's cities," Preuss wrote. "Yet this, in a nutshell, represents most of the problem."

What those critics were saying was that Jacobs hadn't acknowledged the importance of race in her analysis. The places she used as examples all "unslummed" by themselves, without any government help. What made this possible was that the inhabitants had strong social networks, which in one way or another gave them access to the capital needed to either buy or take care of property. In the case of the North End, which Boston's banks had long redlined, members of

The old Bronx Courthouse, 2005. Photo by Alice Sparberg Alexiou.

the tight-knit Italian community loaned money to one another or bartered their work skills. In Greenwich Village the urban pioneers like the Jacobs family were middle class or professionals with access to capital. To quote writer and philosopher Marshall Berman, the picture that Jacobs paints of her ideal, diverse neighborhood is "the city before the blacks got there."

"Her world ranges from solid working-class whites at the bottom to professional middle-class whites at the top," Berman writes in *All That Is Solid Melts into Air,* his 1982 study of modernism. "There is nothing and no one above; what matters more here, however, is that there is nothing and no one below—there are no stepchildren in Jacobs's family of eyes." This latter reference is a gentle swipe at an oft-quoted Jacobs passage about the "eyes on the street" in her ideal neighborhood. Jacobs's vision seems like a mirage when viewed from a later time when, in his words, "millions of black and Hispanic people would converge on America's cities—at precisely the moment when the jobs they sought . . . that earlier poor immigrants had found, were departing or disappearing. . . . Many of them found themselves desperately poor, chronically unemployed, at once racial and economic outcasts, an enormous *lumpenproletariat* without prospects or hopes. In these conditions, it is no wonder that rage, despair and violence spread like plagues—and that hundreds of formerly stable urban neighborhoods all over America disintegrated completely."

Jacobs did have something to say on the subject of race. After acknowledging that racial discrimination and segregation are, in her words, "our country's most serious social problem," she then writes, "I do not mean to imply that a city's planning and design, or its types of streets and street life, can automatically overcome segregation." But she then says that bad design "*can* make it *much harder* for American cities to overcome discrimination no matter how much effort is expended." Later, while discussing unslumming, she says that those who are able to leave ghettos are able to overcome discrimination, "one of the terrible problems of most slum populations." She adds that the most "drastic" of discriminations is that against "Negroes," at that time still an acceptable sobriquet for African-Americans. But, she adds, "it is an injustice with which all our major slum populations have had to contend to some degree." She stays with the subject for two more pages, and finally concedes that race does, indeed, matter:

The effective breaking down of residential discrimination outside a slum, and the less dramatic self-diversification within an unslumming slum, proceed concurrently. If America has now, in the case of Negroes, reached an effective halt in this process and in general entered a stage of arrested development—a thought I find both highly improbable and quite intolerable—then it may be that Negro slums cannot effectively unslum in the fashion demonstrated by slums formed by other ethnic populations and population mixtures. . . . unslumming is at the very least directly—as well as indirectly—inhibited by discrimination.

But this is as far as Jacobs takes the subject of race. In analyzing her words, we must note that she was writing at a time when the white intelligentsia was only just beginning to acknowledge race as a crucial social issue. "Blacks were writing about blacks then, not whites," says sociologist Herbert Gans, who has written extensively on the subjects of race and housing. But soon that would change. In the heated politics of the early 1960s, a time of rapid changes, the civil rights movement was gaining momentum and people were beginning to think about race. In 1963 Harvard sociologists Nathan Glazer and Daniel Moynihan wrote their landmark *Beyond the Melting Pot*. The prior year, Michael Harrington's seminal *The Other America* appeared, introducing the phrase "the culture of poverty."

Harrington devoted considerable space to the discussion of race. He talked of the "vast, silent and automatic system directed against men and women of color." And in a chapter devoted to slums, Harrington nails down an uncomfortable fact that Jacobs only dances around: "Where the ethnic slum once stood, in the 'old slum' neighborhood, there is a new type of slum. Its citizens are the internal migrants, the Negroes, the poor whites from the farms, the Puerto Ricans. They join the failure from the old ethnic culture and form an entirely different kind of neighborhood. For many of them, the crucial problem is color, and this makes the ghetto walls higher than they have ever been."

Jacobs, it is fair to say, did not adequately address race in *Death and Life*. What is more, you can reasonable argue that she never has. In her book *Dark Age Ahead*, published in 2004, Jacobs briefly addresses the issue of people who are displaced when a neighborhood gentrifies. "Affordable housing could have been added as infill in parking lots and empty lots if the government had been on its toes, and if communities had been self-confident and vigorous in making demands, but they almost never were," she writes. Her comment begs the question: but why didn't communities make those demands? And, specifically, what demands? And on behalf of whom? It is appropriate to note that some criticized the West Village Houses because it accommodated only the middle class, not the poor. In other words, not people of color. To state it bluntly, how many white urban pioneers today are fighting to ensure that people of color are not pushed out of their now-gentrifying neighborhoods?

Let us now examine New York City's South Bronx, a black and Hispanic neighborhood that once personified urban blight, through the Jacobs spectrum.

The South Bronx

When President Jimmy Carter paid his now-famous visit to Charlotte Street in the South Bronx in 1977, the wide press coverage he received shined a spotlight on the shameful state of America's cities and turned the neighborhood into a spectacular national symbol of urban blight. Carter was photographed standing on the weedy, garbage-strewn lots surrounded by eight-foot-high piles of rubble that had once been five- and six-story brick walk-ups, many with marble lobbies and facades decorated with elegant granite cornices carved by Italian immigrant masons. The South Bronx had once been a compendium of perfect, Jacobs-prescribed city neighborhoods with such euphonious names as Morrisania and Melrose and Mott Haven, where successive waves of immigrants settled, first Germans and Irish, followed by Italians and then Jews. The short blocks were filled with local businesses: candy stores, Solly Sherman's vegetable and deli market on Charlotte Street, tailor shops, dry cleaners, shoe stores, movie theaters. Children played in the street as people sat on their stoops or in chairs on the sidewalk.

But in the 1960s white people began to flee the South Bronx, and it became a dumping ground for welfare recipients. By the 1970s arson fires were literally burning it to the ground. Between 1970 and 1980 the area lost more than half of its population. Almost all who remained were black or Hispanic. The reasons for the South Bronx's decline were many and complex. They included New York City's 1970s fiscal crisis, which led to a policy of deliberate neglect: in 1976 Roger Starr said publicly that the area was so far gone that it merited "planned shrinkage" rather than attempts to rebuild it.[1] City officials, embarrassed by Starr's bluntness, disavowed his remark. But at the same time, they left the South Bronx to fend for itself. Doing so carried no political risk because, to state it baldly, poor blacks and Hispanics lacked the means and personal connections to fight back—unlike Jacobs and her neighbors in Greenwich Village during the 1960s.

But now, thirty years later, thanks to a combination of government aid and grassroots activism, the South Bronx has come back, and dramatically so. Its burned-out ruins have been replaced—not with high-rises but low-rise infill projects. One of these is Charlotte Gardens, a project that reclaimed the neighborhood that Carter made famous. It was built by a community development corporation, one of many that were now forming in poor areas, both urban and rural, throughout the country. The South Bronx Development Organization was headed by the controversial Ed Logue, whose mega urban-renewal projects had transformed New Haven, then Boston, before he was lured to New York in 1968 by Governor Nelson Rockefeller to run the Urban Development Corporation. Jacobs had frequently and loudly locked horns with Logue. (Later she would say about Logue, "Boy, in my books, he went down as a maniac."[2])

Charlotte Gardens was atypical of infill projects: it consisted of eighteen acres containing eighty-nine single-family private homes built in the midst of the ruins of Charlotte Street. When the houses were completed in 1986, they made a shocking sight: vinyl-sided ranch houses, neatly landscaped with—yes!—lawns and flower beds, surrounded by empty, garbage-filled lots and burned-out, hollow-eyed apartment buildings, like a Levittown dropped in the middle of a dying slum. Critics—and there were many—said that the homes would never be able to survive such a hostile environment. But Charlotte Gardens did survive, and more: most of the homes, which now sell for five times their original price of approximately sixty thousand dollars, still have their original owners. As for the surrounding area, what was once an urban wasteland that was compared to Dresden after the Allied bombing is now a visually interesting mix of new two- and three-story townhouses and old buildings, many of them renovated, interspersed with an occasional still-empty lot.

But every time you turn around, a Charlotte Gardens home-owner said, somebody's building something on a lot, usually an-other townhouse. "When we moved here, in 1986, people told me I was crazy," she said, as she carefully planted mums along the bor-ders of her immaculately cut lawn on a beautiful autumn Sunday. "I was living at the time on the Lower East Side. People who'd run away from the South Bronx were saying to me, 'What do you want to move there for?' But now," she continued happily, "they're telling me, 'I'd like to move back! Do you know of any houses in the area for sale?' But the people living here don't want to sell."

When the Charlotte Gardens project was completed, reactions were mixed. Architecture critics hated the suburban-style houses and faulted the project's low density. They charged that building single-family homes separated by suburban patches of green within an urban landscape constituted a terrible use of urban space. To re-build the Bronx, they said, you need to reestablish high density— something that, thanks to Jane Jacobs's insights in *Death and Life,* people were now regarding as a good thing for cities.

On the face of it, the criticism had merit. Nobody today seriously doubts the necessity of high densities in urban space. But the fact is that Charlotte Gardens has been a huge success, if only for the simple reason that it has given working-class people an otherwise unattain-able opportunity to own their own homes, complete with that patch of grass that so annoys Jacobs but nevertheless remains firmly part of the American dream. Most Americans, both at the time when Jacobs was writing *Death and Life* and now, aspire to live in the suburbs, not in the crowded city neighborhoods that Jacobs so adores.

The very existence of the Charlotte Street houses, offensive as their design is to urban aesthetes and as unsatisfying as they may be to Jacobs, have formed a crucial link in the complex and sometimes imperceptible changes that are now sweeping all through the Bronx. The pioneers who bought the eighty-nine homes settled in, invited their incredulous friends to visit, and thereby got people to think about moving there, too. For those who had never left the South Bronx either because they couldn't or wouldn't, just the sight of those meticulously tended homes elicited a wide range of emotions: some, to be sure, felt resentment or envy, but many surely now were hopeful that their borough was coming back to life. All of which gave the community the incentive to pursue change. Community development corporations were popping up all over the Bronx, like Father Gigante's Southeast Bronx Community Organization, Sebco in Hunts Point, the Mid-Bronx Desperados, Banana Kelly, and Nos Quedamos in Melrose.

The community development corporations were receiving federal money as well as grants from private foundations with which they were building infill housing and renovating buildings in partnership with the city. In other words, the outside aid coming to the South Bronx was in manageable increments and administered locally, and therefore benefiting the community. It was not in the old top-down Title I form that Jacobs called "cataclysmic money."

In this reborn South Bronx landscape, people saw business opportunities. Gutsy individuals raised capital, often from friends and family, to start their own businesses, which they believed could now survive and even thrive. Fast-forward to the present. Vicente Medina, a Mexican immigrant, has converted a grand old bank building in the Tremont section of the Bronx into the three-hundred-seat El Rancho Restaurant, which he opened in 2004. El Rancho represents a step up from the neighboring businesses, Medina told the *New York Times* (September 21, 2004). But Tremont, which had fallen on hard times, is ready for an elegant restaurant, Medina said. To use Jacobs's terminology, the area has unslummed. In this way the South Bronx's rebirth today resembles Greenwich Village in the 1960s, which Jacobs called "the unslummed former slum in which I live."

Except that there is a major difference between these two places, and it has to do with race. Greenwich Village, populated mostly by white people, many of them highly educated and well connected, unslummed by itself. Villagers then had the means and the connections to protect their community, both from the government and private developers.

The South Bronx, poor and nonwhite, does not have the resources of the Villagers. But the good news is that community
groups, in partnership with government, accomplished in the South
Bronx what urban renewal could not.

Nos Quedamos

One such group is Nos Quedamos, which was formed in 1993 after
Yolanda Garcia, a resident of the heavily Puerto Rican Melrose section of the South Bronx, one day noticed some city workers walking around her neighborhood with clipboards, making diagrams
and taking measurements of abandoned buildings. When Garcia,
who with her family had a small carpet business in Melrose, asked
them what they were doing, they told her that the city had plans to
rebuild the neighborhood. Garcia began to investigate. She discovered that the city's plans included razing existing housing to build
a low density, middle-income project. The city was very proud of
the plan, but it had never discussed it with the people living in Melrose like Garcia and her family and all the others who had homes or
small businesses, who had stayed in their neighborhood even as the
Bronx was burning around them. And now they were going to lose
their homes and businesses, not through arson but through urban
renewal.

So in the Bronx in 1993 a scenario was being played out just like
the one Jane Jacobs had described in *Death and Life,* down to the
residents finding out about the city's urban renewal plans only by
accident. And Yolanda Garcia, just as Jane Jacobs had, sprang to action. She and other Melrose residents started Nos Quedamos, "we
stay," so named because plan or no plan, they weren't going anywhere. They pounded on doors, and for two years met at least once
a week in a church basement. They figured out how politics work
and how to get people in city government to pay attention to you.
Nos Quedamos began to register people to vote, thousands of
them. It was 1993, and David Dinkins was running for mayor
against Rudolph Giuliani. He would lose, but in the meantime the

politically ambitious Bronx borough president Freddie Ferrer was telling Dinkins, pay attention to the Bronx because the Latino vote can swing this election.

Nos Quedamos sweated it out, ultimately getting control over the plans to rebuild their neighborhood. Walking through it, you will see a work in progress. Hundreds and hundreds of spanking-new low-income housing units now stand where was once burned-out rubble. Among the little bodegas and storefront churches of 161st Street, a major thoroughfare, stands here and there a still-empty lot, waiting to be built on. But a few blocks over on Brook Avenue, alongside a Catholic church and its adjoining parochial school, you will come upon the new Melrose Condominiums, three-story townhouses with tiny front yards adorned with rosebushes.

Across the street from the condos is a park filled with people, children using the new playground equipment and old men sitting on the benches talking. On the street a group of young men are standing around and admiring somebody's carefully restored 1950s-model bright-red Pontiac convertible. Salsa music is pouring out from a tiny wooden, flag-festooned house tucked into a corner of the park. It is a beautiful autumn day and its small garden courtyard is filled with families. This is the Centro Cultural Rincón Criollo, the city's oldest "casita," where Melrose's many Puerto Rican residents gather to socialize and listen to music.

Taking all this in, you will think, yes, this is exactly what Jane Jacobs had in mind in *Death and Life* when she talked about "mixed-uses" and "unslumming," why some parks work and others don't, how people use streets and sidewalks, and why cities need short blocks. And you will also be reminded why districts need old buildings, a point that Jacobs makes with great emphasis. Not expensively renovated old buildings, she writes, "but also a good lot of plain, ordinary, low-value old buildings, including some rundown old buildings." Because new ideas need old buildings, with their affordable rent. In Melrose there are plenty of old buildings. Many look freshly renovated, with new windows and cleaned facades, but there are still some standing deserted, which means that there is still opportunity for a small businessman or a community group to buy one for cheap and fix it up, then rent it out to residential or commercial tenants, or perhaps in true Jacobs-like fashion, a mixture of both.

At the intersection of Third and Brook avenues stands the old Bronx Courthouse, a massive four-story granite structure. On its front facade sits a wreathed statue of Justice, whom you could see while you were riding the now-defunct Third Avenue El, as if she were watching over you and all the others inside the subway car, immigrants and the children of immigrants, who had escaped the oppression of wherever they had escaped from. Since 1978 this Beaux-Arts structure, now listed on the National Register of Historic Places, stands empty. With its grand scale, the courthouse looks for all the world like the Parthenon of the Bronx.

Gazing upon it, something catches in your throat and you think, why doesn't somebody restore this wonderful building? Why isn't it being used for, say, a school or a museum? A community center? A restaurant? Even, God help us, for retail space? And, if you happen to have a copy of *Death and Life* in hand, you can open it and read about "architectural focal points" and realize the courthouse is exactly what Jane Jacobs means. "Most landmarks and focal points in cities," she writes, ". . . come from the contrast of a use radically different from its surroundings, and therefore inherently special-looking, happily located to make some drama and contrast of the inherent difference." And you will understand that the courthouse is precisely the opposite of the civic centers surrounded by "border vacuums" that she so despises. "The mingled city with individual architectural focal points intimately surrounded by the everyday matrix is in harmony with the economic and other functional behavior of cities."

In fact, for years Nos Quedamos has been trying to acquire the building for the community; they envision using it as a town hall. But for now it belongs to a group of investors who bought the courthouse in 1998 for a song—three hundred thousand dollars, to be precise—at a city auction. Their bid beat out Nos Quedamos's. The group expressed anger, and so did Bronx political leaders, at the Giuliani administration for selling off a city landmark to speculators instead of renovating it for use of the community.

Six years later, the owners, after putting the courthouse back on the market in 2000 for $1.8 million and then taking it off again, were still looking for "the right tenant," somebody with "a high purpose" to fit the grandeur of the building. The owners said they lacked confidence in the many community groups who had approached them, turning down their requests to rent space in the property. Many small businessmen often express interest in moving there. A fruit wholesaler wanted the whole building; he would put a farmers' market right out in front on the sidewalk—something that Melrose badly needs. But no, the owners decided.

"The people close to the area would love to be in the courthouse," one of the owners said. "It has such a romantic aura. But I don't think it would be a good idea to have ten, twenty local businesses in it. Because the neighborhood has upgraded, there's been a lot of development." In other words, the developer seemed to be saying, the courthouse was too upscale for the poor people living in the community.

The ongoing saga of the Bronx Courthouse, with all its layers and ambiguities, is a perfect lens through which to test Jacobs's observations. However it turns out, following this story will help us further understand the process of "unslumming." Does the rebirth of the South Bronx show that gentrification is inevitable? Or does the government have a role to play in ensuring that the poor do not get pushed out of their neighborhoods when real estate starts looking up?

For all the grit and savvy of community groups like Nos Quedamos, the South Bronx still needs the government's help to protect it from being unslummed out of control so that its rejuvenation will also benefit the people who live there, and not merely outside real estate speculators.

Unslumming and Gentrification

The word "unslumming" immediately conjures up another word, one that we hear constantly in the context of cities: gentrification.

The word had not yet been coined at the time Jacobs was writing; it first appeared in 1964 in an article by British sociologist Ruth Glass to describe the phenomenon of middle-class people moving into working-class London neighborhoods and displacing the people living there. "Gentrification" has taken on such strong political overtones that government publications avoid the word, preferring instead the innocuous-sounding phrase "inner-city revitalization." To say that a neighborhood has gentrified conjures up images of yuppie pioneers buying up fabulous old but neglected brownstones in "bad" neighborhoods, then gutting and renovating them to the tune of millions of dollars. Businesses like Starbucks and The Food Emporium then follow. But for the people who were already living there—and note that they are often people of color—gentrification equals dislocation. Community leaders sometimes refer to the process as "hood snatching."

So now we find ourselves at an uncomfortable juncture in our journey through the South Bronx, where we must now pause and ask: what is the difference between "unslumming" as Jacobs describes it and gentrification? Is there a point at which unslumming stops and gentrification begins? Can a neighborhood unslum without becoming gentrified? Or are we really talking about the same thing—is there simply no difference between the two terms? Jacobs, asked numerous times over the years about gentrification, always says that it all comes down to supply and demand. Gentrification occurs when there is too little supply of funky old neighborhoods—for which we can at least in part blame the old urban renewal tactics, which bulldozed them away.[3] But this is hardly a satisfactory response to the problem of gentrification.

Jacobs devoted an entire chapter in *Death and Life* to unslumming. She discusses what causes a neighborhood to turn into a slum, or, conversely, to unslum. Slums, she writes, form when stagnation and "the Great Blight of Dullness" in a neighborhood—the opposite of diversity—drive away those who can leave. Jacobs seems to be saying that people will try to get out of a neighborhood that does not offer them anything good. Slums, she says, are vicious circles that can be disrupted only by breaking what she calls the "link": "too many people move out of it too fast—and in the meantime dream of getting out." She cited, among other neighborhoods, Boston's North End and her own Greenwich Village as examples of successfully "unslummed former slums." A person who now sets foot in either of these neighborhoods today will have a hard time imagining that anybody could have ever thought them slums. Of course, when Jacobs was writing her book these were still pretty grimy places, but nonetheless places where people were happily remaining or deliberately moving into.

Perhaps what happens next in the South Bronx, a place that once personified despair but is now decidedly on its way up, will give us some more insight into gentrification—or, as it were, unslumming. It is a perfect laboratory for testing Jacobs's observations. Let us look at some of the facts of the area's rebirth.

From a low point of 266,603 in 1980, the population according to the 2000 census had increased to 337,120. Jill Jonnes has been studying the South Bronx for more than two decades. In her 2002 book, *South Bronx Rising,* she reports that in 2000 the area had 57,361 new units in rehabilitated apartment buildings and nearly 10,000 units in new two- and three-family townhouses. Moreover, there is now a small community of artists and "immigrants" from Manhattan living in Mott Haven, with its cheap loft space, small historical district of Victorian brownstones, and snazzy new bar called the Blue Ox.

But for all the hope that the South Bronx's rebirth has generated, the area has one of the lowest income levels in the country. Half the population receives public assistance, and one-third of the households earn less than ten thousand dollars a year. Despite the housing boom, the borough's economy is severely depressed. The South Bronx, it seems, is a long way from gentrification.

CHAPTER NINE

Toronto

In June 1968, two months after her arrest at the Lomex hearing, Jacobs and her family moved to Toronto to begin a new life. When asked, she has always said that the Vietnam War was the reason she and her family left New York City for Canada. The Jacobs family were antiwar activists, and visibly so. Six months before her arrival in Toronto, Jacobs had signed her name along with more than four hundred writers and editors to a full-page ad that ran in the *New York Post* announcing that they refused to pay a proposed 10 percent tax increase to finance the war. Besides this, the Jacobses often participated in the protests that by the late 1960s were taking place all over the country with increasing regularity.

At the famous march on the Pentagon in October 1967, the family, along with other demonstrators, clashed with soldiers in gas masks on the Pentagon steps. "They looked like some big horrible insect, the whole bunch of them together, not human beings at all," Jacobs would later recall in an interview with reporter Mark Feeney of the *Boston Globe* (November 14, 1993). The soldiers drove the protestors back with the butts of their rifles, injuring some; afterward the steps of the Pentagon were splattered with blood. Among the 250 people arrested that day were author Norman Mailer and peace activist Dave Dellinger, later famous as one of the demonstrators at

Aerial view of Toronto, Yonge Street, 1973. City of Toronto Archives, Series 35, File 1. Northway-Photomap, Inc.

the 1968 Democratic Convention who would be tried with the rest of the "Chicago Seven."

Jacobs was not hurt, but as she was running down the steps, she, in her words, fell out of love with her country. "It sounds ridiculous," she told the *Globe*, "but I didn't feel part of America anymore."

To oppose the Vietnam War on moral grounds was one thing. For Jane and Robert Jacobs, there was an added incentive to leave the United States: their two sons, Ned and Jim, were eighteen and twenty, and they were going to be drafted. Both had made up their minds that they would go to jail rather than to Vietnam. Faced with their sons' all-but-certain imprisonment, Robert and Jane Jacobs decided in 1968 that the family should head north.

They chose Toronto over other possible choices in Canada after Robert Jacobs made a few exploratory trips there and decided that he liked it. Moreover, there were opportunities for him as an architect to make a living in Toronto, which was experiencing a building boom. He began to hunt for a job and soon found a position as a hospital architect at the prestigious Toronto architectural firm Craig, Zeidler, and Strong, which later became Zeidler Robert, where Robert Jacobs would remain for the rest of his career.

There was doubtless another factor in the family's decision to leave New York, although Jane never stated it directly: the fact is, she was sick and tired of the constant battles she had been waging for years with the city. "It's absurd to make your life absurd in response to absurd governments," she told the *Village Voice* (July 6, 1972). All that fighting took time away from her family and her work. She had started on a new book after her resignation from *Architectural Forum* in 1962 in which she was examining cities as the basis of economies. Six years later, *The Economy of Cities* was still not finished. For Jacobs, living in New York had become a detriment to her writing.

The Jacobs family were just a few of the many Americans who were leaving the United States for Canada because of their opposition to the war. The immigration wave had started in the mid-1960s, and was now increasing dramatically because of the war's escalation combined with ending most draft deferments and introducing a draft lottery, which meant that if you had a low number, you would undoubtedly be called up. The war resisters were by no means the first Americans who fled their country to Canada for ideological reasons. Thousands of pro-British Loyalists had headed north after the Revolutionary War. Now, in 1968, Americans comprised Canada's fastest-growing minority. Some sat in bars, crying from homesickness, and would later take advantage of the amnesty granted under President Carter and return to the United States. But 65 percent of those who came during this wave stayed, becoming Canadian citizens and submerging their American identity as much as they could.[1]

At first the Vietnam War resisters were regarded with suspicion, but by 1968 they were mostly getting a warm reception. Canada had been a strong American ally during World War II and the subsequent Cold War, but Vietnam marked a turning point in relations

between the two countries. The vast majority of Canadians opposed the war; they had their own antiwar movement, complete
with periodic demonstrations in front of the American consulate.
One of the occasional participants was John Sewell, who would
serve as Toronto's mayor from 1978 to 1980.[2]

"Draft dodger," a derogatory term in the United States, suddenly became a badge of honor once you crossed the northern border. And it wasn't just the Canadian on the street who was on your
side. Author Margaret Atwood was at that time married to an
American and an active supporter of resisters.[3] Prime Minister
Pierre Trudeau openly welcomed them, with not only his words
but his actions as well: his government would liberalize the immigration law in 1969. "The status of being a draft dodger doesn't enter at all into our immigration policy," he would state at a Washington news conference in March 1969. "If you're dodging the
draft, you are not even asked about it and you are admitted to the
Canadian border." The exiles' actions, he said, were "dictated by
reason of conscience."[4]

Once they had crossed the border, most of the Americans ended
up in Toronto, where they numbered some 20,000 by the early
1970s. Many lived in the so-called "American ghetto" that had
formed near the University of Toronto, an area that included the
Annex, Jacobs's neighborhood. They had their own newspaper,
Amex (The American Expatriate in Canada), published from an
office on the campus and filled with such tidbits as how to get Canadian teaching credentials and a reminder that November 14, 1970,
was National Draft Resistance Day. "A rep will come from the U.S.
to pick up our cards that are turned into the office. Cards will then
be mailed to Washington en mass," the ad reads. "Turn in your
draft card by 6 p.m., Wednesday, November 13th. Hurry!"

New arrivals could go directly to the offices of the Toronto Anti-
Draft Programme (TADP), which deliberately used the British
spelling of "program." TADP was the de facto nerve center of the
American exile community. Located in an old house on Spadina
Road near the university, it guided you through your immigration
paperwork. You could also pick up your *Manual for Draft-Age*

Immigrants there; thousands of copies were mailed to the United States in 1968 and 1969.[5] The organization could also help you find temporary lodging; if you were really desperate you could always crash at free-spirited Rochdale, an educational cooperative filled with students and whoever else wandered in. Rochdale was housed in a brand-new high-rise building at 341 Bloor Street West. Started by a group of Americans and Canadians as a well-intentioned experiment in alternative learning, Rochdale soon degenerated into what one local politician called "an eighteen-story flophouse" that was frequently the target of drug raids.[6]

There was another significant component of the American immigration to Canada during the late 1960s: members of the American intelligentsia, like Jane Jacobs and other journalists, editors, and writers, as well as a plethora of PhDs, of which the United States was producing far too many. Most of these newly launched academics couldn't find teaching jobs in their homeland and were happy to fill the many vacant positions at the now-expanding Canadian universities, which as a result were becoming increasingly Americanized. The American professors felt ashamed of their country for its actions in Southeast Asia as well as at home—this was a time of massive unrest on college campuses, its most famous and tragic example being the National Guard's killing of four students at Ohio's Kent State University in May 1970. They taught Canadian students about America with a decidedly anti-American slant, thereby feeding a growing Canadian antipathy toward all things American.

Opposition to Vietnam was not the sole reason for this antipathy. Canada was increasingly chafing at its powerful neighbor's growing domination of just about everything Canadian, not only the culture but above all the economy. Prime Minister Trudeau made independence from the United States a cornerstone of his foreign policy. "We're a different people from you and we're different people because of you," he said during a 1968 Washington press conference. "Living next to you is in some ways like sleeping with an elephant. No matter how friendly and even-tempered is the beast . . . one is affected by every twitch and grunt. It should not therefore be expected that this kind of a nation, this Canada, should project itself onto the international scene as a mirror image of the United States."[7]

The assertions of Trudeau, the witty and wildly popular prime minister, delighted Canadians and of course irritated Americans. But it was not that simple. His words, however eloquent, were hardly enough to free Canada from domination by its powerful neighbor. Mixed in with Canadian resentment was, and continues to be, an obsession with all things Yankee. The denizens of late 1960s Toronto realized that the Americans with their sassy attitudes and colorful counterculture were infusing Toronto with new life. The old "Toronto the Good" had been known chiefly for its Anglo dullness. You couldn't order a drink on a Sunday unless it was to accompany your dinner, and some bars, the so-called "beverage rooms," had separate entrances labeled "men" and "women with escorts," in effect barring woman from the premises. At the University of Toronto, women were not allowed to enter Hart House, the student union. But soon such archaic customs would be in the past.

Toronto in the late 1960s was changing fast, and it wasn't only because of all the Americans now living there. A flood of newcomers had been arriving because of the opening of Canada's doors to non-Commonwealth immigrants that began in the late 1950s: first Italians and Greeks, followed by Portuguese, then Chinese, Indians, Pakistanis, and other Muslims from such diverse places as East Africa and Malaysia, and numerous other nationalities. Together, they were turning Toronto into a multicultural delight of interesting ethnic neighborhoods, filled with grocery stores and restaurants offering foods from every part of the world. At first the Anglo establishment viewed the new immigrants with suspicion. But by the late 1960s, Toronto was proud of its newfound diversity. The old Toronto the Dull had turned into Toronto the Exotic.

When they arrived in Toronto, the Jacobs family moved into a rented bottom-floor flat of a house in the Annex, a multi-ethnic, mixed-use neighborhood of private homes interspersed with apartment houses located right off a main thoroughfare. It is the kind of cozy urban residential neighborhood that doesn't exist in Manhattan anymore.

The Annex is now thoroughly gentrified, and home to many writers and other intelligentsia. But in 1968 the area was, as they say, "in transition," somewhat scruffy, with many of its brick houses being used as rooming houses. In short, it was the perfect Jane Jacobs neighborhood.

And Toronto was thrilled to have her. *Death and Life* was widely read and admired in Canada, and now its author was actually living there. "Why would one of North America's leading authorities on the design of cities, whose writings have stirred the minds of town planners, architects and civic officials around the world, pick Toronto as her new home?" wrote a *Toronto Star* reporter (December 23, 1968). "My husband said there were possibilities here and room and hope," Jacobs told the *Star.* "He was right—this is a city of hope, and I love it." These were halcyon days in Toronto, which was feeling great about itself, sometimes to point of smugness.

American cities, on the other hand, were getting lots of bad press. Think New York, or Chicago, or Detroit, and the immediate associations were crime and riots, air pollution, and racism. No doubt about it, U.S. cities were in trouble. In addition to the continuing flight of the white middle class to the suburbs, the Nixon administration was now cutting aid to the cities due to the soaring costs of the Vietnam War. "Filth, fear and fashion," trumpets a headline on the front page of the Toronto's other newspaper, the decidedly staid *Globe and Mail,* in 1969. The story, about the fashion industry, has a New York dateline, and opens with these words: "This city is tearing itself and its people apart." Then the reporter breathlessly continues:

Everywhere you walk—and you're warned not to walk much—the stench of garbage and drains and the filthy subway mixes with the body odor of human fear. There's panic at the idea of what would happen if the ghetto rebellion coalesced, or all the students rioted, or all the muggers came out the same night.... The New York accent grows shriller every year. . . . Consider, then, the plight of the clothing designer who expects to create beauty in this atmosphere of ugliness (January 1, 1969).

Contrast us, Torontonians in effect were boasting, with New York. Toronto's crime rate was negligible. What Toronto considered slums didn't look anything like the slums in American cities. Toronto didn't have the tortured relations between blacks and whites that were now being played out in the States and caught on camera. The images of race riots and burning cities were being watched, to the embarrassment of Americans, all over the world. Many of Canada's new immigrants were black, from the Caribbean and Africa, and Canadians felt that they were doing a much better job of welcoming them as well as all the other new immigrants, whatever their race, than the Americans were, then or ever. In the United States, Jacobs has often remarked, immigrants are made to feel ashamed of not having an American background. But not so in Canada. Americans, she says, speak of a "melting pot," a concept she finds destructive. For Canadians, Jacobs says, the ideal is a "mosaic."[8]

The United States and the mess it had made out of its cities was now serving as an "early warning system" to Canadians, said Jacobs in 1968. The suspense is unbearable, she said, while waiting to see whether Canada will repeat the United States' mistakes. Jacobs had it right: Toronto was changing physically, and fast.[9] But what all these changes would add up to in the end was anybody's guess. On the face of it everything seemed to be getting better. Downtown now boasted glamorous modern buildings like Mies van der Rohe's steel-and-glass-towered Toronto Dominion Centre and Viljo Revell's New City Hall, with a public square complete with an ice rink, a space so well thought out that it became, in the words of journalist Robert Fulford, "the great living room of Toronto."

But with no historical preservation laws yet on the books, the building frenzy also had the potential to do the city a lot of damage. Massive old Victorian buildings like the Old City Hall and the elegant Union Station occupied now-valuable land, and were now being threatened with demolition to make way for new development. As were Toronto's many shabby but often interesting neighborhoods, which now represented potential gold mines to investors.

Already old Edwardian and Victorian houses were falling to the wrecking ball and being replaced with high-rise apartment buildings. And it was not only private developers who were snatching up properties. The city had designated twenty-seven neighborhoods as blighted in a 1956 pamphlet titled *Urban Renewal: A Study of the City of Toronto.*[10] By 1968 several of these neighborhoods had already been expropriated. One, Regent Park South, had been razed during the late 1950s and 1960s to build a high-rise Le Corbusier–inspired public housing project that soon became a crime-ridden failure. The city was now busy trying to gain title to additional areas in order to "renew" them—that is, to tear them down and rebuild. As to exactly how, there was no legal necessity to consult with the people who were living in those "blighted" neighborhoods before drawing up plans and implementing them.

There was also now another potentially city-destroying trend: suburbanization. Despite the growing appeal of downtown, in contrast to the decay in American cities, Toronto's suburbs were nevertheless expanding and sprawling fast. The inevitable result was that more and more people were driving cars. Traffic was becoming a real problem in downtown. The most obvious solution was to build expressways, just as the Americans had done, even though Canadian municipalities did not have the resources of their American counterparts; there was no equivalent of the Interstate Highway Act in Canada.

Toronto already had one expressway in the city proper. The Gardiner, named after the first chairman of Metro, the cigar-chomping Fred Gardiner, had been built during the 1950s. It was an elevated monstrosity that ran near the shore, creating dead and darkened space below and around it and cutting off views of Lake Ontario. Public opinion at the time of the Gardiner's construction was decidedly pro.[11] And really, what was the alternative? How else to handle all the cars that people were driving to their jobs in the city from their new suburban homes? The Gardiner project had dragged on for years, not fully completed until 1966. It stood now as an assault on all the senses.

All of these issues felt depressingly familiar to Jane Jacobs in 1968 as she settled in to her new life.

The Spadina Expressway

And then, within a few months of her arrival, she learned to her dismay that another expressway was now in the works. When finished, it would have six lanes and connect downtown Toronto with the suburbs. And there was more: the house in which she and her family were renting an apartment sat right in its path.

The Spadina Expressway would eliminate 900 homes; throughout the city construction would cause major traffic disruptions, increase pollution, and destroy some of Toronto's ravines, a distinct feature of the city landscape.[12] The irony was overwhelming. How could it be that after years of expressways battles in New York, the Jacobs family was now finding themselves literally face to face with the Canadian version?

In fact, plans to build the Spadina had been approved in 1962 with virtually no opposition.[13] The idea had first come up during the 1950s after the formation of Metropolitan Toronto, Metro, as it came to be called, which created another layer of government joining the then-separate towns and suburbs into one entity to deal with common issues like roads and sewers. By 1968 construction on the Spadina had already begun, albeit only two miles' worth plus an interchange (in Jacobs's words, "poised for imminent attack upon a wide swath of raw earth and for the subsequent invasion of still unviolated ravine and pleasant communities to the south").[14] That much had already cost Ontarians $70 million, and the estimate for the completed project, which would include a subway line down the middle of the roadway, ran as high as $222 million.

And there was more: the Spadina would be only one artery out of five planned expressways that would crisscross and suffocate the city. That fact came as no surprise to Jacobs. Experience had taught her that officials always tried to, in her words, sneak in expressways just one piece at a time so that nobody would notice, or if someone did finally wake up to what was happening, it would be too late to stop it. And this was exactly how Metro Council had been advancing the Spadina project, which had been moving in fits and starts, bit by bit ever since the 1950s. At times the project had lain dormant for years, causing people to forget about it. Now, in 1968, Toronto traffic commissioner Sam Cass was bragging that no place in the city would be further than three-quarters of a mile from a traffic ramp, wonderful news to all the commuters from the suburbs.[15]

But this was 1968, an economic boom time in Toronto, and there were plenty of people who liked living in the city, many of them intellectuals and young professionals who were buying up old homes and fixing them up. They were also getting their neighbors to join residents' associations. These homeowners had no intention of moving to the suburbs. In 1965 a group of them had come together as the Civic Action League, Civac. All you had to do was look across Lake Ontario to Buffalo to see the damage caused by an expressway that runs through a city. These citizens of Toronto weren't going to let the same thing happen to their city. Civac was headed by a young man named David Crombie, who would in 1969 be elected an alderman and in 1972 mayor of Toronto.

And there were other groups who opposed the Spadina. It would cut through some of Toronto's most expensive areas, where local watchdog groups known as ratepayer associations had long been looking out for themselves.[16] And in poor and working-class neighborhoods, community organizers were coming in and galvanizing the citizens.

These different groups opposed the Spadina and began meeting all over the city, trying to figure out ways to stop the project that was going to wreck their city.

One of the neighborhood organizers was Bobbi Speck, a young mother who lived in the Annex. Speck was a New Yorker who had married a Canadian in 1966 and moved to Toronto. In 1968 she learned that the Spadina was going to be built right through her neighborhood. She and a few other Annex residents began to dig around, asking questions. They went to their local civic organization, the Annex Ratepayers, which told her that there was no use taking on the city over this. The battle, they told them, had already been fought ten years prior. But Speck was not deterred. She began to organize the opposition, hosting weekly meetings in her home and pasting posters on the trees that lined the blocks containing information about strategy meetings that were now being held in neighborhood homes and public venues. Speck now began to hook up with other neighborhood organizations around Toronto. This was the state of affairs when Jane Jacobs, Speck's neighbor, first heard about the Spadina Expressway.

One day soon after she had moved to Toronto, Jacobs attended one of Speck's strategy meetings. None of Jacobs's new neighbors who were present in Speck's house that day had yet met her. So nobody there recognized the new face at their meeting, a gray-haired woman with thick black glasses. Speck recalled nearly forty years later that they talked about possible ways to thwart the city's will. "We were going on gut instinct," she said. "But in the back of our minds, we were thinking, we don't know what the hell we're doing!" Jacobs, after listening to her neighbors, got up and explained to the group how to fight an expressway. "It was stunning," Speck said. "I was thinking as she was talking, this woman is incredible! She has everything down pat! Her thoughts came out in paragraph form, and put our instincts into a broader context." Speck wondered who the speaker was. Afterward, Speck approached her.

"You're so knowledgeable about all these things," Speck said. "I hope you'll get involved with this fight."

"That's why I'm here, dear," Jacobs replied. Before walking out the door, she added her name to a list that Speck had left for interested people to sign.

When the meeting was over, Speck picked up the piece of paper and perused the names on the list. When she saw the name Jane Jacobs, she couldn't believe it. The famous writer, Speck now realized, was not only her neighbor, but offering help to defeat the Spadina.

One day a *Star* reporter came to a neighborhood meeting, which resulted in a front-page metro-section story in April 1969, complete with a photo of Speck holding a telephone receiver to her ear ("She's organizing a protest against Spadina Expressway"). The story was like a lightning rod. Immediately Speck began getting a lot of phone calls. Many of them came from furious residents of North York, who wanted the Spadina because it would, they believed, drain off the traffic that was now clogging their streets. But more calls came from people who were opposed to an expressway running through their neighborhood, not the Annex but other neighborhoods like the Kensington market area and others south of Bloor Street. What a relief it was for these various groups to find one another, and they coalesced into the Stop Spadina—Save Our City Coordinating Committee (SSSOCCC). The faculty and students at the University of Toronto also became actively involved, often hosting organizing meetings at the campus. SSSOCCC was under the leadership of sociology professor Allan Powell, and among its supporters was the iconoclastic and influential University of Toronto professor and writer Marshall McLuhan. ("Toronto," McLuhan said, "will commit suicide if it plunges the Spadina Expressway into its heart.") [17]

It was during this time that Jacobs and McLuhan met and became friendly. She admired his intellect, even though she found him difficult to talk to (as did everybody else) because "he would say something interesting or outright brilliant which I would have liked to pursue with him and test out a little bit, but instead he would flit—or so it seemed to me—to a different idea, and from that to still another." Soon after their meeting, he asked her to write a script for a film about the harm that expressways cause cities, and she agreed. [18]

Jacobs gave her active support to SSSOCCC, but stayed in the background. For the next four years, SSSOCCC activists fought hard. They mobilized supporters, held meetings at the University of Toronto, and staged demonstrations in highly visible places so as to maximally embarrass public officials. One meeting had been billed as a debate between Jacobs and an official who was pushing for the expressway. SSSOCCC had sent invitations to several public figures, including Sam Cass. But nobody accepted. Jacobs ended up making a speech; the entire story appeared on the front page of the *Star* metro section, complete with a close-up photo of Jacobs captioned "Jane Jacobs: Expressway 'just stupid'" (January 25, 1970).

On New Years Day 1970 at the just-opened St. Lawrence Centre for the Arts, the mayor's reception was interrupted by about twenty protesters carrying a twenty-foot sign. They were quickly booted out, but not before Ned Jacobs, nineteen, the younger Jacobs son, had sung the first stanza of a song he'd written, "The Bad Trip," to the accompaniment of his guitar.[19] Here in Toronto, just as in New York, activism was for the Jacobses a family matter. Jimmy Jacobs, Ned's older brother, also did his part for his newly adopted country, leading a group of protestors down Spadina Road as he played the bagpipe. The marchers carried a coffin to symbolize the expressway, which they threw into an excavation ditch at the end of their march.[20]

The Spadina Expressway fight had become a kind of culture war, pitting suburbanites against city dwellers. Tempers were rising. Sometimes SSSOCCC posters at the university announcing meetings were ripped down. But by 1969, the tide of public opinion was turning against the Spadina. In its lead editorial on January 13, 1969, the traditionally pro-business *Globe and Mail* was calling on the government to reexamine its plan to build the expressway. ("It ignores one thing: people.") "The case against the Spadina Expressway isn't guesswork," wrote a Toronto architect in a signed editorial that appeared in the *Star* (January 20, 1970). "It has precedents in every major American city in which there are downtown expressways. . . . If you still need to be convinced, ask Jane Jacobs." Reporters frequently quoted Jacobs in their stories. Sometimes the byline was hers. "Surely the government in so up-to-date a City Hall must know all about the expressway disaster-lands in Boston, Philadelphia, New York, Buffalo, Detroit, Washington—the battles and demonstrations, mounting over the years, by increasingly desperate victims," Jacobs wrote in the *Star*.

Jacobs was making Toronto's politicians nervous. Appearing at a public hearing on the expressway, which Jacobs called a "sham" and a "charade," she proceeded with ad hominem attacks on the individual officials. Committee members, all of them men, "sat bolt upright during Mrs. Jacobs's speech." One accused her of "rabble-rousing."[21] A little more than a year later, in June 1971, the Spadina

Expressway project was abandoned. Nearly $70 million had been spent on it, but politicians could not do otherwise. The SSSOCCC had forced the issue all the way up to the provincial level, which was ultimately where it was decided. And 1971 was an election year.

"If we are building a transportation system to serve the automobile, the Spadina Expressway would be a good place to start," the just-elected Progressive Conservative Ontario Premier Bill Davis said to the Ontario Legislature. "But if we are building a transportation system to serve the people, the Spadina Expressway is a good place to stop." Its demise also spelled the end for the rest of Toronto's proposed expressway network.

The SSSOCCC celebrated its hard-won victory with a meeting at Convocation Hall, where participants viewed *A Burning World*, the polemical film that McLuhan had made with Jacobs's help. It was filled with images of cars streaming along expressways, and, Jacobs later said, "bore no relationship at all to our original script." Jacobs also conducted her own private ritual to mark the end of the Spadina fight. She collected a bag of tree seeds from her backyard and scattered them in the "Ditchway," as Torontonians had come to call the excavated remains of the expressway that was literally stopped in its tracks.

"There it sits—its raw earth baking in the sun," wrote Ron Poulton in the *Toronto Telegram* (July 15, 1971). "The expressway-that-might-have-been is a platinum monument to a change of philosophy. When the pragmatist with his bulldozer clashed with the dreamer and his pen, something happened that had never occurred on such a scale in the city's history. The heavyweight lost and the flyweight won. And the pattern was cut for a city for people instead of a city for cars." Suburbanites and their representatives were furious. Toronto's economic future, they insisted, would be bleak without new roadways to handle the increasing numbers of cars. But their predictions were wrong.

With or without Jane Jacobs, the Spadina would have been defeated. But the fact that she was in Toronto speaking out against it raised the level of discourse and gave the anti-expressway movement added legitimacy.

The Golden Age

The SSSOCCC's influence did not end with the Spadina's defeat in June 1971. Many who had been active in the expressway battle, including Allan Powell and David Crombie, now turned to local politics either as candidates themselves or behind the scenes. For the 1972 municipal election, they formed a coalition with other groups who, like them, opposed high-rise structures and runaway development. The result was that thirty-seven-year-old alderman David Crombie was elected mayor, and eleven out of the twenty-three city council seats went to the so-called "reform candidates."²² This time marked the beginning of what later was remembered as Toronto's "golden age," when local community groups not only continued to thrive, but also had the ear of their local elected officials.

One spring morning in 1973, Jacobs and others demonstrated in a rundown part of St. Jamestown where a developer had gotten a permit to demolish some houses that dated from the nineteenth century. In their place were plans to build three high-rise apartment buildings for low-income tenants. The protestors, Jacobs later made it a point to say, "weren't against low-income housing; they were against big plans . . . that bit by bit had been destroying the diverse fabric of the city."²³

The crowd stood and watched as a bulldozer began to rip up one of the houses. What could they do? There seemed to be no means within the law to stop the demolition. And then Jacobs remarked that city code prohibited the tearing down of a building unless it was surrounded by a fence. So the demonstrators began to take down the wooden fence around the house that was being demolished. They made neat piles out of the boards. In the meantime, somebody called city hall. When an inspector arrived, he ordered the demolition halted. Mayor Crombie then weighed in, putting in a call to the provincial housing authorities, because it was they, not the city, who had the power to stop the project. And they stopped it.²⁴

The city purchased the property and came up with an alternative plan: high-density infill housing. The original houses were preserved, and new structures were squeezed into what were the backyards. Dundas-Sherbourne, as the development is known, was the first of many infill projects that now dot Toronto.

So while the building frenzy continued, it did not go unchecked. In 1973, during the construction of the 1,815-foot CN Tower, a telecommunications tower that is now the symbol of Toronto and to date the tallest free-standing structure in the world, the city voted a forty-five-foot building height restriction for downtown. Everybody was talking about "saving the neighborhoods," and therefore now-gentrified areas like Cabbagetown were preserved. Mixed use was encouraged; neighborhoods that had been slated for urban renewal were now successfully fighting back.[25] All of which helped enhance the already-stellar reputation of "The World's Newest Great City," as *Time* magazine trumpeted on its cover.

Throughout the "golden age," Mayor Crombie, who would serve three consecutive two-year terms, and Crombie's city hall successor, the left-leaning and controversial John Sewell, and others involved in Toronto's planning went to Jane Jacobs for advice. But they did so on an informal basis. Jacobs did not occupy any official position in city government. She shunned publicity. Jacobs and her husband had bought a house on Albany Avenue, where she had a life that seemed just like anybody else's, sitting on her porch and chatting with her neighbors. Often she was seen on the street, wheeling her shopping cart or standing in line for a movie. And she continued to write.

Still, this private citizen was a public figure. She was, for example, very much involved in planning the St. Lawrence Neighbourhood, a mixed-use development that combined three-story row houses with low-rise apartment buildings. St. Lawrence was built during the late 1970s on abandoned industrial property near Lake Ontario. The project, admittedly, is dull to look at for the same reason as its closest New York equivalent, the West Village Houses: both were planned from the ground up and therefore lack the charm of neighborhoods that evolve on their own. Moreover the St. Lawrence situation—alongside Jarvis Street and the Gardiner Expressway—makes for an ugly and noisy environment. As for the houses, their design feels awkward. You have to walk down a flight of stairs from your front door to your living room. Still, the complex is widely considered an outstanding example of successful public housing: it mixes not only uses but incomes. Robert Fulford calls it "the tour de force of the reform era."[26]

Architect Alan Littlewood, who worked on the St. Lawrence project with both Jacobs and her husband—Robert Jacobs oversaw the environmental study—described a scene that took place one night about the Jacobses' dinner table that shows the nature of Jane Jacobs's contributions to the project:

> I had taken off on an architectural diatribe about the virtue of buildings that possessed the ability to turn corners. I was terribly concerned about the quality of the streetscape and had zoomed in on this one detail as being crucial. Jane [responded] that . . . I was missing the point. What I should be thinking about were things such as the appropriate widths of the pavement . . . the relationship between the buildings and street; the number and nature of doors and stoops; the variety of uses along the street. . . . She pointed out all this between the main course and dessert. . . . I went into the office . . . the following day with . . . instructions for major revisions to the way we were to approach the design of St. Lawrence.[27]

In Canada, Jane Jacobs was a star. But in the United States she was starting to fall off the radar screen. Not that she didn't have American admirers. Old-time Villagers continued to remember with immense gratitude that she had saved their neighborhood. Planners and students of urban history read and marveled at her insights in *Death and Life,* which had within a few years of its publication become the authoritative book on cities, widely cited by academics and used in planning theory courses in universities across the United States and Canada.

But little by little, the larger American public was forgetting her name. *New York Magazine* did a story in 1976 about the wonderful West Village that read like a rip-off of *Death and Life:* "an equalizer of economic circumstances . . . unexpected people mix, sort of like

La Ronde. . . . The West Village is different—geographically, mentally, visually. Villagers simply call it 'living on a human scale.'" But the article did not even mention Jane Jacobs. Only rarely did her name crop up anymore in the American press.

In 1970 she gave a lecture at New York City's Ninety-second Street Young Men's Hebrew Association that got coverage only in a neighborhood newspaper. She advised the mostly young audience there to break at least one rule a day. For example, she said, you might try burning your draft card, or deserting the military. Or you could refuse to pay your subway fare. "Our first duty is to misbehave and to keep misbehaving in order to destroy authority," she told the cheering audience. She also dismissed the then-ubiquitous warnings of a coming population explosion as nothing more than a cover for the deliberate extermination of black Americans.[28] Given the paranoia of the Nixon years, it seems certain that Jane Jacobs, outspoken as she was, had an FBI file.

And Jacobs galled not only the American establishment, but a lot of her former admirers in New York as well. After immigrating to Canada, she took to publicly castigating her former home. She had dedicated *Death and Life* to New York. Now, in the 1970s, New York was going through a terrible time. By the middle of 1975, more than thirty major corporations would leave New York, as Jacobs's former mentor William H. Whyte Jr. documented in *New York Magazine* (September 20, 1976). Bankruptcy seemed like a real possibility, but President Gerald Ford told New York not to expect a Washington bailout, inspiring the irreverent *Daily News* headline "Ford to City: Drop Dead." And there was Jane Jacobs, telling the *Village Voice* in 1972 that yes, indeed, New York was going down the tubes; in fact, she said, it "may already have run out of time." Nothing like her new home, Toronto, which she just loved, because it was "the way New York used to be. We just had to get out of New York."

She insisted that she didn't feel guilty about leaving even though she regularly received mail from New Yorkers begging for her help in saving their neighborhoods. "They want my help," Jacobs told the *Voice*, "but they don't seem to realize that it's up to them to do the fighting. You know, I don't really blame the predators, I blame the victims who do nothing. Vietnam would never have been possible without the cooperation of the people who never marched."

For Jane Jacobs, New York belonged to the past. She had completed her second book, *The Economy of Cities,* soon after arriving in Toronto. In it, she returned to ideas about cities and economics that she had first toyed with in *Death and Life* and developed them further.

CHAPTER TEN

Economist without Portfolio

Why do some places get rich, but not others? This crucial question, which economists have yet to answer satisfactorily, formed the subtext of two lectures that University of Chicago economist Robert Lucas delivered at Cambridge University in the spring of 1985.[1] In "On the Mechanics of Economic Development," Lucas, who would win the Nobel Prize for economics in 1995, argued that places that thrive do so mostly as the result of what economists call "human capital." This vague term means individuals' skills and knowledge, comprising everything from the most basic, such as knowing how to read, up to designing space stations and everything in between.

Lucas was now proposing a mathematical model for economic growth that factored in human capital—even though, Lucas conceded, the term was neither measurable nor directly observable. Human capital, he said, was "simply an unobservable magnitude or force, with certain assumed properties, that I have postulated in order to account for some observed features of aggregative behavior. . . . We can no more directly measure the amount of human capital a society has, or the rate at which it is growing, than we can measure the degree to which a society is imbued with the Protestant ethic." Nevertheless, Lucas continues, this force, "admittedly

Jane Jacobs in Toronto, 1968. Frank Lennon, *The Toronto Daily Star.*

unobservable, has also been used to account for a vast number of phenomena involving the way people allocate their time, the way individuals' earnings evolve over their lifetimes, aspects of the formation, maintenance and dissolution of relationships within families, firms and other organizations, and so on." Lucas was now focusing specifically on what he called the "external effects," or "spillovers" of human capital: how improvement in an individual's skills and knowledge that makes him more productive also makes the people he interacts with—in the classroom, in the office, on the assembly line, and so on—more productive. But these external effects, Lucas concedes, are hard to measure.

When Lucas was developing his hypothesis, he read Jacobs's 1969 book *The Economy of Cities.* Her book, Lucas realized, was all about the external effects of human capital, and it helped his ideas take shape. "As Jacobs has rightly emphasized and illustrated with hundreds of concrete examples, much of economic life is 'creative' in much the same way as is 'art' and 'science,'" Lucas said in his Cambridge lecture. "New York City's garment district, financial district, diamond district, advertising district and many more are as much intellectual centers as is Columbia or New York University."

In other words, Lucas's equations were an attempt to account for something that companies have long known: it is in cities where they most thrive because it is cities that draw the most creative and competitive minds. In cities is where people feel what they call the "electricity," where they rub elbows and "do lunch." Ideas get hatched during those midtown lunches. When industries move out of New York and relocate to, for example, South Carolina because of all the money they will presumably save, the results usually disappoint. Often the companies return. In the end it seems there is no substitute for human contact, despite Marshall McLuhan's warnings in the late 1960s about the imminent disappearance of cities in an age where we are all electronically linked.

Lucas's insights started economists talking among themselves, and eventually caused a paradigm shift in their thinking. From now on, they began to think about knowledge as a force in economic growth. "All economic growth since the industrial revolution is due to ideas," Lucas says. "But growth theory for years ignored the force of ideas. For Jacobs, this question is the center of everything."[2] Today, twenty-plus years after Lucas's Cambridge lectures, economists at Harvard, MIT, and the University of Chicago write papers that cite her and test her theories. Jacobs's work, Lucas says, taught him to look around and see things that economists routinely miss. "Jacobs," he says, "shows that most of the ideas come from the ground, not R and D departments."

Besides *The Economy of Cities*, Jacobs has written three books on economics: *Cities and the Wealth of Nations, Systems of Survival,* and *The Nature of Economies.* As was the case with her foray into urban planning, she was writing about economics from the outside with absolutely no training, having wandered into it unintentionally. The subject pops up from time to time within the rich layers that constitute *Death and Life*. For example, she tells us in chapter seven that cities nourish all sorts of ideas and businesses because economic activity is one of the effects of diversity, according to her a sine qua non for all cities. "Cities," she wrote, "are the natural homes of supermarkets and standard movie houses *plus* delicatessens, Viennese bakeries, foreign groceries, art movies, and so on, all of which can be found coexisting, the standard with the strange, the large with the small. . . . The diversity, of whatever kind, that is generated by cities rests on the fact that in cities so many people are so close together, and among them contain so many different tastes, skills, needs, supplies, and bees in their bonnets."

But cities do not generate new businesses just by existing. "They generate it because of the various efficient economic pools of use that they form." Her observation finally led her to ask, why do some cities thrive, while others decline? This question marks the starting point of *The Economy of Cities,* which picks up the thread she started weaving through her first book. "This book is an outcome of my curiosity about why some cities grow and why others stagnate and decay," she states as the very first sentence. Afterward she continues in her characteristic fashion to analyze the underlying economic order of cities.

In this way Jacobs found herself writing about economics. Her research consisted of reading, gathering lots of newspaper and magazine clippings and stuffing them into folders, and jotting notes down on legal pads, lined notebook paper, index cards, even the backs of envelopes. This had been her method all her writing life. Over the years, when something interests her, she once told an interviewer, she has learned to trust her instincts. Once her mind gets hold of something, she surrenders to the idea, clinging to it and examining it until she feels satisfied. She writes, she has often remarked, to explain things to herself. It doesn't matter what direction she finds herself traveling. Supremely confident, she goes willingly anywhere her restless mind leads her.

And now, how absolutely brazen of Jacobs, daring to venture into such a rarified discipline as economics. As with *Death and Life,* her new book included few footnotes, no citations, not even a bibliography. And just as she had examined urban planning from a perspective entirely her own, Jacobs was now looking at economics through her black-rimmed glasses and giving it her own spin. Conspicuously absent in her book are the terms economists use to talk to one another, like "capital accumulation" and "business cycle." But she doesn't need them. Unversed in the economists' language, Jacobs invents her own. One could argue that after producing the magnificent *Death and Life,* she had earned the right to write about economics or just about anything simply by the strength of her intellect and the force of her diction. In *The Economy of Cities,* her characteristic carefully crafted prose often soars into poetry.

She examines economies through her favorite angle: cities. None of the economic theories could explain why cities exist. "If we postulate only the usual list of economic forces, cities should fly apart. The theory of production contains nothing to hold a city together," says Lucas. "A city is simply a collection of factors of production—capital, people and land—and land is always far cheaper outside cities than inside. Why don't capital and people move outside, combining themselves with cheaper land and thereby increasing profits?"[3] Because, Jacobs had already told us in *Death and Life,* it is cities where ideas are incubated. And now, the premise of her new book was that everything springs from ideas. Or, as economists would say, human capital. It follows that businesses deliberately locate in cities because businesses need something that is intangible and cannot be measured: human ingenuity, she calls it, which is just another term for ideas. Ideas, the basic elements of economic growth, are nurtured in cities.

Economic growth comes from ideas, ideas grow in cities, and therefore cities cause economies to grow: this is the gist of the Jane Jacobs universe. Her hypothesis about cities as the primary factor in economic growth led her to question another longstanding assumption: that agriculture preceded the establishment of cities. Jacobs was now claiming that just the opposite was true: cities must have predated agriculture. All rural work, she argued, must have originated in cities. She has no archaeological evidence for her bold statement, which she attempts to prove through logic, walking us step-by-step through an imaginary ancient city that she calls New Obsidian.

Never mind the purely rhetorical foundation for her argument: in the Jane Jacobs universe, the city is the most basic unit of our civilization simply because this is what she believes as her own article of faith. All life springs from the city, just as the ancient philosophers believed that speech and reason and words—*logos*—formed the basis of everything in the world. Jacobs ignored the then-common assumption that economies grow mostly because of what happens at their highest levels, in and around large corporations. No, no, no, says Jacobs. Economists have got it all wrong. On the contrary, economic growth begins and continues in cities.

These statements serve as an introduction that leads right into the heart of the matter. "How do cities really grow? What can it be that creates and recreates city economies?" Jacobs asks at the end of the first chapter. Answering this question is the point of the book. "Cities are not just great lumps of chaos. They are a form of very intricate, very wonderful order, and they seem like chaos mainly because we do not understand this order nor the processes by which it works," Jacobs had said in a speech she gave in England while she was working on her book.[4] By the second chapter, she is attempting to crack open the process: cities, based on her own observations, "are places where adding new work to older work proceeds vigorously." She cautions us that the new work doesn't arise out of nowhere. "New work arises upon existing work; it requires 'parent' work." Her beautifully crafted sentence sounds simple, but contains complex ideas that she, no economist, expands upon not with mathematical formulas but by telling us stories.

To illustrate how work leads to more work, she uses the wonderful example of bra manufacturing. In the 1920s, a New York dressmaker, Ida Rosenthal, began making bras in order to make her dresses fit the customers better. Rosenthal went on to found the Maidenform company. The bra—what a delightful image! Who would have thought that the bra could serve to explain such an important economic principle!

Jacobs uses images that she finds in the most ordinary sources: the telephone book, the newspaper:

This process in which one sort of work leads to another must have happened millions of times in the whole history of human economic development. Every newspaper reports it. From only a few days' gleanings in the women's pages, one learns that a cleaner of suede clothing is now starting to bottle and sell her cleaning fluid for people who want to clean their own suede; a chest and wardrobe manufacturer is starting, for a fee, to analyze what is wrong with one's household or office storage arrangements; a playground designer is starting to make and sell equipment for playgrounds and nursery schools; a sculptor is starting a line of costume jewelry; a designer of theatre costumes launching himself as a couturier; a couturier is starting a boutique. (*Economy of Cities*, 53–54)

Jacobs loves lists, which in her hands turn into a figure of speech, one of the many that she uses to tell her story of how economies work. What a tremendous advantage she has over economists, whose tools are limited and unintelligible to anybody but other economists. Jacobs's tools, a combination of logic sweetened with carefully crafted words, charm us and therefore convince us.

Adam Smith, Jacobs asserts with breathtaking certainty, had it all wrong when he talked about "the division of labor" as the chief source of economic growth. On the contrary, she argues, economies stagnate when work stays within given categories. Adam Smith's famous example of the pin factory, Jacobs shows us, contains a major fallacy: pin-making was not a division of anything, but an example of new work spun off from old, in this case the manufacture of wire carding combs. Adding an additional few steps to making the bristles used in the combs resulted in a new product: pins. "The fact that Smith's mistake was subtle and casual has only rendered it the more obfuscating and durable," Jacobs observes, and then adds (italics hers): "*Division of labor, in itself, creates nothing.*" The only thing that comes of it is "operating efficiency," which, she claims, actually kills development.

Cities need chaos in order to thrive economically. Whenever you attempt to straitjacket cities into organized units, they stagnate. Chaos, she implies, is the function of a healthy city. But that chaos, she has earlier told us, has, paradoxically, an underlying order. "Under the seeming disorder of the old city, wherever the old city is working successfully, is a marvelous order for maintaining the safety of the streets and the freedom of the city. It is a complex order. Its essence is intricacy of sidewalk use, bringing with it a constant succession of eyes," Jacobs wrote in *Death and Life*. She now extends her fascination with disorganized order from sidewalks to the economies of cities. In her subsequent works, most of which would also deal with economics, she would continue to play with the idea of organized chaos.

How a place behaves economically determines whether or not it is a city.[5] A city, she writes in the appendix of *The Economy of Cities* in her only attempt to define the term, is "a settlement that consistently generates its economic growth from its own local economy." Any place where this occurs becomes a city. A city starts to grow when it begins to export the products that it manufactures, like saddles from sixteenth-century Birmingham, England, along with other local products that support the first products, like the hardware used in the saddles. A city's exports necessitate its importing goods needed for the manufacture of exports. The city will eventually start to manufacture the imported goods at home for practical reasons — "import replacements," she calls the process, an old concept that economists call "import substitution."

In this way, Jacobs found as she studied and compared different industries in different cities around the world as she was writing her second book, cities thrive. When the components of the process multiply, a city experiences "explosive growth." She sees a city economy as a reciprocal system, like that of a living organism, an idea she had already touched on in *Death and Life*. There she had devoted the entire final chapter to a discussion of cities as organisms, consisting of complex and intertwined relationships. Now she was picking up the thread of this idea in *The Economy of Cities,* where she explains that a city grows from within like any living thing. If any part of its reciprocal process stops, so does the entire system. This is what happens when cities stagnate. She cites the examples of Detroit and her hometown of Scranton, both of which once enjoyed "explosive growth."

Scranton began to decline after World War I, and furnished a perfect environment for Jane Jacobs to begin her lifelong thinking about cities.[6] Iron ore from the nearby hills was the first export from the Lackawanna Valley hamlet that in the mid-nineteenth century would become Scranton. "This is a marvelous place," a reporter wrote in the *Wilkes-Barre Advocate* in 1844. "Only two years ago it was a wilderness. . . . But the eye of speculation and improvement was on it, and a furnace was erected between the hills and upon the stream. The mines for coal to be used . . . are within a biscuit toss of the doors of the furnace, and the ore is obtained on the opposite hill." The iron ore was smelted in the blast furnaces of the Lackawanna Iron Works, a company started in 1842 by two Scranton brothers. At first they produced pig iron—blocks of unrefined iron—and nails, which were loaded onto mule-driven wagons that traveled to the canals where the iron was unloaded into barges and then sent to "rolling and puddling mills" where the "pigs" were converted into wrought iron. But these first two exports did not prove profitable. Moreover, the local ore was of poor quality, necessitating that better-grade ore be imported to Scranton's furnaces from New Jersey, New York, and Pennsylvania's Lebanon County.

Scranton's "explosive growth" began only after George Scranton started a business venture in 1845 that amounted to a classic Jacobs-style example of import replacement: he had the idea to manufacture iron railroad tracks, also called "T" rails, a basic necessity for America's railroads, which were now expanding across the continent. At the time, T rails were manufactured only in England, from where they were imported at great cost and inconvenience. Scranton, then, was right on target. His gamble paid off handsomely. He convinced the New York & Erie Railroad, which at the time desperately needed English T rails to make good on a state contract, to back the Lackawanna Iron Works's expansion financially. At the same time, in a lovely example of a Jacobs "reciprocating system," the railroad also contracted with Scranton for twelve thousand tons of T rail. Lackawanna Iron Works transported the rails by mule wagon and canal boat to Binghamton, New York, from where they were distributed.

The company began to prosper and issued stock, thereby attracting capital. Men in search of work—among them were many Welsh, Irish, and German immigrants—found their way to the newly incorporated city, now called Scranton. The workers built crude houses for themselves out of lumber from the local sawmill on "Shanty Hill," just across Roaring Brook from where the furnace was located. Their wives and daughters worked in mills that produced textiles, which become another Scranton export. After Lackawanna Iron Works supplied the newly formed Delaware Lackawanna & Western Railroad with T rails, Scranton convinced the railroad, which ran between Hoboken and Buffalo, to build its office and shops in Scranton.

In 1908 DL&W erected the gorgeous Lackawanna Station, designed by an American architect trained at Paris's École des Beaux-Arts. The exterior, faced with Indiana limestone, was topped with an eight-foot-wide bronze clock flanked with concrete eagles. The station's Italian marble interior was decorated with a series of faience panels, each tile depicting a scene along the DL&W route: the Hoboken ferry slips, the Delaware Water Gap, Lake Hopatcong in New Jersey. Arriving in this glorious interior, travelers had easy access to the hotels, restaurants, and taverns that were now opening up in downtown Scranton as businessmen, enticed by the railroad's presence, began investing their money in this up-and-coming city. Banks and other businesses filled up elegant granite office buildings. Rich people had places in Scranton to eat elegant meals and play cards. The most luxurious hotel belonged to the Caseys, two Irish immigrant brothers, and was designed by the same architect who did Lackawanna Station.

From the rail yards just a stone's throw from the passenger station, the DL&W shipped out the region's coal and iron and T rail, thereby encouraging the increased mining of Scranton's anthracite coal, which soon overtook iron and steel as the city's number-one export. Anthracite, hard and clean-burning, was superior to the softer, bituminous coal of nearby areas. To advertise anthracite's fine qualities, the DL&W created the image of Phoebe Snow, a Gibson Girl in a white dress. The imaginary Phoebe, traveling from Hoboken to Buffalo, one end of the DL&W railway line to the other, claimed: "Upon the trip to Buffalo, My gown stays white, From morn till night, Upon the road made of anthracite."

Lackawanna Iron Works now began to manufacture locomotives for the railroads. Other locomotive companies set up shop in Scranton, with its ready supply of raw materials. In 1881 one of the Scranton scions broke off from Lackawanna Iron Works and opened a steel mill that produced steel T rail, which was superior to the iron product. In 1891 the new company merged with the original one, becoming the Lackawanna Iron and Steel Company, which by 1894 was producing one-sixth of America's steel. Besides its two furnaces in Scranton, Lackawanna Iron and Steel Company operated five furnaces in Pennsylvania and one in New Jersey, from where steel was shipped to Scranton and there made into rail.

But Scranton's lack of good iron ore in the end did in its major industry. In 1902 Lackawanna Iron and Steel Company left Scranton for Buffalo, a place that offered a ready supply of good-grade iron ore. Despite Scranton's loss of its iron industry—along with 2,500 jobs—its main export, anthracite coal, in combination with railroads that shipped out the coal, kept the city's economy going. But Scranton's "reciprocating system" began to break down after World War I, when Jane Jacobs was a small child and the coal industry was starting its decline. The anthracite coal had been mined out, leading to massive unemployment. During the Depression, Scranton fell on hard times.

When World War II began, the owners of the *Scranton Tribune* led a successful drive to bring in war-related heavy manufacturing, a story that the twenty-seven-year-old Jane Butzner wrote up and sold to the *New York Herald Tribune* in 1943. "For the first time in U.S. history, a mining town whose veins of mineral wealth have been worked out is avoiding a ghost town fate," she begins exuberantly, and then goes on to describe Scranton's new industries, which included manufacturing wings for B-29 bombers, piston rings, and radio parts. But war industry offered Scranton only a brief respite from its decline, which resumed after the war when the combined effect of cars and the Interstate Highway Act practically annihilated the railroads.

Incredibly, today Scranton does not have any train service. And with the exception of one former steel factory that still produces ammunition for the United States Army, there is no heavy manufacturing. The long-abandoned Scranton brothers' fifty-foot-high blast ovens still stand, their scorched walls rising up beside Roaring Brook like an ancient Roman ruin next to the hill from where the first coal that fired them up was excavated. Lackawanna Avenue, Scranton's main street, with its wonderful granite and terra cotta office buildings that date from the Gilded Age, is listed in the National Register of Historic Places. But there are big chunks of downtown that look decrepit. Buildings stand unoccupied. After five o'clock few people are on Scranton's streets.

During the 1980s the old Lackawanna rail yards, which had been abandoned, were turned into Steamtown, a museum showcasing what was once a millionaire's private train collection. The city of Scranton along with private investors had acquired the collection and moved it from Vermont to Scranton. The hope was that the museum would revitalize the city. But the project soon ran out of money and Steamtown seemed destined to go belly up, until Scranton's veteran congressman Joseph McDade, the longtime ranking Republican on the powerful House Appropriations Committee, stepped in and saved the day. Using the deal-making skills for which he was well known, he pushed through legislation that had Steamtown declared a national historic site, and under the jurisdiction of the National Park Service. Many in Washington objected, and not only to the $66 million cost. As appealing as the train collection seemed—among its twenty-nine steam locomotives and eighty-six cars was "Big Boy," at 1.2 million pounds the biggest locomotive on earth, built to haul military supplies over the Rockies during World War II—it had no particular historical significance and no connection whatsoever to Scranton or coal mining.[7]

Steamtown opened in 1988, accompanied by a lot of hype from local business groups about how the new national park was going to help bring back Scranton. Five years later several blocks of century-old buildings along Scranton's main street were demolished to build an adjoining mall, where you can now sit in a tacky food court and get a great view of the old rail yards, and watch the tourists hop on vintage train cars for brief runs, as if taking rides at a theme park. A brass plaque is affixed to the mall's main entrance, announcing that the structure is dedicated to Joseph McDade, "who helped make this dream a reality." The mall, McDade and local politicians insisted, would together with Steamtown be great for Scranton. Most local businesspeople agreed. So did the local newspaper, the *Scranton Times-Tribune,* which as a result didn't bother to talk to any of the people who were operating businesses in the stores that were going to be demolished.

Joseph X. Flannery, a *Tribune* columnist, called Jane Jacobs in Toronto to hear her reaction. Furious, she typed up a letter that she sent to city officials. "Far from enhancing or strengthening Scranton's downtown, a mall development is guaranteed to be destructive economically, visually and socially," Jacobs wrote.[8]

The stores were dynamited on a Sunday morning. Hundreds of people went down to watch. The crowd's mood was upbeat, as if they were taking part in a festive celebration. After the mall was completed, two longtime and locally-owned department stores located right across the street—one, Scranton Dry Goods, was where Jacobs as a child had played on the escalator—soon closed. They could not compete.

So what has been the upshot? Steamtown admittedly attracts visitors, sometimes by the busload. But plopping down a tourist attraction, especially one that provides no tax revenue, together with a suburban-style mall in the middle of a struggling old downtown is hardly the stimulus needed to bring a long-stagnating economy back to life. People don't go downtown to shop at a mall; on the contrary, they crave the little mom-and-pop store as an antidote to all the giant retail chains that now blight the landscape. As for McDade, even as the mall was being built, he was fighting a federal indictment charging him with illegally accepting money and gifts from defense contractors, who in return received lucrative contracts in his district. After an eight-year battle he was acquitted, and retired from Congress in 1998.

But the mall notwithstanding, downtown Scranton is starting to come back to life. The former DL&W train station, from where the last train left in 1970, has been renovated into an elegant hotel. Mayor Christopher Doherty has been working with local civic and business leaders to make the area once again attractive to business, creating tax-free zones and grants for projects to restore facades. As a result, small businesses have opened—a day spa, a toy store, several upscale restaurants—and a few large corporations have relocated parts of their operations to Scranton. One, VaxServe, a division of Aventis Pasteur, the world's largest vaccine manufacturer, moved into the former Woolworth building, now beautifully renovated.

Some of the new entrepreneurs are even remodeling their buildings to include residential space. Ken Marquis, who owns an art and frame shop that occupies what used to be the laundry building of the Casey Hotel, torn down in 2001, made the top three floors into luxurious lofts. Before he had finished the construction, the lofts were rented. Two of his tenants are artists, of which Scranton now has a growing community. Marquis, who had never heard of Jane Jacobs, says he likes the idea of mixing commercial and residential spaces. So does the mayor, who says he wants Scranton to be a city where people both live and work.[9]

So far, so good for Scranton. But suburban sprawl continues unabated throughout Pennsylvania and its cities continue to decline.[10] Most of Scranton's jobs are not downtown, unemployment is high, and many of its young people are leaving. These facts hardly escape the notice of Mayor Doherty. But he is undeterred. He told the *Scranton Times* (April 25, 2004) that he sees the city as a "regional" downtown, the center of a 65- to 100-mile radius that draws retirees and telecommuters, or people who need to be in Philadelphia or New York only once or twice a week. Would that Doherty's optimistic vision come to pass. The chances of it happening are impossible to gauge, but seem a lot less likely if people cannot hop on or off a train in Scranton.

Jacobs had done it again. When *The Economy of Cities* came out in 1969, it charmed the critics. They could not resist the sheer audacity of what she said, and, most of all, the complete confidence with which she said it. "Her work will stand (or fall) upon the sheer internal strength and consistency of her reasoning," wrote architect James Marston Fitch in *Architectural Forum* in a review that was critical but also admiring. "A theory of economic life and the role of healthy cities so outrageous as to seem at once simplistic and profound. To be kept in anticipation of the attempted rebuttal that has not yet appeared," said the Christopher Lehmann-Haupt in his annual list of "twenty books I'm keeping in my library."

The rebuttal expected by Lehmann-Haupt never appeared. Once again, Jacobs was shaking up an entire discipline, writing about a subject into which non-academics just did not venture. How were academics to respond to the oft-outlandish statements that she wrote in her book, uninhibited by colleagues and peer reviews? There is no one cause for poverty, she remarks at the end of a discussion on the paradox of why cities need to be inefficient if they are to work well. Poverty is simply the absence of wealth. Or her notion that waste recycling was not just economically feasible, but potentially a gold mine, creating endless possibilities for spin-off work? (She picks up this point again in her later work *The Nature of Economies*.) Or her contention that "services will become the predominant organizational work"?

It was as if her sheer chutzpah had rendered economists speechless. Many privately dismissed Jane Jacobs as an amateur, even a nut case. Noted Harvard economist Edward Glaeser, who has often cited Jacobs in his work, once remarked that his colleagues "damned *The Economy of Cities* with words like 'imaginative,' 'creative,' 'original.'" But whether economists liked it or not, what she said mattered. *Death and Life* had changed the way we perceive cities, establishing her as one of the most important and creative thinkers of her day. Now the chattering classes were reading her second book, on economics, which meant that the economic establishment could not ignore her. After *The Economy of Cities* appeared in 1969, Jacobs spoke at the American Economic Association's annual meeting. Her session, says Robert Lucas, was standing room only.

From here on, Jacobs, whose first book had made us realize that we had deep feelings about cities, would write about economics. And, as she had done for cities, she turned the usual assumptions about economics upside down. Economic growth, the experts believed, was tied mostly to what happened on the highest levels—what happened in and around megacorporations. But Jacobs saw things differently. The Jacobs perspective breaks down huge entities, whether they be cities or economies, into its smallest units, which tend to evade just about everybody's eyes but hers. Jacobs was now showing us that we can only understand economies by studying the smallest and most mundane things that happen all around us, every day. All we need to do is know to look for them. She contends that economists, imprisoned by their theories, do not.

Just as she had condemned the entire profession of city planning in *Death and Life* and thereby infuriated professionals in the field, she was now subjecting economists to the same Jacobs treatment. Economics, she writes in the first chapter of her next book on the subject, *Cities and the Wealth of Nations,* is "a fool's paradise" that so far has failed us. No school or theory is spared her tongue-lashing. By the end of that first chapter, she is on the way to reinventing the entire science: "It would be rash to suppose that macroeconomics, as it stands today, has useful guidance for us. Several centuries of hard, ingenious thought about supply and demand chasing each other around, tails in their mouths, have told us almost nothing about the rise and decline of wealth. . . . Choosing among the existing schools of thought is bootless. We are on our own."

It is cities, not nations, that form the basic entities of economic life, argues Jacobs. Regions that lose their ties with cities stagnate. This is the central thesis of *Cities and the Wealth of Nations,* which puts forth other equally audacious arguments. Jacobs has no use for nations; almost all, she writes, come into being by force. By implication, nations are an unnatural entity. "The mystique of the nation," she writes, "is the powerful, gruesome glamour of human sacrifice." About this nobody could argue with her. She continues on unfettered, arguing that nations undermine cities, the sine qua non of the Jane Jacobs universe.

Cities and the Wealth of Nations was published in 1984, and picked up where *The Economy of Cities* left off. Fifteen years had separated the two books; during that time she'd written *The Question of Separatism,* where she argued in support of Quebec's secession, a very touchy issue in Canada at the time that most public figures preferred to avoid. She based her Quebec argument on her firm belief that smaller is better. But this time she took her premise beyond local governments and applied it to entire nations. Using the example of Norway's peaceful secession from Sweden in 1905, she maintained that Quebec's succession would benefit all involved, both politically and economically. Now Jacobs was picking up the subject of economics again in *Cities and the Wealth of Nations,* where she argued that the only way for any nation to avoid economic stagnation is to break down into small units. She even called for separate currencies, for example for Quebec and Ontario. "I don't know why there's so much fear about separate currencies—it's a manufactured terror!" she remarked in a 1997 interview with the Canadian Broadcasting Corporation.

Transplanting factories or building dams in underdeveloped regions here or abroad, she correctly observes, fails to stimulate growth. "Development cannot be given," she writes. "It has to be *done.* It is a process, not a collection of capital goods." She calls huge aid programs transplanted into what we now call "developing nations" or subsidies given at home in the form of welfare "transactions of decline." For all their good intentions, such transactions only exacerbate the stagnation and poverty that they are supposed to alleviate. "In its very nature, successful economic development has to be open ended rather than goal oriented, and has to make itself up expediently and empirically as it goes along." She offers us a panoply of examples: "The first successful railroad in the world was an amusement ride in London. Many of us can remember when plastics were used for little except toys and kitchen gadgets, and for piano keys as a lower-cost replacement for ivory."

"Open-ended drift," she calls the process, which sounds like a description of how she writes her books. Her mind knows no restraints and is uninhibited by dogma or theories, resulting in ideas that meander all over the landscape, touching on so many subjects that it is impossible to trace the progression of her thinking through the years in a straight story line. But Jacobs insists that "drift" has an underlying order, like what biologists observe in natural ecologies. Once again, Jacobs is playing with her by-now-familiar images of order and chaos, which she has already applied to cities and city economies. Now she is extending the metaphor further, to economic development on the large scale. Jacobs stops at nothing, trying to break down huge entities into "unexamined, but obviously intricately interconnected, and surely understandable, relationships."[11]

The Death and Life of Great American Cities, The Economy of Cities, and *Cities and the Wealth of Nations:* these books together form what I call Jane Jacobs's Urban Trilogy, an idea for which I am indebted to writer and Harvard professor Howard Husock. Jacobs's trilogy should be read in sequence. "This book is an attack on current city planning and rebuilding," reads the first sentence of *Death and Life,* the starting point for a discussion about cities that Jacobs would extend over nearly twenty-five years through all three books, down to the last two sentences of *Cities and the Wealth of Nations:* "Societies and civilizations in which the cities stagnate don't develop and flourish further. They deteriorate."

Today, the most fashionable economic theories incorporate mathematical models to measure how ideas affect economic growth. For the uninitiated, it's pretty dry stuff. It all started with Robert Lucas's 1985 paper, and Lucas read Jacobs while working on his theory. All work, Jacobs tells us in *The Economy of Cities,* begins with ideas. When people exchange ideas, work multiplies, leading to economic growth, leading to more work, which has a multiplying effect leading to more growth. And so on. The examples she gives of the process—the bra industry in New York, the bicycle industry in Japan—read like poetry.

So it turns out that in economics, just as in anything having to do with cities, Jacobs was prescient. Now, a generation after the publication of *The Economy of Cities,* ideas that she made accessible to everybody through her skillfully crafted words are reduced to mathematical form by economists. But standard economics textbooks do not mention Jane Jacobs. With the exception of the few leading economists such as Lucas who cite her in their work, the fact is that most of their lesser-known colleagues have never heard of her. They do not read her. Therefore it is difficult to assess Jacobs's influence on economists.

Now, when people mention Jane Jacobs, they think of cities. But after her 1984 book *Cities and the Wealth of Nations,* she would focus her thoughts elsewhere. Her writing came to a temporary halt. Except for a children's book, *The Girl on the Hat,* she would not publish another book for eight years. In 1992 she produced *Systems of Survival,* a dialogue on the moral codes concerned with making a living. From then on, she would no longer focus on cities in her writing.

Systems of Survival had its seeds in the work Jacobs did for Energy Probe, a Toronto-based organization that she helped found in 1980. Energy Probe called for the privatization of Ontario Hydro, the state-owned utilities company, as well as other public holdings such as the postal service, the rail system, and public transportation.[12] Jacobs would remain actively involved with Energy Probe until the late 1990s. During her time with them, she would think hard about the role that the public and private sectors played in economies.

She tried out some of the ideas she was percolating at a 1987 seminar on "the ethics of making a living," along with members of the theology and philosophy departments at Boston College, a Jesuit university. Jacobs rarely spoke in public, but Richard Keeley, associate dean at the college's Carroll School of Management, had been determined to bring her to his institution. He had placed *Death and*

Life in the college's curriculum, making it required reading in an undergraduate program that, faithful to the Jesuit tradition, combined philosophy, theology, and social activism.

Keeley had heard Jacobs speak in 1980 in Boston at a conference on "Great Cities of the World." There, in Faneuil Hall, in the presence of a select group of invitees including mayors from all over the globe, she had taken on two powerful men: the world-famous architect Moshe Safdie of Harvard University, who had just talked about the constraints having to do with energy, transportation, and community participation on designers and planners, and James Rouse, the mega developer of Boston's Quincy Market and Baltimore's Harborplace. "What we need is what I call 'Big Human Plans,'" Rouse had said in his address, invoking the famous architect Daniel Burnham. Small plans, Rouse had added, are the mark of feeble imagination, an inability to envisage the "new, compelling, rational images of what a city could be."

Then it was Jacobs's turn to speak. First she apologized to the audience because her speech would not be a prepared affair like her predecessors'. No, hers would be "piecemeal," just like life. "Life is an ad hoc affair, and has to be improvised all the time," she said. Big plans, she said, throwing a not-so-subtle dart at Rouse, "stifle the emergence of future, alternative courses of action. Believe me," she concluded, throwing another dart, this one at Safdie, "cities are not going to be humanized by building new urban models at Harvard." The audience applauded loudly, and Safdie gave her a kiss on the cheek.[13]

After the 1980 conference Richard Keeley wrote Jacobs a letter, inviting her to participate at a Boston College conference on the ethics of making a living. She turned the letter over and typed her polite refusal on the other side of the paper. Jacobs guarded her privacy carefully. When she appeared in public, it was usually in support of a civic cause. Moreover, Jacobs had a particular antipathy for academics, both as a concept and the people who made a living off it. Her discomfort with academia probably stemmed in part from her negative experiences with formal schooling, as well as the criticism she endured over the years from people like Mumford and city planning officials. Because she had no college degree, they had accused her of lacking the proper qualifications to write *Death and Life;* tough as Jacobs appeared on the surface, these personal attacks must have hurt deeply.

And now, even after so many years of accolades that she had received about her writings, her position on credentials had not softened. "I'm not a professor. I barely finished high school!" she once snapped at an economist who addressed her as "Professor Jacobs" during a public discussion devoted to *The Economy of Cities.* On principle, Jacobs refused, and continues to refuse, all honorary degrees that universities offer her from time to time. Among the rejected are the University of Toronto and Harvard. Obviously unimpressed by even the classiest of institutions, she will not bend. Academic credentials, she believed then and continues to believe, are only a symbol of knowledge, obfuscating its substance.

Jacobs's stubbornness did not deter Keeley. In the end he convinced her to come to Boston College, where Jacobs subsequently took part in a lively symposium that helped her to articulate the ideas behind *Systems of Survival,* a Platonic dialogue between six fictional characters who struggle to define the ethical basis of earning a living. In this context she explores what roles the public and private sectors should play in order to attain a goal that she never explicitly states but nevertheless implies: the greatest good for mankind. In other words, the Platonic arête.

Systems of Survival is written as a dialogue, although that had not been Jacobs's intention. She had begun the book using her customary narrative form. But as she worked, something seemed not right to her. She then decided to let the characters speak directly to one another. In this way she came to use the dialogue form, which made her characters come alive. They then began to assert themselves in ways that she hadn't expected, Jacobs told Canadian Broadcasting Corporation interviewer Peter Gzowski in May 1993. Jacobs had originally set the story in Toronto. But the characters had now become so assertive that she decided to turn them into New Yorkers. Because Torontonians, Jacobs told Gzowski, unlike New Yorkers, are too polite to say what is on their minds. And once the characters had been relocated to New York, they began to argue and then everything went along fine.

Both in form and substance, *Systems of Survival* constantly invokes Plato. Armbruster, one of the book's characters, pulls *The Republic* off his bookshelf and quotes passages that illustrate some of the ideas that Jacobs is pushing. At that point, she told Gzowski, she realized that she'd better "go back and read the old philosophers.... So I began reading. And I was astounded to find that I was reinventing the wheel!"

The main thesis of *Systems* is that two "moral syndromes," the guardian and the commercial, govern all work and must remain separate. Jacobs's idea echoes Plato, who mentions guardians of the law and merchants in *The Republic* and later *The Laws;* in both works, Plato aims to define which tasks belong to which citizens of his ideal state. In Jacobs's ideal society, guardians—by which Jacobs, like Plato, means government—must above all shun trade because it leads to corruption. On the contrary, the commercial sector must absolutely embrace trade; the desire for profit is what drives people to do business with one another. But merchants, unlike governments, must shun force; otherwise, how could two people trust each other enough to conduct business?

Combining the guardian and the commercial institutions can result in what Jacobs calls "a monstrous hybrid," something bound to fail. Organized crime, Jacobs shows, is one example of a monstrous hybrid. Another is communism, which she long condemned, doomed to fail by the very fact that guardians were trying to run commerce and therefore ran it into the ground. According to Jacobs, industries don't belong with guardians. When a Dallas television reporter asked Jacobs in 1994 what was the greatest intellectual discovery of the twentieth century, Jacobs's response was that "communism and socialism didn't work. I think it is something so obvious. Although some say no, it was just that there were bad leaders."[14]

Systems of Survival was Jacobs's first best seller. But it only made the Canadian lists, where it remained for an impressive twenty-six weeks. In the United States her book was all but ignored. Still, she felt gratified; her aim in writing it, according to Larry Solomon, an old friend and cofounder of Energy Probe, was to spur public debate over the issues of private and public ownership. As it did. When it came out, *Systems* provided fodder for numerous Canadian radio and television shows. The term "monstrous hybrid" got picked up and was bandied about by writers and journalists, including the eminent writer Robert Fulford. Clearly her book had hit a nerve in Canada, and no wonder: Canada's firm tradition of paternalism and all that goes with it—government ownership of utilities and regulation of areas such as health care—was ever more going head-to-head with a growing trend toward privatization.

But the book's success was also due to the fact that it was by Jane Jacobs, who could do no wrong in Canada.

CHAPTER ELEVEN

The Quintessential American

During the first week after Jane Jacobs arrived in Toronto in 1968, she and her family had three minor scuffles with the law.[1] First, the police reproached Jane and Robert after finding their ten-year-old daughter wandering the streets early one morning. She was, she told them, merely exploring her new neighborhood. Jane then had a second encounter with the law after, of all things, jaywalking. Finally, Robert's car was stopped because his mirror was blocked by piled-up furniture in the back seat.

So at the time Jacobs wondered whether she, an American, was just too independent minded to find happiness in Canada, where people were so polite and, it seemed, so obedient? The Canadian ideal is, after all, peace, order, and good government. Contrast that with the United States, where the constitution promises "life, liberty, and the pursuit of happiness."

But never mind the differences. The Canadians adored Jacobs. Walking down an Annex street one day with her shopping cart, she realized that she was happy.[2] Jacobs became a Canadian citizen in 1974. What a polite, sane place Canada is, she'd written to her mother as she was going through the naturalization process. Jacobs marveled at how the application form for citizenship listed "getting along well with your neighbors" as one of the duties of Canadians.[3]

Jane Jacobs and Toronto mayor David Miller, 2004. José San Juan, City of Toronto.

In becoming a Canadian, Jacobs had to give something up: she could no longer define herself by standing up to authority as she did when she lived in the United States, first as a child in Scranton and later as a writer and activist in New York. In Canada, Jacobs quickly entered the inner circle of politicians and professionals, and remains there today. Her influence in her adopted city is considerable. People say that David Miller, Toronto's current mayor, won a hotly contested election in 2004 because of Jacobs's support. In Toronto she is from time to time publicly feted, as in 1997 when a group of her devotees sponsored a month-long celebration of her titled "Ideas That Matter," complete with conferences and presentations.

Afterward the sponsors set up a think tank by the same name to further her teachings. Ideas That Matter, funded by financier and philanthropist Alan Broadbent, publishes a quarterly journal and sponsors symposia to which various members of the intelligentsia are invited to discuss Jacobs's ideas. And every year, Ideas That Matter gives out the Jane Jacobs Prize to somebody who "contributes to the fabric of Toronto life in unique ways that demonstrate the ideas of Jane Jacobs." The Ideas That Matter group includes civic leaders and professionals in the fields of architecture and urban planning, all of whom gaze at her, up on her pedestal, as if she were some ancient Pythian goddess sitting on her tripod in Delphi. They form a fiercely protective wall around Jacobs, carefully screening those who seek to talk to her.

The fact is that among Canadians who know her work, Jane Jacobs is immune to criticism. You can't write a newspaper or magazine story about anything having to do with cities without quoting her. "The urban guru," her acolytes call her. Over the years, says the *Toronto Star*'s longtime urban affairs columnist Christopher Hume, when Jacobs has taken positions that his paper disagreed with, rather than say so it has remained silent. Jacobs's near-divine status irritates some people, including members of the academic community, who justifiably criticize her works for being woefully short on analysis. She is, says David Hulchanski, a professor of social work at the University of Toronto and director of its Centre for Urban and Community Studies, guilty of "extreme empiricism." "You can't just leap from observation to sound byte," Hulchanski says. True enough. But that is precisely what Jacobs is so good at. Leave it for the academics to do the analyses. But for a good read, go to Jacobs. It's all about the power of her prose. And then add to that the fact that she is a wise old woman, a status that in Canada apparently commands respect—in stark contrast to the United States, where youth is idealized.

When Jacobs's book *The Question of Separatism*, which supported Quebec's sovereignty, came out in 1980, passions over the issue were running high. The first Quebec referendum had just been defeated by a vote of 60 percent to 40 percent. Yet no one criticized Jacobs. At least not in public. But behind the scenes it was a different story. "The view was that she didn't know what she was talking about, and not being helpful in a difficult situation," says Richard Gwyn, the *Toronto Star*'s longtime political columnist, who nonetheless describes himself as a "big fan" of her. Another Jacobs devotee, David Crombie, agrees. "Her Quebec book is ahistorical," he says. "She has no understanding of how Canadian history works." But Canadians chose to ignore Jacobs's foray into the morass of Quebec separatism. By all accounts, few outside Quebec read *The Question of Separatism.*

Likewise, nobody publicly challenged Jacobs over her support for the privatization of Ontario Hydro. In fact most Canadians still associate Jacobs and her ideas with the left. Clearly, they either don't know, or don't want to know, what she really believes about privatization. We have already seen that she is not interested in ideologies. If you try to pin her down, your hand might get slapped. An interviewer once asked her, what are the limits of regulation? Her answer: "You have to look at specific things, and they change over time."[4] Jacobs cited the example of Toronto, which once upon a time had no outdoor cafes because of regulations made at the time when the city's streets were full of horse manure. A good regulation, Jacobs said, is "knowing why it is in there and when it is no longer necessary."

The interviewer persevered. "When you start talking about the big role of government and that it messes around too much in people's lives sometimes," he said, "is there a danger than one can become too free-enterprise, that one is forgetting the social network that government can provide?"

And she snapped, "You are putting words into my mouth. I never said that government was messing around too much in our lives. I said it was doing stupid things. That's not the same thing at all. It may be doing too little in our lives and still be doing stupid things. It's not an ideological thing."

As if it were that simple. People still marvel at Toronto, but its golden age belongs to the past. The 1970s "save the neighborhoods" campaigns halted the construction of high-rises and hastened the gentrification of once-working-class neighborhoods such as Cabbagetown. Today, there is a desperate need in Toronto for public housing. Homeless people, once seen in only a few areas on the edges of downtown, are now everywhere, camped out on corners and on doorsteps. On these issues, Jacobs is silent.

But Canadians forgive her. "Our Jane," CBC journalist Peter Gzowski (who died in 2002) affectionately called her. Indeed, Canadians think of her as a Canadian. But this is a paradox, because she is a quintessential American. "A deeply American Canadian," journalist Robert Fulford called Jacobs in a conversation with this author.

Canadians accept a much greater role for the government in their lives, and therefore have a much greater sense of personal limits than their neighbors to the south. In contrast stands Jacobs, who loves nothing more than to assert her, and anybody else's, independence. Especially when it comes to cities. In 1997 the Metro government was dismantled and the city of Toronto was forced to amalgamate with surrounding areas, a move vociferously opposed by Jacobs and others. At the time Jacobs even said publicly that Toronto should think about separating from Ontario. Because of the structure of Canada's government, cities have much less autonomy than their American counterparts.

Since then, the Ideas That Matter organization has sponsored conferences where Jacobs has met publicly with mayors to look at ways to empower cities. But when the mayors stress the importance of working hand-in-hand with the federal and provincial governments, they raise Jacobs's hackles. "I think you have an ingrained mindset of dependency," she scolded the mayors of Toronto, Winnipeg, Vancouver, Calgary, and Montreal at the 2001 conference in Winnipeg. "You must somehow gather the self-esteem not to be apologetic about yourselves."[5]

Without minimizing her genius, it is nonetheless fair to say that the optimism underlying Jacobs's work is completely American in nature, and sometimes verges on naiveté. "She has made the point that a sense of independence and of control over one's life is essential to satisfaction and productivity," the architectural critic Paul Goldberger once said of her in the *New York Times* (April 28, 1996). Jane Jacobs, who grew up a doctor's daughter in Scranton, Pennsylvania, in a grand old house as a Yankee with roots reaching back before the Revolutionary War and a family tradition that included Southerners who voted Republican, can well take personal freedom for granted. But somebody born in a more uncertain part of the globe—the former Yugoslavia or the war-torn areas of Africa— cannot.

Jacobs, we recall, tried unsuccessfully to set *Systems of Survival* in Toronto. But she soon found that characters from Toronto were too polite to speak their minds. So she moved them all to New York, where they found their voices. Which seems only fitting. New York, after all, is where Jane Jacobs found her voice and wrote her greatest work.

Planners and anybody who is connected with urban studies know and acknowledge how much Jane Jacobs's thinking changed theirs. Cities, her passion, moored her. Starting from cities, we have seen her thinking branch out in many directions. When her ideas intersect with others, she has the ability to stop and observe. Most people, when they think too hard, think themselves into confusion. Jacobs, we have seen, is not like most people. At the point where most people give up, she sees nuance, studies it, separates out the strands, continues to think. Finally, she writes.

Paradoxically, there is an undisciplined quality to her thinking process. Ever the outsider, she is unfettered by the rules or vocabulary of any given discipline or the necessity to support herself solely through her writing—Robert had a long and productive career as an architect, which is fortunate because Jacobs's books were not of the sort that makes their writer wealthy.[6] Jacobs, the autodidact, has let her mind go in whatever direction it pleases, so much so that it is impossible to describe her ideas in a single story line. In an increasingly specialized world where publishers demand academic credentials for writers who want to publish books in a given field, there are few like Jane Jacobs anymore.

She has never stopped writing. After *Systems of Survival* she took a break from economics, traveling to Alaska to retrace the steps of her great-aunt Hannah Breece, who many years earlier had left Jacobs her memoirs. Upon her return, Jacobs edited her aunt's work, which was then published in 1995 as *A Schoolteacher in Old Alaska,* a forthright and wonderfully detailed account of one woman's experiences on the frontier.

In 2000, Jacobs returned to economics with *The Nature of Economies,* another dialogue between the characters who first appeared in *Systems of Survival.* They rehash ideas running through all of her previous books, comparing economic life to ecosystems. In 2004 *Dark Age Ahead* was published, a polemic about what Jacobs sees as potentially fatal flaws in our civilization. These two books received mixed reviews. Some critics faulted them for their lack of focus, and rightfully so. Once Jacobs no longer used cities as the springboard for her writing, it meandered. The dialogue form in Jacobs's hands was serviceable, nothing more. It is fair to say that these later works do not in any way measure up to her great urban trilogy.

But if Jacobs had only written *Death and Life,* that book alone would have been enough to establish her genius. We have seen that its publication led to shelving large-scale urban renewal programs, helped kill the Le Corbusier–style "tower in the park" housing project design, and made "mixed use" zoning mainstream. During the 1970s, as Jacobs was helping Toronto to be remade into a place that visitors envied, a young man named Neil Goldschmidt was elected mayor of Portland, Oregon. Goldschmidt, who would later become President Carter's secretary of transportation, had read *Death and Life* and loved what Jacobs had to say. Two years after his election in 1972, Goldschmidt, fearlessly declaring war on automobiles, killed a proposal to build a freeway, instead pushing through a mass transit system of buses and light rail. Today "the Rose City," as Portland is called after the fragrant flowers that grow all over in the city's many gardens, stands as a model for planners with its densely populated mixed residential and commercial center, and public transportation that people actually use instead of their cars.[7]

For all that, over the years Jacobs has often complained that despite the accolades her ideas have received, they have not really changed the world. In one sense she is right. Sprawl continues unabated, blighting the landscape with monotonous office parks and empty suburban streets lined with cookie-cutter homes, pushing us toward inevitable ecological disaster as we consume ever more fossil fuels in our SUVs. Toronto may be "the city that works" but two-thirds of the city's five million inhabitants live in suburbs, which occupy 95 percent of the city's area. Former mayor John

Sewell has compared Toronto to "Vienna surrounded by Phoenix." Smart growth is a catchy phrase, but for now it only gets lip service. For now, many North American cities continue to lose population and jobs.[8]

And if we look at what is happening around us, as Jane Jacobs has done all her life, the unmistakable conclusion is that North Americans still perceive owning a private, detached home in the suburbs with a car parked in the driveway as the fulfillment of their dreams. (Note that Canada's suburbanization happened on a less dramatic scale than in the United States, where everything tends to go to more of an extreme than anywhere else.) And for all the excitement over revitalized downtowns and the so-called "SoHoization" of former industrial neighborhoods, most of those who are choosing to live in these newly "vibrant" neighborhoods, to use a favorite Jacobs adjective, are retirees or young professionals without children.[9] Few choose to live and raise their children in the densely populated city environment that Jacobs idealizes.

All of which raise the question, are Jacobs's ideas about cities still relevant today? How will the global digital network affect community, which has been under siege particularly in the United States since the growth of suburbs and highways after World War II? The reality of the Internet and virtual "communities" make the notion of what makes for a city, always a puzzle, harder and harder to solve. But connection with others is a basic human need. That more and more Americans are attending church on Sunday shows that virtual community does not suffice to fill that need.

Community, it seems, must be physical as well as metaphysical. There is, after all, no substitute for downtown, still a cherished place in our collective imagination to judge by such golden oldies as "New York, New York" and "I Left My Heart in San Francisco." The lyrics to these songs do not evoke images of Levittown. Jacobs's insights, it turns out, are just as relevant today as when she wrote *Death and Life,* a fact that brings us back to the subject of Jane Jacobs and change.

Changes happen all the time, although sometimes in such small increments that we cannot perceive them with our eyes. In like manner, ever since Jacobs wrote *Death and Life,* her ideas have been shaking people up, who then tell other people about them, so that her influence is felt in many niches that are linked together into a vast, interlocking network.

"I think you have underestimated the impact your last two books have had," David Osborne, author of *Laboratories of Democracy* and an expert in development economics who worked as a senior advisor to Vice President Al Gore, wrote to Jacobs in 1988. "You would be surprised how many of the best people in the development field have read your work. In a quiet way—totally outside the (largely irrelevant) academic world—you have had a profound influence on practitioners of development. When I find someone who knows how to think about development, I often ask if they have read your books. Ninety percent of the time, the answer is yes. There is often a sense . . . of membership—a small fraternity of the enlightened."[10] During the 1980s recession, Osborne says, officials were beginning to realize that big projects like convention centers and stadiums did nothing to revive local economies. International development specialists are also waking up to this fact; at the World Bank, experts cite Jane Jacobs. They realize that micro-loans for starting little local businesses, many involving traditional women's work, help developing countries grow their economies. Traditional mega-aid schemes like building dams or factories, it turns out, do not.

In the early 1980s Oregon resident Alana Probst read an excerpt from *Cities and the Wealth of Nations* in the *Atlantic Monthly* during an airplane flight, and she could barely contain her excitement.[11] Probst, in the fourth generation of a logging family, was then working with a community development organization in Eugene. There and all over Oregon, the collapse of the logging industry was destroying the economy, dragging down the businesses and the lives of those who depended on logging. Predictably, local industry leaders said that luring a large company into Eugene would solve the region's problems.

But Probst and her group were instead thinking about ways to stimulate the small businesses that still remained. She had the idea that if businesses used locally made instead of imported supplies, it would create jobs. It was simple common sense. They had been testing their idea, with unexpectedly good results. She had never heard of the term "import replacement." After reading the excerpt, Probst immediately contacted Jacobs by mail. Jacobs responded with practical advice and contacts that helped Probst to continue her work on a larger scale.

Throughout her long life, Jacobs has always lent her support to those grassroots causes she deems worthy. Individuals fighting huge civic projects that they perceive will blight their cities often write to her for advice. And they get it. Laura Hall, an urban designer furious over a proposed six-lane freeway through Santa Monica, California, met Jacobs in 1997 and asked her advice on what to do about it. How, Hall wanted to know, had Jacobs survived the attacks on her by conventional planners after the publication of *Death and Life?* Jacobs answered that all of the people who came out to join her in her battle against the Lower Manhattan Expressway after her book was published proved to her that she was not alone. "You advised me," wrote Hall, "to go back to my community and speak out and write." [12] Hall followed Jacobs's advice. She started a movement against the freeway, picked up the support of the Environmental Defense Fund, and won her battle.

Examples of Jacobs's influence are endless: a police officer who taught at New York City's Police Academy made the chapters on sidewalk safety and "the curse of border vacuums" in *Death and Life* required reading for his course. The book is the bible for adherents of the New Urbanist movement that, perceiving the hunger that people have for community, is the force behind the design of such places as Seaside, Florida, and other new communities that mix retail and residential. The goal is for everything to be within walking distance, or at least accessible to public transportation.

The writer and philosopher Marshall Berman talks at length about Jacobs in his wonderfully original book about modernism, *All That Is Solid Melts into Air.* Since the nineteenth century, writes Berman, modernists have used the street "as the medium in which the totality of modern material and spiritual forces could meet, clash, interfuse and work out their ultimate meanings and fate." In the 1960s, Berman says, Jane Jacobs dug up the street image that had been buried by the modern architectural movement personified by Le Corbusier, and resurrected it for all time with her stunning passages in *Death and Life.*

And so on. Jacobs's insistence that her ideas have not changed the world much strikes this writer as disingenuous. Moreover, the change often happens in small ways, not just in the sense of grassroots movements like Alana Probst's in Oregon, but even smaller, at a level that cannot be seen by the casual eye. But we know that it is happening nonetheless because we can see its effects, even if it translates for the time being only into something metaphysical, like ideas. Developers may continue to build suburban developments on what was once farmland, and many of the occupants of the new homes are still driving SUVs, but perceptions are changing. Everybody knows that energy sources are not limitless, and nobody believes that we can continue our profligate lifestyle indefinitely.

We have seen that Jacobs's ideas intersect with many areas. In 1997, during a five-day Toronto conference attended by hundreds of people celebrating her contributions, Jacobs, sitting on stage dressed in one of her usual outfits consisting of a large denim shirt, jeans, and jogging sneakers, talked with an interviewer about how she sees the world. "I think we are misled by universities . . . into thinking that there actually are separate fields of knowledge," Jacobs said solemnly. "[But] no, they link up . . . everything is a seamless web . . . and it's a very functional thing not just a poetic expression."

To illustrate her point she used the example of fractals, like the old Dutch Cleaner can with its picture of woman holding a can with a picture of her holding a can, and so on and on. Her point is that everything starts at the smallest level. "If you remove the big thing," Jacobs said, "you can still have the little ones, but not vice-versa. The big thing would be hollow. So once you know fractals you live in all of them at once—I live at 69 Albany Avenue and also the Universe." One of her few superstitions, she said, is wishing upon a star. "It's my way of praying—and at that moment I'm in my home, the universe, and I'm connected."

A lifetime of thinking had now led Jacobs straight into what is popularly called "the new science," a radical change in scientific thinking that has taken shape within the last two decades. In other words, we are talking about one of Thomas Kuhn's paradigm shifts, mentioned earlier in connection with the changes brought on by Jacobs's *Death and Life*. In the world of science, traditional theory has it that the universe operates according to certain mathematical laws. But this view is now being challenged by chaos theory, so-called because, it turns out, knowing those laws does not necessarily predict what happens. Just like building Le Corbusier–inspired housing projects does not solve the pathology of poverty. In fact, the design only makes the lives of the people living there worse. In other words, what was once thought to be order is chaos—behind which there is a complex order that results from the interweaving of many components. Just like Jane Jacobs envisions cities.

NOTES

Introduction

1. Joseph P. Fried, "Demise of Radio Row Is Still Causing Static," *New York Times,* February 18, 1968.
2. Lewis Mumford, "The Gentle Art of Overcrowding," *New Yorker,* May 20, 1950.
3. Obituary of Robert H. Jacobs by Sid Adilman, *Toronto Star,* September 19, 1996.
4. The story about the check to Consolidated Edison comes from a newspaper clipping, *New York World Telegram* (no date), Jane Jacobs Archives, John J. Burns Library, Boston College (hereafter referred to as Jacobs papers).

Chapter One: From Scranton to New York

1. Information about Dr. John Decker Butzner, and quotes by him, come from the following sources: "Widow of City Physician, Bess Butzner, Celebrates 90th Birthday," *The Scrantonian,* June 15, 1969; obituary, *Scranton Tribune,* December 23, 1937; Mark Feeney, "City Sage," *Boston Globe,* November 14, 1993; Jane Jacobs as quoted in Max Allen, *Ideas That Matter,* 133, 150; Jonathan Karp, "Jane Jacobs Doesn't Live Here Anymore," *At Random,* Winter 1993 (cited in Allen, *Ideas That Matter,* 13–14); interview with Jane Jacobs by James Kunstler, *Metropolis,* March 2001. That Dr. Butzner delivered his daughter is apparent from Jacobs's birth certificate, which he signed as the attending physician.
2. Jacobs, *The Economy of Cities,* 160.
3. Jacobs, *The Economy of Cities,* 129–130; 159–163; 202.
4. Details and anecdotes about Jacobs's childhood, including quotes by her, come from: speech by Jacobs on May 7, 2004, in Greenwich Village, New York City; Adele Freedman, "Jane Jacobs," *The Globe and Mail,* June 9, 1984; Kunstler, *Metropolis* interview; Karp, "Jane Jacobs"; "Jade Writes Potpourri," *Scranton Times,* March 22, 1995.

5. This quote, and the information about her ancestors, comes from a 1952 interrogatory of Jacobs by the U.S. State Department. Jacobs papers, MS95–29, box 11, folder 6.

6. All information about Hannah Breece comes from Jane Jacobs, ed., *A Schoolteacher in Old Alaska.*

7. "I was so damn glad . . .": quoted in the *New York Times,* May 6, 1963. Details about her experiences immediately following her graduation, including her first years in New York City, come from a biography Jacobs wrote on November 22, 1961, for *Architect's Journal,* reprinted in Allen, *Ideas That Matter,* 3. Jacobs discusses her aunt Martha Robison in her book *Cities and the Wealth of Nations,* 124–129. The details about the "Agony" column come from a speech by Toronto planner Joseph Berridge, who quoted Jacobs at a Boston College symposium, November 19, 1993.

8. "Just flabbergasted by the number of people . . .": quote, as well as the detail about surviving on Pablum, is from Jacobs's *Metropolis* interview with Kunstler.

9. Quote is from Jacobs's speech, May 7, 2004.

10. Facts and figures on New York's housing conditions during the Depression come from: *New York Panorama: A Companion to the WPA Guide to New York City; New York Times,* March 3, 1935 and July 7, 1937; Richard Plunz, *A History of Housing in New York City;* Kenneth T. Jackson, ed., *The Encyclopedia of the New York City,* s.v. "Tenements," "Public Housing." The figure of a million and a quarter New Yorkers on the dole was reported in 1931 by the journalist Lorena Hickok, cited in Ric Burns et al., *New York: An Illustrated History,* 417.

11. Karp, "Jane Jacobs."

12. Jane admired the crafts shops and other details: Jacobs's speech, May 7, 2004. For the anecdote about Jacobs sitting on the building roof: Karp, "Jane Jacobs."

13. The facts about Romany Marie and "Mother" McAvoy come from their respective obituaries, *New York Times,* February 23, 1961 and November 12, 1940. About Greenwich Village, see Ross Wetzsteon, *Republic of Dreams.*

14. The passages from *Vogue* are quoted in Allen, *Ideas That Matter,* 35–37.

15. Details about Jacobs's Columbia studies come from Karp, "Jane Jacobs." Her quote "I was allowed to continue getting an education" comes from her bio for *Architect's Journal.*

16. The facts about Jacobs's sexual harassment at *Iron Age,* as well as her quote about her boss, are contained in her response to a 1949 State Department questionnaire. Jacobs papers, MS95–29, box 11, folder 6.

17. Biographical information about Robert Jacobs comes from

Jane Jacobs, *Systems of Survival*, 227, and a letter by Jane Jacobs to R. Davis of the Seaside Institute, September 16, 1997, Jacobs papers, MS02–13, box 2, folder 1. Quotes by Robert and Jane Jacobs told to Mark Feeney, *Boston Globe*, November 14, 1993.

Chapter Two: Urban Blight

Information about postwar suburbanization comes from Kenneth T. Jackson, *Crabgrass Frontier*, chapter 13, "The Baby Boom and the Age of the Subdivision," and chapter 14, "The Drive-In Culture of Contemporary America." Facts about New York's public housing come from Richard Plunz, *A History of Housing in New York City*. Details about the West Village during the post–World War II period come from my conversations with Arthur Stoliar, January 2004.

1. Replies by Jacobs to State Department questionnaires: Jacobs papers, MS95–29, box 11, folder 6.
2. Details about Jacobs's work at *Architectural Forum* come from her May 7, 2004, speech in Greenwich Village, as does the quote "Always be suspicious of magazines . . ." Another source is Peter Blake, *No Place Like Utopia*.
3. See Robert Fishman, *Urban Utopias in the Twentieth Century*, 184–185.
4. Le Corbusier's quotes come from his book *When the Cathedrals Were White*, 42, 51, 55, 87, 90.

Chapter Three: Urban Renewal

1. Kunstler, *Metropolis* interview.
2 Kunstler, *Metropolis* interview.
3. "It soon became obvious to me . . .": Jacobs bio in *Architects Journal*.
4. Sources for facts and figures about East Harlem in the 1950s: conversations with Gene Sklar and Judy Kirk Fitzsimmons, February 2004; Union Settlement Association Records, Columbia University Library; Union Settlement Association Records, Burke Library, Union Theological Seminary; *The WPA Guide to New York City*; Plunz, *Housing in New York City*; Stern et al., *New York 1960; New York Times*, October 4, 1949.
5. Ellen Lurie's reports: Union Records, Columbia University Library, box 35, folder 7. William Kirk's letters: Union Records, Columbia University Library, box 24. Quoted with permission of Judy Kirk Fitzsimmons. Some anecdotes about Kirk are from my conversations with Judy Kirk Fitzsimmons.

6. Kisseloff, *You Must Remember This,* 370.
7. Jacobs, *Death and Life,* 95.
8. For descriptions of Greenwich Village's heyday, see Wetzsteon, *Republic of Dreams.* For NYU as property owner, see *New York Times,* December 8, 1957.
9. See Caro, *The Power Broker,* 707.
10. Sources for Robert Moses and the Washington Square Southeast project: Plunz, *Housing in New York City,* 289; Fred J. Cook and Gene Gleason, "The Shame of New York," *The Nation,* October 31, 1959. Facts about the abuse of Title I in New York come from Cook and Gleason. For Robert Moses's relationship with the New York Archdiocese, see Caro, *The Power Broker,* 741. For Moses's relationship with the press, see Caro, *The Power Broker,* 979; Cook and Gleason; Gay Talese, *The Kingdom and the Power.*
11. For the saga of Moses and the Cross Bronx Expressway, see Caro, *The Power Broker,* chapters 36–38.
12. Jacobs's interview with Leticia Kent was conducted in October 1997 for the Greenwich Village Society for Historic Preservation. Jacobs papers, MS02–13, box J.
13. Jacobs recalling that sometimes people would refuse to sign petitions and other details are from the Kunstler *Metropolis* interview, where Jacobs also quotes Moses's remark about "a bunch of mothers."

Chapter Four: The Housewife with No College Degree

The facts in this chapter about the life of William H. Whyte, including his relationship with Jacobs, come from his preface to *The Exploding Metropolis,* his obituary in the *New York Times,* January 13, 1999, and my telephone conversations with Alexandra Whyte. The information at the end of the chapter about Jason Epstein, Nathan Glazer, and their relationship with Jane Jacobs and each other is based on my interview with Glazer on April 28, 2004, in Cambridge, Massachusetts, as well as several e-mail exchanges, and e-mails from Epstein.

1. "All right, I'll do it . . .": *Metropolis* interview by Kunstler. Jacobs's Harvard speech is reprinted in *Architectural Forum,* June 1956.
2. "I had hypnotized myself . . .": *Milwaukee Journal,* July 8, 1962.
3. Fred Kent, president of the Project for Public Spaces, in a telephone conversation with me on January 9, 2004, quoting Jacobs immediately after a conversation he had had with her.
4. Richard A. Miller, "Lincoln Center: 'a new kind of institution,'" *Architectural Forum,* August 1958.

5. New School speech: Jacobs papers, MS95–29, box 25, folder 8.
6. Whyte's memo: Jacobs papers, MS95–29, box 25, folder 8.
7. The anecdote about the two professors comes from Jacobs's interview by Claire Parin, May 28, 1999. Jacobs papers, MS02–13, box J.
8. Jacobs's letter to the Rockefeller Foundation is printed in full in Allen, *Ideas That Matter,* 47–48.
9. Jacobs's quote is from the *Milwaukee Journal,* July 8, 1962.
10. Information about Jason Epstein is from Jacobs's letter to Ann Godoff of Random House, September 18, 2001. Jacobs papers, MS02–13, box 5, folder 3.
11. For Anchor Books, see Epstein, *Book Business,* and Cerf, *At Random.*
12. Fred Kent, quoting to me from his recent conversation with Jane Jacobs, January 2004.

Chapter Five: *The Death and Life of Great American Cities*

1. *New York Times,* August 27, 1967.
2. For Lewis Mumford and the Regional Planning Association of America, and other facts about Mumford's life, see Donald L. Miller, *Lewis Mumford: A Life.*
3. The newsletter is quoted in Stern et al., *New York 1960,* 865.
4. Kunstler, *Metropolis* interview. The anecdote about driving with Mumford into the city also comes from Kunstler's interview.
5. Miller, *Lewis Mumford: A Life,* 486.
6. On zoning, see the article in Jackson, *Encyclopedia of the City of New York,* and Klemek, "Urbanism as Reform," chapter 4.
7. Quote comes from James Glantz and Eric Lipton, *City in the Sky.*
8. The 1944 study on New York's population density was undertaken by the Committee for City Planning and Zoning, New York City Housing Department Library, Citizens Housing Council, New York.
9. Thomas Jefferson, *Notes on the State of Virginia:* query 19, "Manufacturers."
10. Fishman, *Urban Utopias,* 163.
11. Louis Sullivan's quote about Boston is in Morton White and Lucia White, *The Intellectual Versus the City,* 192.
12. Marchus Cunliffe, *Spectator* (no date), Jacobs papers, MS95–29, scrapbook 2.
13. *New York Times,* November 5, 1961.
14. O'Harrow's remarks are reprinted in *Planning,* September 1986.
15. Jacobs papers, MS95–29, box 13, folder 6.
16. *Forth Worth Dodge Construction News,* May 22, 1962. Jacobs papers, box 27, folder 2.

17. *American City*, May 1962. Tronzo quoted in the *Pittsburgh Press*, February 22, 1962. Both are reprinted in Allen, *Ideas That Matter*, 50–51.

18. Jacobs's response to the complaints about her remarks on Boston are contained in her letter to Arnold Nicholson, associate editor of *Saturday Evening Post*, dated October 23, 1961. Jacobs papers, MS95–21, box 11, folder 6.

19. The account of the MOMA panel with Jacobs and Logue is by Walter McQuade, *The Nation*, March 17, 1962.

20. Regarding Lewis Mumford quotes: "insolent chariots" from his 1958 essay "The Highway and the City," reprinted in a Mumford essay collection by the same title. His attacks on Robert Moses: "Restored Circulation, New Life," 1955 *New Yorker* "Sky Line" essay reprinted in *From the Ground Up*. Letters: "Your analysis . . . of Lincoln Center . . .": Mumford to Jacobs, May 3, 1958, reprinted in Allen, *Ideas That Matter*, 95; "There are half a dozen publishers . . .": Mumford to Jacobs, January 4, 1958, Jacobs collection, MS95–29, box 13, folder 6; "I have grappled with Jane Jacobs's stimulating and awful book . . .": Mumford to Frederic Osborn, Hughes, ed., *The Letters of Lewis Mumford and Fredric J. Osborn;* "the paper burned . . .": Mumford to David Liebovitz, October 10, 1962, cited in Miller, *Lewis Mumford: A Life*. Mumford letters quoted with permission of Robert Wojtowicz.

21. Telephone conversation with Herbert Gans, March 16, 2004.

Chapter Six: The West Village and Lomex Battles

The material about the fights that Jacobs led in Greenwich Village comes from the following sources: my discussions with Greenwich Villagers Arthur Stoliar, Avram and Carmen Greiss (January 2004), and John Simon (March 2004); Jacobs's 1997 interview with Leticia Kent; *Death and Life*, 124–125; May 7, 2004 talk by Jane Jacobs in Greenwich Village; and accounts in the *New York Times, Village Voice, Villager,* and *New York Herald Tribune*.

1. On Micove, see *Village Voice*, December 7, 1961; *New York Times*, April 28, 1961. Jacobs's contention about Schwab is in her interview with Leticia Kent.

2. *Villager*, March 2, 1961.

3. Caro, *The Power Broker*, 867–879.

4. The story about Lester Eisner was told by Jane Jacobs at her Greenwich Village talk, May 7, 2004.

5. Sources for the account of the Save the West Village campaign are: Leticia Kent interview; *New York Times,* March 3, 14, 27, April 3, May 9, 1961; *Villager,* March 16, June 6, 1961.
6. Sources for the account of the so-called "riot" October 1961 at City Hall are: Jacobs's Leticia Kent interview and May 7, 2004 talk; *New York Times,* October 19, 1961; *New York Herald Tribune,* October 19, 1971; Citizens Union press release October 20, 1961; Mayor Wagner papers, folder titled "Housing—West Village," La Guardia College, New York City, cited in Klemek, "Urbanism as Reform."
7. Leticia Kent interview, also the source of much of the information about the Lomex fight. Other sources: my conversation with Arthur Stoliar; *Village Voice,* August 20 and December 12, 1962; *New York Times,* December 7, 1962; *Villager,* January 31, 1963; Stern et al., *New York 1960,* 259. On SoHo, see Kostelanetz, *Soho.*
8. Kunstler, *Metropolis* interview.
9. Mumford's letter is quoted in *New York Times,* December 5, 1962. After Lomex's defeat, Jacobs's letter to Mumford: Mumford Collection, Annenberg Library, University of Pennsylvania.
10. Moses's speech quoted in the *Villager,* January 31, 1963. On the waning of Moses's power, see Caro, *The Power Broker,* 1078.

Chapter Seven: More Battles

1. James Baldwin, interview by Dr. Kenneth Clark, "The Negro and the American Promise," *American Experience,* Public Broadcasting System, Spring 1963.
2. For example, Frances Piven, Columbia University School of Social Work, as quoted in Richard Schickle, "New York's Mr. Urban Renewal," *New York Times,* March 1, 1970.
3. See Wilson, *Negro Politics,* 188–189, 254–255; and Hirsch, *Making the Second Ghetto,* 251.
4. Starr, *The Living End,* 103.
5. Jacobs's interview with Blake Harris, *Government Technology,* August 2002.
6. Transcript of the National Housing Council conference on cities, 1962. Jacobs papers, MS95–29, box 24, folder 8.
7. Kuhn, *The Structure of Scientific Revolutions,* chapter 8, "The Response to Crisis."
8. Plunz, *Housing in New York City,* 290–291.
9. Jacobs, at her May 7, 2004, talk. She said that this remark was overheard by one of the committee's "moles" at the planning office.

10. *New York Times,* October 29, 1963. On the destruction of Penn Station and the passing of the landmarks law: *Village Voice,* August 13, 1964; *New York Times,* October 19, 1964. Also see Burns et al., *New York: An Illustrated History.*

11. *New York Times,* June 2, 1963.

12. Conversation with Margot Gayle, New York City, October 2004.

13. *New York Times,* February 11, 1966.

14. Gratz, *Cities Back from the Edge,* chapter 13, "The Soho Syndrome," 303.

15. Sources for the Seward Park High School meeting on Lomex that took place on April 10, 1968: Leticia Kent interview; *Village Voice,* April 18, 1968; Jacobs's talk on May 7, 2004; written account by Margot Gayle, June 4, 1988, based on a telephone conversation she had with Jacobs, in the Jacobs papers, MS95–29, box 25, folder 7.

16. Reprinted in Allen, *Ideas That Matter,* 74–78.

17. Jacobs's letter to her mother is printed in full in Allen, *Ideas That Matter,* 72–73.

18. *New York Times,* April 18, 1968.

19. Quoted in Stern et al., *New York 1960,* 261.

20. See Marshall Berman, "Buildings Are Judgment," *Ramparts* 13 (March 1975): 33–39.

Chapter Eight: Race, Gentrification, and the South Bronx

Statistics about the Bronx come from New York City Department of City Planning, 2000 census community district summary. Information about Nos Quedamos comes from my conversations with Yolanda Gonzalez, Petr Stand, and Ron Shiffman. On gentrification, see Lance Freeman and Frank Braconi, "Gentrification and Displacement," *Journal of the American Planning Association,* Winter 2004. Freeman, a Columbia University professor and expert in housing and urban poverty, finds that so far research on this question has wielded inconclusive results. Still, "most of it suggests that a relatively small percentage of housing moves can be attributed to displacement, and there is little evidence that implicates neighborhood gentrification in the process." On the South Bronx's comeback, see Robert Worth, "Guess Who Saved the South Bronx? Big Government," *Washington Monthly,* April 1999. Also Brian Francis Sahd, "Community Involvement in the South Bronx: A Historical Analysis of Participation in Planning and Development from the 1960s to the 1990s," PhD dissertation, Columbia University, 2000.

1. Jill Jonnes, *South Bronx Rising,* 298–299.

2. Kunstler, *Metropolis* interview.
3. Interviews with Roberta Brandes Gratz, *Tikkun,* May/June 2001, and *Metropolis* interview with Kunstler.

Chapter Nine: Toronto

Much of the material in this chapter came from my conversations with the following people: journalists Robert Fulford, Christopher Hume, and Richard Gwyn; Bobbi Speck; former Toronto mayor David Crombie; Jim Lemon, Shoukry Roweis, Larry Bourne, David Hulchanski, and Frank Cunningham, all of the University of Toronto; Larry Solomon.

1. See John Hagan, *Northern Passage,* for a study of American war resisters in Canada.
2. John Sewell, *Up Against City Hall,* 10–13.
3. Hagan, *Northern Passage,* 72.
4. *New York Times,* March 26, 1969.
5. The figure of 20,000 expatriates comes from Hagan, *Northern Passage,* 66, as does the information about TADP, 73–82. Regarding the draft manual: Hagan, 253, and the *New York Times,* February 11, 1968.
6. *Globe and Mail,* unknown date, 1970.
7. Robert Fulford, "Canada Wants Out," *New York Times Magazine,* April 21, 1974; Trudeau quoted in the *New York Times,* March 26, 1969.
8. Speech by Jane Jacobs, Amsterdam, 1984. Jacobs papers, MS02–13, box I.
9. See Robert Fulford, *Accidental City,* and John Sewell, *Shape of the City.*
10. Sewell, *Up Against City Hall,* 20.
11. Sewell, *Shape of the City,* 177; Fulford, *Accidental City,* 51–66.
12. "The pursuit of paralysis," editorial, *Globe and Mail,* January 13, 1969.
13. David Nowlan and Nadine Nowlan, *The Bad Trip,* 70.
14. *Globe and Mail,* November 1, 1969.
15. These facts about the Spadina come from: the *Globe and Mail,* January 13, 1969; Sean Marshall, "The Expressways of Toronto," *Transit Toronto,* http://transit.toronto.on.ca; Sewell, *Shape of the City;* David Nowlan and Nadine Nowlan, *The Bad Trip.*
16. Lemon, *Liberal Dreams,* 262–263.
17. McLuhan is quoted on the inside cover of David Nowlan and Nadine Nowlan, *The Bad Trip.*
18. "Making a Movie with McLuhan," *Antigonish Review* 74–75 (Summer/Autumn 1988): 127–129.
19. *Toronto Star,* January 2, 1970.

20. Photo in Allen, *Ideas That Matter,* 117.
21. *Toronto Telegram,* April 7, 1970. Reprinted in Allen, *Ideas That Matter,* 116.
22. Sewell, *Shape of the City,* 181–182.
23. Allen, *Ideas That Matter,* 124–125.
24. For the account of the St. Jamestown house: Jane Jacobs, radio transcript, CBC, October 20–24, 1997; *Globe and Mail,* April 2, 1992.
25. See Sewell, *Shape of the City,* 191. For accounts of successful neighborhood fights against urban renewal in Toronto, see Sewell, *Up Against City Hall.*
26. See Fulford, *Accidental City,* 73–74 and 83–90, for a full account of the St. Lawrence project. See also Roberta Brandes Gratz, *Cities Back from the Edge,* 331–333.
27. Allen, *Ideas That Matter,* 203–204.
28. Clipping from *East Side News,* Union Settlement papers, box 14, folder 2, Columbia University Library.

Chapter Ten: Economist without Portfolio

1. Lucas's speech was published as "On the Mechanics of Economic Development," *Journal of Monetary Economics* 22 (1988): 3–42.
2. Lucas lecture, Toronto, June 21, 2004. My understanding of how economists have integrated Jacobs's ideas is also based on my conversations via e-mail with Robert Lucas and David Warsh, former columnist for the *Boston Globe* and currently editor of economicprincipals.com.
3. Lucas, "On the Mechanics."
4. The lecture was given February 2, 1967, at the Royal Institute, and is reprinted in Allen, *Ideas That Matter,* 90–91.
5. Letter from Jacobs to Matthew Frederick, July 31, 1995. Jacobs papers, MS95–29, box 12, folder 4.
6. Facts about Scranton's iron industry come from: Daniel Perry, *Scranton's Historic Furnaces,* Pennsylvania Historical and Museum Commission, 1994; and the exhibits at Steamtown.
7. For the Steamtown controversy, see: Gratz, *Cities Back from the Edge,* 199–203; Kelly Kissell, "National Park at Train Yard Is Focus of Debate," *Los Angeles Times,* February 9, 1992; Mike Shoup, *Pittsburgh Post-Gazette,* September 4, 1994.
8. Quoted by Joseph X. Flannery, "She Wrote the Book on City Planning," In My View column, *Scranton Times-Tribune,* February 17, 2001.
9. Ruth Corcoran, "Scranton's Own Soho Flourishes between Lackawanna and Spruce," *Northeast Pennsylvania Business Journal,*

January 1, 2005; Telephone conversation with Ken Marquis, April 2005.

10. Christine Fanning, "Urban Pioneers," *Northeast Pennsylvania Business Journal,* November 1, 2004. Fanning cites a recent study by the Brookings Institute.

11. Jacobs, *Death and Life,* 439.

12. Larry Solomon, one of Energy Probe's founders, in a conversation with the author, January 3, 2005.

13. Jacobs's quotes at the 1980 Boston "Great Cities" conference come from "At the Edge of the Great City," an unpublished article by Richard Keeley.

14. Jacobs papers, MS95–29, box 35, folder 2; videotape of "Conversation with Jane Jacobs."

Chapter Eleven: The Quintessential American

1. Jacobs's interview with Paul Wilson, *Saturday Night,* March 1, 2000.

2. Jacobs, as quoted by Boston College historian Thomas O'Connor at a conference about Jane Jacobs at Boston College, November 19, 1993.

3. Jacobs's letter to her mother is reprinted in Allen, *Ideas That Matter,* 143.

4. Blake Harris, interview with Jane Jacobs, 2002, *Government Technology,* www.govtech.net.

5. The quarterly *Ideas That Matter,* 2, no. 1: 20.

6. Karp, "Jane Jacobs."

7. In 2004 Goldschmidt's achievements were irrevocably tainted after a tenacious reporter at an alternative weekly published a series of stories documenting that while Goldschmidt was governor, he had a sexual relationship with a teenage girl. The reporter won a 2004 Pulitzer Prize.

8. See, for example, Bruce Katz, "Reviving Cities: Think Metropolitan," Brookings Institution Policy Brief 33, June 1998.

9. See Timothy Egan, "Vibrant Cities Find One Thing Missing: Children," *New York Times,* March 24, 2005.

10. David Osborne, letter to Jane Jacobs, Jacobs papers, MS02–13, box 11, folder 8. Quoted with permission of David Osborne.

11. The information about Alana Probst comes from Probst's essay, "Why I Believe Jane Jacobs Wrote a Book Just for Me," in Allen, *Ideas That Matter,* 185–187.

12. Laura Hall, letter to Jane Jacobs: Jacobs papers, MS02–13, box 2, folder 2. Quoted with permission of Laura Hall.

SELECTED BIBLIOGRAPHY

Allen, Max, ed. *Ideas That Matter: The Worlds of Jane Jacobs*. Owen Sound, Ontario: Ginger Press, 1997.

Berman, Marshall. *All That Is Solid Melts into Air*. New York: Penguin, 1988.

Blake, Peter. *No Place Like Utopia*. New York: W. W. Norton, 1993.

Burns, Ric, James Sanders, and Lisa Ades. *New York: An Illustrated History*. New York: Alfred A. Knopf, 1999.

Caro, Robert. *The Power Broker*. New York: Random House, 1974.

Cerf, Bennett. *At Random*. New York: Random House, 1973.

Epstein, Jason. *Book Business*. New York: W. W. Norton, 2001.

Fishman, Robert. *Urban Utopias in the Twentieth Century*. Cambridge, MA: MIT Press, 1982.

Fulford, Robert. *Accidental City: The Transformation of Toronto*. New York: Houghton Mifflin, 1995.

Gans, Herbert. *The Urban Villagers*. Updated edition. New York: Free Press, 1982.

Glanz, James, and Eric Lipton. *City in the Sky: The Rise and Fall of the World Trade Center*. New York: Times Books, 2003.

Gratz, Roberta Brandes. *Cities Back from the Edge*. New York: John Wiley & Sons, 1998.

Hagan, John. *Northern Passage: American Vietnam War Resisters in Canada*. Cambridge, MA: Harvard University Press, 2001.

Harrington, Michael. *The Other America*. New York: Macmillan, 1962.

Hirsch, Arnold R. *Making the Second Ghetto: Race and Housing in Chicago 1940–1960*. 2nd ed. Chicago: University of Chicago Press, 1998.

Howard, Ebenezer. *Garden Cities of Tomorrow*. 1898. Reprinted with preface by F. J. Osborn and essay by Lewis Mumford. Cambridge, MA: MIT Press, 1965.

Hughes, Michael, ed. *The Letters of Lewis Mumford and Frederic J. Osborn*. New York: Praeger, 1972.

Jackson, Kenneth T. *Crabgrass Frontier: The Suburbanization of the United States*. New York: Oxford University Press, 1985.

———, ed. *The Encyclopedia of New York City*. New Haven, CT: Yale University Press, 1995.

Jacobs, Jane. *Cities and the Wealth of Nations*. New York: Random House, 1984.

———. *Dark Age Ahead*. New York: Random House, 2004.

———. *The Death and Life of Great American Cities*. New York: Random House, 1961. Reissued by Vintage Books, 1992.

———. *The Economy of Cities*. New York: Random House, 1969. Reissued by Vintage Books, 1970.

———. *The Nature of Economies*. New York: Random House, 2000. Reissued by Vintage Books, 2001.

———. *The Question of Separatism*. New York: Random House, 1980. Reissued by Vintage Books, 1981.

———. *Systems of Survival*. New York: Random House, 1992. Reissued by Vintage Books, 1994.

———, ed. *A Schoolteacher in Old Alaska: The Story of Hannah Breece*. New York: Random House, 1995. Reissued by Vintage Books, 1997.

Jonnes, Jill. *South Bronx Rising*. New York: Fordham University Press, 2002.

Kisseloff, Jeff. *You Must Remember This: An Oral History of Manhattan from the 1890s to World War II*. New York: Harcourt Brace Jovanovich, 1989.

Klemek, Christopher. "Urbanism as Reform: Modernist Planning and the Crisis of Urban Liberalism in Europe and North America, 1945–1975." PhD diss., University of Pennsylvania, 2004.

Kostelanetz, Richard. *Soho: The Rise and Fall of an Artists' Colony*. New York: Routledge, 2003.

Kuhn, Thomas S. *The Structure of Scientific Revolutions*. 2nd ed. Chicago: University of Chicago Press, 1970.

Kunstler, James. *The Geography of Nowhere*. New York: Simon & Schuster, 1993.

Le Corbusier. *Towards a New Architecture*. Translated by Frederick Etchells. New York: Praeger, 1960.

———. *When the Cathedrals Were White*. Translated by Francis E. Hyslop Jr. New York: McGraw-Hill, 1964.

Lemon, James T. *Liberal Dreams and Nature's Limits: Great Cities of North America Since 1600*. Toronto: Oxford University Press, 1996.

Miller, Donald L. *Lewis Mumford: A Life*. New York: Wiedenfeld & Nicolson, 1989.

———, ed. *The Lewis Mumford Reader*. Athens: University of Georgia Press, 1995.

Moses, Robert. *Public Works: A Dangerous Trade*. New York: McGraw-Hill, 1970.

Mumford, Lewis. *The City in History*. New York: Harcourt Brace, 1961.

——. *The Culture of Cities*. New York: Harcourt Brace, 1938.

——. *From the Ground Up*. New York: Harcourt Brace, 1947.

——. *The Highway and the City*. New York: Mentor Books, 1953.

New York Panorama: A Companion to the WPA Guide to New York City. Guilds' Committee for Federal Writers' Publications, Inc., 1938. Reprinted with introduction by Alfred Kazin. New York: Pantheon Books, 1984.

Nowlan, David, and Nadine Nowlan. *The Bad Trip: The Untold Story of the Spadina Expressway*. Toronto: Anansi, 1970.

Plunz, Richard. *A History of Housing in New York City*. New York: Columbia University Press, 1990.

Riis, Jacob A. *How the Other Half Lives*. New York: Dover, 1971. Reprint of the 1901 edition published by Scribner's and Sons, 1890.

Sewell, John. *The Shape of the City*. Toronto: University of Toronto Press, 1993.

——. *Up Against City Hall*. Toronto: James Lewis & Samuel, 1972.

Starr, Roger. *The Living End*. New York: Coward-McCann, 1966.

Stern, Robert A. M., Thomas Mellins, and David Fishman. *New York 1960*. New York: Monacelli Press, 1995.

Talese, Gay. *The Kingdom and the Power*. New York: New American Library, 1966.

Wetzsteon, Ross. *Republic of Dreams: Greenwich Village, The American Bohemia, 1910–1960*. New York: Simon & Schuster, 2002.

White, E. B. *Here Is New York*. New York: Curtis, 1949.

White, Morton, and Lucia White. *The Intellectual versus the City*. New York: Mentor Books, 1964.

Whyte, William H., Jr., ed. *The Exploding Metropolis*. Reprint of Time, Inc. 1957 edition. Berkeley: University of California Press, 1993.

Wilson, James Q. *Negro Politics*. New York: The Free Press, 1960.

The WPA Guide to New York City. Guilds' Committee for Federal Writers' Publications, Inc., 1939. Reprinted with introduction by William H. Whyte Jr. New York: Random House, 1982.

INDEX

ABOUT THE AUTHOR

Alice Sparberg Alexiou is a journalist and author. She holds degrees from Columbia and Fordham Universities in classical literature and journalism. Alexiou is an editor at *Lilith* magazine and has contributed articles to numerous publications, including the *New York Times*. She lives in Long Island, New York, with her husband. They have two sons.